The Finance Mentors' Ledger

Practical Advice To Remain Relevant
And Have Meaningful Careers In
Finance & Accounting

Compiled by Andrew Codd

AUTHOR'S LEGAL DISCLAIMER
This book presents a wide range of opinion about a wide variety of topics related to having a career in the accountancy & finance professions. These opinions reflect the research and ideas of the author, or those whose ideas the author presents. The author and the publisher disclaim responsibility for any adverse effects resulting directly or indirectly from information contained in this book.

Why this book?

To explain the title of this book, *The Finance Mentors' Ledger: Practical Advice To Remain Relevant And Have Meaningful Careers In Finance & Accounting,* I have to go back to 2005.

On the value of mentors

At the time I didn't really see much use in having mentors. I had just qualified as an accountant and couldn't see where they could help with what I was going through? How could they know the latest developments, tools and techniques in finance better than me, I mean I'd just qualified, right? Then a chance ten-minute encounter changed my mind. It was in the lobby of a Holiday Inn Hotel where I met my first proper mentor Vincent. As we sat together over coffee I felt the weight of frustrations from working sixty-hour weeks, in a role I hated, for a boss who I felt was out to get me, suddenly lifting and having a ray of hope that there was a better way. Vincent had shown me, on the back of a napkin, a model, a structure, a way to have a meaningful career in Accounting & Finance, contribute value to others, as well as how to have a life outside of it. If only I had realised the power of mentors sooner.

Since then you could say a lot has changed in our profession. We've accelerated away from what some had called the computer age into the fourth industrial revolution, or Industry 4.0 with its cognitive computing power which is threatening to digitise & commoditise a lot of the work that was once the realm of traditional finance professionals & accountants. Depending on your viewpoint, having a career in accounting & finance right now can either be one burdened with overwhelming anxiety or a greenfield laden with so many opportunities.

On the value of debits and credits

This book also represents a ledger of sorts because the mentors are depositing their experiences (i.e. like a debit entry due to an increase in assets) and conversely, the readers are drawing down on these assets (i.e. a credit entry). My genuine belief, and it's why we created the **#SITN** (Strength in the Numbers) podcasts, is that:

- Most of the answers to our biggest challenges in Accounting & Finance are already there in our profession if we just shared our stories and journeys in trying to overcome them;

- By doing so we will develop even more mentors who overtime will increase not only the overall debits being deposited (increasing our assets), but also our ability to draw from these, so increase the credits too.
- And ultimately all these debits & credits will improve our ability and potential to create more influence and value by solving the most meaningful problems of the organisations within our communities and so ensure that Society is better off overall.

In Finance & Accounting we can make a genuine positive impact on our World. So how can you get the most out of this book?

Getting the most out of this book

I firmly believe that the quote on the cover of this book, from Sir Isaac Newton best sums up the power of having mentors. They are giants, with useful stories and insights that can help give us some hope when we feel overwhelmed and frustrated. Additionally, their hard-won lessons can help us see over the fence as to what potential paths exist and give us a better focus, direction and perhaps some useful first steps we can take to get closer towards our goals.

On the mentors in this book

Given the value our finance and accounting profession can deliver it means that we are both a global and increasingly mobile community. So whilst the 79 mentors in this book are drawn from around the world and its chapters are structured around their country of origin, their experiences travel far and wide.

8	Africa
10	Asia & Australasia
23	Americas
38	Europe
79	**Total**

One-third of the mentors are female; and two-thirds are male. Combined the mentors have over 2,000+ years of experience in accounting & finance, so you could say all the way back to when abacuses and clay tablets were the main tools of our profession.

In this book the various mentors will talk a great deal about their experiences within accounting & finance as well as with the business, operations, sales, HR, the relationships between them, and also the implications for your career. They will speak about financial planning & analysis, business partnering, strategy, systems, controls, compliance, analytics and leadership. About professional development, personal branding, the impact of digitalisation via technologies like data management, visualisation, artificial intelligence and the robotisation on our profession.

On the dangers of the cave

However, none of those things will make any difference to you or your career unless you remember to do one thing:

Come out from your cave.

The cave has always been finance & accounting's Comfort Zone. It has been that safe space where most of us start our career journeys from. How many accountants qualify, get their letters, and then think, *"Thank goodness, I don't have to study for exams again."* The cave is an analogy for all of our existing knowledge, systems, tools, processes, training, experiences, relationships, qualifications that don't evolve and so keep us in the dark, tucked away from the change that is going on just outside our caves. The cave is also a reference to the tools and concepts we're still using today, such as: variance analysis; standard costing; Du Pont ratio analysis; McKinsey's budgeting concept as well as double-entry bookkeeping and Excel spreadsheet VLOOKUPs that were all developed to work in prior industrial revolutions & eras.

Some of the more curious cave dwellers in our profession might have ventured nearer the cave entrance, or just outside it. They might have heard noises about digital disruption; or value creation; business partnering; analytics; getting a seat at the table; the socially intelligent accountant; lean accounting; and so on. But when they go back into their caves what they hear is *"but that's not the way we do it around here,"* or *"there's no way we'll find the time and budget to do that"* because their colleagues have been too busy overloaded meeting deadlines, crunching numbers, gathering & cleaning data, churning out the reports, reacting to requests for ad-hoc analysis the executives wanted yesterday, and ultimately doing more with less as leaders view finance as a cost centre and overhead causing a drag on the bottom-line.

But staying in our caves can be dangerous. We all want to be comfortable, but we'll pay a high price if we don't follow the example of our cave dwelling ancestors who bravely stepped out of their caves. According to the psychologist Jordan Peterson, they did this to improve their ability to deal with and cope with what's going on outside their caves. Because like our ancient ancestors, if we don't possess this better understanding then we will cease to be relevant, we become extinct or at best an endangered species within our organisations.

On the call to learning

However, this call to arms is not a call to do battle. It's a call to learning. This book and the mentors' advice within it gives some perspectives on how to feel, think, and act differently as well as more productively, with more humanity than our existing skills and understanding allow. It makes venturing out from our caves a little less scary and provides some tried and tested paths for us to leverage the opportunities that are outside.

Today's world is a difficult place. Humankind and our profession have experienced more change in the past twenty years than it has in the 4,000 that preceded them.

From Accounting with Clay Tablets to Cloud & Cognitive Computing

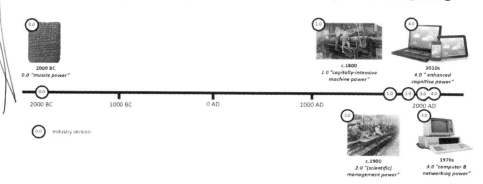

Our traditional power bases of guarding access to the financials and being the only ones capable and trained to interpret the numbers, which have served us so well for so long, have eroded. Nowadays, more operational leaders are becoming financially literate and have more self-service access to the financial and non-financial data that have been democratised by IT. Even geographical, social and economic boundaries are coming down with the advancement of outsourcing and offshoring. The rules of what we've been used to are constantly changing.

However, as accountants and finance professionals we know that people and our organisations cannot live without boundaries, without structure, without rules. For most of our profession's existence we've been about audits, compliance and controls as a way of preserving and safeguarding value in our organisations. Unfortunately, in a world of accelerated change the old rules that have underpinned our profession so well are getting swallowed up in the insatiable vortex of change.

The result of all this disorder can be unsettling, where confusion reigns and with less and less traditions to hold on to. That's why you won't find the advice of these mentors in any mainstream textbook or accounting syllabus. You won't find it on a generic Google search, LinkedIn blog post, or in an article complied by a paid content writer (well at least in a way that's specifically applicable to real accounting & finance practitioners). The advice is built from real world experiences and hard-won lessons. It is far from the fictious exercises and case studies asking you to perform a trial balance on XYZ plc, or reconcile the suspense account of ACME Inc when at business school or university.

On bridging the gap

If we want to answer the question on how best to have meaningful and rewarding careers, in a profession that has stood the test of time. It is unlikely that the answer is going to come from the traditional resources and training received based on what was the norm in prior industrial eras. And even if we did draw from such resources they would be of little use in helping us figure out the right paths to take and assess how to best interpret the threats and opportunities of tomorrow. We can't change the world out there, it has a momentum all of its own. Fortunately, we don't have to because we can begin much closer to home. We can begin with ourselves, with what we can control, and that starts by using this book in the right way.

The mentors in this book can step in and show you the paths they've taken, how they've survived and thrived through this period of accelerating change. And 'the path' to take is an apt analogy because this book, by design, is meant to be a useful companion guide. The advice is broken down into practical steps and real stories, so that you can first walk through them in your mind's eye first before setting off on your own journey outside your cave. This book is really about:

Bridging the Gap.

Between the "outside" and the "inside." Between the world "out there" and your inner world. And if used correctly, a bit like a reference guide, not to be read cover to cover but rather when you need to find a particular answer, this book can become that bridge. The bridge between you and the world. The bridge that can take you from where you are now and get you closer to the career you desire.

In terms of how this book enables the building of that bridge it has been organised in some key ways:

- At the start of each chapter you'll find #hashtags that highlight the key topics in each chapter.
- Every guest mentor's profile indicates where you can best connect with them: LI=LinkedIn, TW=Twitter & WS=Website.
- The material has been thoroughly indexed so you can navigate to key pages efficiently.
- There is a create-your-own-index section where you can put the key insights, pages & make notes that are relevant and personalised to you.
- A curated recommended resources list of books, articles, papers, websites & videos with links to save you searching for them.
- The last paragraph of each mentor is dedicated to their best bit of advice received or given. Reading these alone will accelerate your ability to bridge the gap.

In such a way the book is designed to make you both more productive and discover more meaning in your career. The advice has been distilled and deconstructed from thousands of minutes of podcasts and interviews to enable you to make a difference for those around you, whether they be colleagues, customers, leaders, your organisation and communities.

Let the journey begin

The lesson to learn from all this is simple. We can only improve our careers in finance & accounting and create the necessary impacts we desire if we first understand how such a world is constructed, how it works, and the rules of the game. However, the final quote on the back cover of this book from Bruce Lee is also important. The mentors in this book provide us an accessible means to better study the world and how we can thrive in it. It's their way, drawn from reflections on their own experiences & circumstances that are unique to them. To truly get the most out of this book it is important that you absorb what is useful for you and construct a career that is also uniquely your own. So enjoy taking the first steps out from your cave, bridging the gap to the career you desire and making this experience uniquely your own.

All the best,
Andrew Codd
Cork, Ireland

Dedication

To Katie, my soulmate and best mentor I've ever known.

Table Of Contents

AFRICA

"You'll be surprised, if you just you start talking to people, you'll understand the business a lot better and you'll actually understand their pain points."

Arno Wakfer
LI: arnowakfer
WS: financevaluecreation.com

Tags:
#value creation #business partnering #automation #data visualisation #data analytics #financial modelling #business insights

ARNO WAKFER is a finance professional with over 15 years commercial experience as CFO, controller, manager as well as in finance business partnering & leadership roles across various industries, in well-known organisations such as Dimension Data, Autodesk, MoreGolf & GIBS Business School. During his career in both South Africa & Australian Arno has led financial strategy development, built high-performance finance teams, implemented business improvements & facilitated change management programs.

Arno holds a CA designation, is a certified financial modeller and valuation analyst and lives in Brisbane, Australia with his family.

On the importance of values in business and making time for planning

Values are very important in business. There is no point you having a vision or mission statement and you then hire people who don't share the same values, vision & mission statement. Because you're going to get some going left and other ones going right, you're not going to go in the same direction. So it's just getting the right people on the bus, that share the same values. And then you need people that can actually execute strategies. A lot of small businesses, they don't have time to plan, because they are running around to make revenue and pay salaries but if you don't plan you're planning to fail.

Small businesses have a very different beat to the larger corporates. They don't have that free time to work on the business, they're always working in the business, and for me as an accountant it's about getting people out of the business and saying, *"Listen let's work on the business and let's see how we can improve it."* My career has always been focussed on business improvements. Nothing is perfect there's always room for improvement.

On the usefulness of business partnering

Earlier in my career I was just managing finances from my desk. I didn't interact, I didn't engage, I was just pushing out reports. It was analysis paralysis I was just looking at detail, detail, detail. And eventually I thought what's the point at looking at the detail if I can't get input from people, in case I'm missing something, maybe I'm missing trends. As a new accountant, I don't really understand the business, I don't understand how the divisions operate, what their processes are? I think that was the mindset shift for me, is to engage through business partnering. You'll be surprised, if you just you start talking to people, you'll understand the business a lot better and you'll actually understand their pain points.

On the two customers of Finance and the importance of conversation

Finance has got two customers: internal customers and external customers. The internal customers are all the departments which have specified their needs. We need to give them reports, actual versus budget, help them better improve their systems and processes and all those things. And then obviously there are external ones, it's more about if you know your customers' needs, such as giving them billing statements or things like that. So we've got a big opportunity in finance of servicing a large stakeholder base and it all starts with a conversation. It's like typically when I tell people on LinkedIn, if someone sends me an invite to connect and you don't start a conversation what's the point of connecting in the first place. Just talk to people, find out what they're doing and how you can help service their business better and that's what at the end of the day we do. Finance serves People, that's what we do.

On why reporting isn't adding value and why automation is exciting

There's this thing that automation is going to take away the all the jobs of finance & accountants, which it won't. And the reason I say that is because what will happen is all the repetitive tasks and monthly reporting, those things will be automated which is a great thing. What's going to happen is it's going to free up a lot more of finance to actually roll up their sleeves and actually start talking to people and engage in doing proper business partnering and creating value. If you're just pushing out reporting you're not adding value because reporting uses historical information, you're just telling what happened in the past. So it's freeing up that time to work on predictions, to work on systemisation, to work on growth, to work on strategy, and to do what I call, to become a co-pilot to driving future business performance. That's what finance is, we're co-pilots, we steer the plane in a way with executives, with the leadership of an organisation.

On why finance professionals need to be visible and how to do this

I do think Finance needs to be more engaging, but you do need to get out of your comfort zone, and you need to be seen, you need to be visible. You need to walk around, you need to let people see you, introduce yourself. You'll be surprised if you can put a name to a face, it changes everything. Obviously with technology you can do conference calls, use Zoom meetings. So when I say be more visible, I really mean so people can hear from you more often, not just on a month end when you send a report. Communicate more often, let people just hear and see you, and for me that's key. They shouldn't just see you once a month.

On the best criticism he ever received and how it helped

I actually received criticism one day but it was the best thing because it put me on a journey to prove them wrong. I think you need to take things with a pinch of salt, you can't worry too much about what other people think of you or what you think they think of you because most times they are not thinking that, so worry about yourself.

Getting back to the story, one day I was sitting in a Boardroom and one of the directors said, *"you can't do that because they'll eat me for lunch."* I thought okay, *"So are you saying that I don't have the capacity to do it or the talent?"* He said *"Both!"* Then I thought, okay, well that's a challenge I'm going to take up, so thanks for the advice, although it's negative, but I'm going to turn it into a positive. A few months down the line I implemented the solution, so for me sometimes you need that bit of a push or drive to prove people wrong.

On why automation is making us lazy

Automation is making us lazy, because we're actually not looking at the reports, we're assuming that they are correct and not checking if the design is wrong or if there is garbage-in garbage-out. So every now and again do your checks. Something that's wrong and that's automated is going to cause you real problems so always have checks and balances, and validation controls in place. Automation is not a once off exercise, technology is constantly developing.

Best bits advice to a younger finance professional

The advice I would give to the younger generation or to myself if I was fifteen years younger is, *less is more*, don't go too much into the detail, rather instead look for trends and warning signals, you'll cut out a lot of analysis paralysis. Look for things that stand out and you'll be surprised that's where there'll be problem areas. The second thing is be your own competitor, don't compete with anyone else, compete with yourself and that's very important because as soon as you start comparing yourself with other people you are not going to get anywhere in life. Improve, Improve, Improve, always try to do your best and improve. Last thing is, as I've said before, nothing is perfect. There will always be room for improvement because in my career I always wanted to get things out perfect and spending so much time at it that you end up losing the plot. So then I said I'd rather get something out because at least then people will look at it quick and give feedback. Questions will come out sooner and that goes for life in general, nothing is perfect, we all know that.

Recommended Resources

Documentary: The Corporation (2003) (link)

Book: *Work Less, Make More: The counter-intuitive approach to building a profitable business, and a life you actually love (2017)*, by James Schramko (link)

Book: *What Is Your WHAT?: Discover The One Amazing Thing You Were Born To Do (2013)*, by Steve Olsher (link)

Podcast: Superfast Business (link)

Podcast: #SITN Strength in the Numbers Show (link)

Website: Finance Value Creation (link)

"We describe value as being at the intersection of the problem and the solution whose measure is the relative importance of the problem to the stakeholder."

Carol Hachandi Lupiya
LI: carol-hachandi-lupiya
WS: theoutperformer.co

Tags:
#business partnering #enablement #value creation #strategic objectives

CAROL HACHANDI LUPIYA is a Partner for the African Region at The Outperformer who design, integrate and facilitate performance and change-focused programs for accounting and finance teams, many who are heavily impacted by structural change, technology advancements and the need to be 'relevant' in the way they work with their business.

Carol holds a CGMA designation and is based in Johannesburg, South Africa.

On not putting olives in someone else green salad
My experience as a consultant is that you walk through the client's door with zero knowledge about their problem and environment, muddle through solution development and walk out as an expert to that challenge. However, I was not 100% sold on the consulting approach of predefined solutions that we would present as a plug and play approach to resolve client challenges. I recall being told by my client that we were forcing her to have olives in a green salad because that was our understanding of how a salad should be and all she wanted was, lettuce, cucumber and tomato in her salad. So at that moment I actually changed the way I looked at consulting and I went and researched on how to be more stakeholder centric as a consultant and finance business partnering provided that link.

Great consulting is really nothing about what I (consultant) have to offer to you, but instead discovering where you (client) are in your work and how far can I take you towards achieving your strategic objectives.

On how to make business partnering work

Even though it's been around for a few decades the business partnering concept and business partners in many finance teams are still stuck with the old way of working where they're not operating at the desired strategic business partner level. You hear sentiments such as, *"Oh! We don't have enough time to partner because we're busy with month end, or too busy with budgets, or too busy resolving accounting discrepancies and other finance related issues."* So my work in these situations is helping shift the needle towards business partnering by co-designing programs that help them get the focus right.

I'll give you an example of one of our clients who was challenged with these task-focused activities, leaving them no time for anything else. I consulted with them and coached them towards getting a better context of the strategic objectives to solve stakeholders' core problems, top-down, and by the way this is where the ball gets dropped. When business partners do not understand the organisational strategy they'll have challenges convincing stakeholders to focus on the higher value activities that unlock sound decision making and better performance. So this client was shocked at how enlightened their stakeholder became when we worked with them to link their day-to-day activities to their objectives. The conversation immediately transcended beyond what is the balance of my budget to what should I be concentrating on to achieve this objective.

On a definition for value creation

And this brings me to the point of value creation. Value is very subjective and one cannot be prescriptive about it. At the Outperformer, we describe value as being at the intersection of the problem and the solution whose measure is the relative importance of the problem to the stakeholder. In other words, if your report is not helping stakeholders make decisions or resolve challenges then it is not of value to them.

On mistaking effort for value

The best mix for me that has worked for clients is in identifying and distinguishing between enablement activities and value creation activities and balancing those. I was invited to a meeting by one of my business partnering clients who was presenting a report to their stakeholder, and I wished for the life of me I had declined that meeting. The business partner was outraged, because after spending a lot of time gathering information and putting the report together the stakeholders only looked at a paragraph of the eight-page report. So we had to go back to the drawing board with my client and what emerged was that they had not understood what their stakeholder needed from the report. This is another challenge facing many business partners and many finance people where effort is mistaken for value. I worked with my client helping them make a distinction between enablement and value creation and this was a bitter pill to swallow for my main stakeholder, because at the end of the session we discovered that almost the entire team was currently engaged in enablement activities and no real focus on value creation activities.

On how to best mix value creation with enablement

Enablement happens when business partners in their roles work to effectively and efficiently standardise recurring written processes, automate reports, build models. In other words creating capacity and capability for ourselves to better serve our stakeholders. You need to clean up your own house first then once you've cleaned it up move on to adding value and value creation, which is successfully facilitating and helping stakeholders to navigate and overcome business challenges using the right tools, technologies and assets to meet their objectives. I might sound like a broken record here but I would like to emphasise that it is important to understand what challenges your stakeholders are trying to solve, otherwise you end up assuming you're right and you give them a wrong solution like my client was outraged when his stakeholders only looked at one paragraph of the eight-page report.

So there are three key questions that one needs to ask to check if they're making an impact with their stakeholders and where the value lies:

1. Is the value in the time you took to create a report or the discussion you have about it?
2. Is the value in the standardisation and automation of the reporting process or the way you distil reports in an individualised way to help stakeholders find meaning in the data?
3. Is the value in the budget process or the way you use the budget to help the business make better decisions?

If you think about it and if I bring you back to the concept of finance business partnering it's not all about the soft skills of communication and presentation in isolation. It goes beyond that, it's a holistic and ongoing contextual consultation with business stakeholders to help them achieve their objectives and overcome their highest priorities. The result is a culture of general partnership and high performance and you'll appreciate that having such a culture of business partnership takes time. That is why business partnership is not a quick fix, otherwise you end up band-aiding over what's not working already.

On the best bit of advice Carol has ever received

My mother would say whatever your hands find to do, do it with all your heart and your soul. In summary give it 100% to whatever you're doing, whether you're washing dishes, whether you're presenting at a seminar, whatever it is give it 100%.

Recommended Resources

Book: *When Coffee and Kale Compete: Become great at making products people,* by Alan Klement (link)

Website: The Outperformer (link)

"What you have to always understand is that the business is in business because of the customer. So even as a finance team you also have to ask yourself, so who is my customer? Who am I in business for?"

Chidimma Eghagha
LI: chidimmaeghagha

Tags:
#global #customer-oriented #emotional intelligence #communication

CHIDIMMA EGHAGHA is currently a member of the reporting operations team at the Royal Bank of Canada, which is Canada's largest bank and one of the biggest in the world based on market capitalisation. Her track record adding value in the financial services industry stretches back over the two decades and not just within Finance & Accounting but also from her time leading Customer Service teams. Originally qualifying with an ACA from the Institute of Chartered Accountants of Nigeria, Chidimma also is a CPA of Canada and holds an MBA from Manchester Business School.

On the biggest change in switching between North Africa & North America
Definitely things are different. First of all you have different laws that apply here in Canada, they're different from what we have back home. The work styles are also a bit different to back home, as an accountant you're expected to be a master of everything but here I see that you are expected to specialise in a particular area. For me that was the biggest change I experienced professionally the fact that here you have to specialise in one particular arm of finance, like analysis or tax, you don't just do everything. But back home as an accountant you are expected to be like a Jack-of-all trades. There's a deeper level of professionalism expected from you here. You're expected to show more depth to your work than probably we were expected to do back home and that requires quite a bit of time.

On specialising in an area of finance & accounting

The first and most important step you need to take in specialising is knowing what your strengths are. What is it that you love doing? Are you the one who is more comfortable working with figures behind the scenes, crunching the numbers? Or are you someone who likes to interface with people helping partner with the business? Because that helps you choose what stream of accounting you really want to focus on. If you're someone who prefers to work by yourself with a system and then crunch out the numbers you probably want to go for more of an analyst role where you're looking at data and churning out reports. Or if you're like me, I prefer to meet the people and support the people directly. So you can go for a business facing role.

On questions to ask when deciding on an area to specialise in

The first thing for me was knowing what my strengths were and then knowing what area of accounting I wanted to specialise in. Ask yourself what is it that I like to do? What is my work style? What style works best for my personality type? Once you've figured those out then the others are relatively easier to deal with, because accounting is a profession where you can apply your technical skills in different areas. For me the most important thing is knowing what you want to do, what gives you satisfaction and joy, then you can apply your skills to those areas.

On the importance of thinking like a Second Grader

Over the years I've had to learn how to communicate accounting terms in words that are very simple for the layman to understand. So there's something I tell myself, which is if I cannot explain a concept in a way that a second grader would understand, then that means I myself haven't got a full understanding of it. Currently now with the whole IFRS implementation there's just so much to digest and communicate. Likewise over the years in supporting the business I've had to like come up with templates, come up with terms, come up with ways in which leaders can manage their portfolios and make it very simple, something simple that you don't need to be a CPA to be able to use it. I've had to break down the IFRS requirements into very simple steps that business leaders can use and apply in their own portfolios. It's not something you can achieve in a day but overtime it's something you can keep making it better and better.

On demystifying the numbers and their impact on the bottom-line

Before I moved to Canada I was heading the team that provided full cycle accounting and back office support for electronic banking. The country had come up with a new monetary policy where they wanted to reduce the amount of cash in the system. They were encouraging people to go to electronic platforms, but because of previous experiences, there being lots of cases of fraud or poor service, customers were not really attuned to getting the product. The challenge was that most of the business leaders I was supporting were used to making their income from the traditional banking services, loans, current accounts, etc... but they couldn't see how getting a customer to have an ATM card or getting a retail customer to get a POS terminal could really impact their bottom line. They really couldn't see the connection between that. So I had to come up with a template that basically took just the one ATM card first of all and showing them how one ATM card could translate into a certain amount of money in terms of percentages from the point it's sold up to the point of continuous usage. I used a simple example of a customer that does $1000 of transactions on a daily basis on their POS, and showed them how much money they're getting on a daily basis, multiplied that by 30 days of a month, multiplied that by, let's say, 30 customers they were able to sign on. After putting together that presentation and sending it out to the business leaders I could see that there was interest, they really wanted to know more about the electronic banking space. I didn't go into all the details of all the other costs and everything, but I just took it to the barest minimum they could get. We then started building on that simple understanding and at the end of the day we were able to increase the revenue from electronic banking by 60% just by applying this new revenue model.

On the importance of communication and how to do it right

The ability to communicate is not just expressing your own views but also in trying to understand the other person's point of view, that's the best way that you can provide support for any business or team. You have to see the whole 360 degrees point of view. I don't think that there's just one right way to solve a problem. Accounting is full of principles and standards, we always tend to feel like there's just one way to do this, but over the course of my career I've found out that there's always different ways to arrive at the solution. As accountants we have to be flexible and open-minded enough to look at things from different perspectives.

On one simple thing to do to be more flexible and open-minded

The best way you could be more flexible and open-minded is just to listen. When I say listen, like really listen to people, really listen to the business, really listen to the teams that we're supporting and try and see things from their point of view. Not with a mindset of I already know how this should be solved, but from could there be another way? The world is going digital and we're having computers and software replacing the work that accountants do right now. The only way I feel that we can still remain relevant is if we are flexible enough to provide more support for business teams and you can only do that by understanding fully what is required from you by your partners.

On what Finance can learn from customer service teams

What you have to always understand is that the business is in business because of the customer. So even as a finance team you also have to ask yourself, who is my customer? Who am I in business for? And whatever you're doing, your processes and your operational flow should be in favour of the customer, not in your favour. As finance professionals we get so caught up with our procedures and our concepts that we forget the reason we do all of this in the first place is to support and make it easier for them and not more difficult.

On the best bit of advice Chidimma has ever received

A manager told me that the only way you can advance professionally and do that fast is if you learn how to work with people. I found that to be very true. You can be ambitious, you can think you can push, but I strongly believe that you cannot achieve your full potential in isolation. You need to be able to work with people, as well as collaborate and learn to understand people. The only way you can build that is by developing your emotional intelligence. You have to be able to read people, know how to work with them, and know how to bring out the best in them. When you do that you become a better person yourself and you're also able to become the best that you can be.

Recommended Resources

Book: *Lean In: Women, Work, and the Will to Lead (2013)*, by Sheryl Sandberg (link)

"If you want to learn how to become a trusted business partner look around in your own life and find one or two, and emulate them."

John Stretch
LI: john-stretch
WS: johnstretch.com

Tags:
#business partnering #trust #automation #value creation #career

JOHN STRETCH has an accounting & finance career covering five decades. He began as a partner in the consulting division of a Big 4 accounting firm before breaking away to form his own consulting practice. Nowadays John develops content on relevant topics in financial management and business strategy. His online e-learning libraries, blogs and case studies can be viewed at johnstretch.com. John can also be found writing blogs, magazine articles and books. His work has been published by Microsoft, CFO magazine, professional institutes, and in business school journals.

John holds a CA (SA) designation, a Masters in Financial Modelling, and is based out of Johannesburg South Africa.

On how to be a trusted business partner

With a lot of accounting going to be automated there's this whole story about being a trusted business partner. There's all this correspondence, people writing papers, on what do you need to do to become a trusted business partner, you must be able to contribute at the strategic level, etc.... . My view is that not everyone is born to become a trusted business partner. If I look back on my career, I can only hone in on two people, in two different organisations, both international organisations who really played the part. They were what I would call trusted business partners. They were qualified accountants, but they could walk into any area of their business, in any part of the world, and people would immediately accept them and listen to them and so on. It was much more about personal characteristics and the ability to get on with people. If there was a technical issue or a technology issue that people wanted to explore and they didn't get the knowledge. Well go and find the knowledge, so source it somewhere. You don't have to be an expert on every element of strategy or if you need to know about scenario planning go and find a scenario planner. It's much more about knowing how to make the moments work and the process. So I say to people if you want to learn how to become a trusted business partner look around in your own life and find one or two, and emulate them.

On the key traits required of a trusted business partner

If you look at the characteristics you're going to find fundamental things like, they're not scared to travel, so they travel a great deal. That trusted business partners are quite happy to go up to India to see how the factory there is doing and so on. They are quite happy to speak in extemporary and in public. They work unbelievably hard in short bursts. For example, they'll go to the factory in India, where there's a feasibility study to be done, they'll work for 17 or 18 hours for 3 to 4 days, and they'll get the thing done, they'll get on the plane and come home. That builds trust like you can't believe.

On fearsome accountants

We are producing these wonderful fearsome accountants that I come across from time to time. I'm talking about people with an honours or Masters in statistics or mathematics. They know how to code, they can just do the most phenomenal things. I mean I was talking to these two youngsters who work in a bank. They said people come to us with an idea for a new banking product or how to sell a new variation. We ask them to make 6 PowerPoint slides explaining their idea, email it to us and within 3 hours we've made you an app. It's a rough app, but it's an app that works. Now we can go and test it out on customers and clients inside the bank, whatever it is. That is phenomenal. Compare that to sitting down and doing a feasibility study or a market survey, or whatever. It's just so powerful and those are the kind of people that are coming into our profession.

On what type of things should we be learning for the future

I can't see any reason why middle-aged accountants can't learn to code. The courses are available for free on the Internet and if you can learn to code you can actually start to build apps and that's the future.

On why should we should embrace automation

When we hear about how routine accounting functions are going to become automated in the future and management accounting is all that's left, I say, don't fight that, become part of it, become part of that automation and master it. Go along on the journey and embrace it because otherwise you will be left behind. When Excel, laptop computers and desktops first came in there were a whole load of finance directors in my country in their 50s who just ducked the whole question of becoming computer literate. Within five years they were out of a job and I think that is going to happen here as well.

On the importance of reflecting on yesterday

The first thing I do every day when I hit my desk is write down the 3 most important things that happened to me yesterday and reflect on them for 5 minutes. Then I develop my plan and my priorities for today, and my To-Do-List. I also live with and have a personal 18-month rolling forecast of me, that's my business and my personal life in mind, and family life and so on that I update rigorously on the first of every month.

On the best advice John ever received

Strangely enough it was three words, *"You're too cheap."* There is a supermarket chain in our region which was started by an amazing entrepreneur many years ago. He's grown it up now to where he's got 20,000 employees and I was in the financial director's office one day where we were discussing how best to develop incentive schemes for the management group. The chairman, as he was then walked in and stood against the wall as we carried on with our conversation. Once we had finished he said to me, *"That was interesting young man. I just wanted to tell you, you're too cheap."* And he walked out. Then I said to the financial director, *"What on earth does he mean? Am I wearing the wrong tie or something?"* Well the financial director, he looked at me and said, *"Don't even think about putting your fees up."*

So I went away and reflected on that and I thought about the other consultants this big organisation employed, the marketing people that they used, the advertising people, the legal advisers, the brand builders, the human resource outsiders, and so on, as well as who they were. Now most of these consultants were internationally or nationally known figures. I was pretty sure if I was charging X dollars a day for my consulting, they were charging 3 or 4 or even 5X. So I really took that as a mission. I sat down and thought, *"Okay, if I'm too cheap, how do I become 5X? What would I need to be able to do to be able to charge 5X?"* It was things like, my client was a grocery retailer and I went on a mission to read every single annual report that was published in English, of any grocery retailer across the world. And you pick up the most amazing things. You can then walk into a meeting and say, *"Do you know what Walmart are doing with their incentive schemes?"* And people say they don't know. You become a thought leader and build an expertise in that.

Recommended Resources

Book: *Business Adventures: Twelve Classic Tales from the World of Wall Street,* John Brooks (link)

Book: *The Millionaire Next Door: The Surprising Secrets of America's Wealthy Paperback,* Thomas J. Stanley; William D. Danko (link)

Article: *CFO Magazine* (link)

"And so when I look at finance partnering I was fortunate to have developed those skills in investment banking. As opposed to being an auditor, where you're kind of looking at what happened, as an investment banker you're trying to talk about something that's less tangible because it's looking forward."

Lance Rubin
LI: cashflowmodelling
WS: modelcitizn.com

Tags:

#financial modelling #investment banking #partnering #relationships #communication #resilience #FMI #Excel

LANCE RUBIN is founder and CEO of Model Citizn and over the last two decades has built a strong reputation throughout the industry of being a highly accomplished and lateral thinking financial modeler. Lance was even referred to by one of the global industry leaders in financial modelling as one of the most tech savvy financial modellers. Lance qualified as a chartered accountant in South Africa & Australia, is an ex-Investment Banker, ex-CFO of a fintech start-up, currently Group CTO of SequelCFO, partner of the accounting & finance careers platform The Outperformer, as well as the Director of BGC Consultants.

Lance is currently based out of Melbourne, Australia although is a regular traveller working with clients and conducting data analytics visualisation and financial modelling training worldwide. He is also an approved trainer with the Financial Modeling Institute (FMI).

On the skills brought across from investment banking into finance partnering

Quite clearly it is financial modelling, that's the number one skill I relied on heavily to add value to my partnering relationships. I had to build 3-way models (Income Statement, Balance Sheet and Cashflow Statement) and I had to build them quickly and accurately. My models were being audited by an accounting firm, so I didn't have the luxury of using hardcoded numbers and copying and pasting at the last minute. It had to be built efficiently and the balance sheet had to balance. I spent a lot of long hours doing it. It does take a lot of time to build a good model but now I use technology for the models we build. These models are still built in Excel but are highly automated in the build and roll-forward process using add-ins.

On why it's important to get out of the model and build relationships

I'd say financial modelling was the first skill set that I leveraged, but then I had to take myself out of the model to go see clients and do deals. I think the communication and building relationships with customers was the next most important skill that I applied to partnering, because as an investment banker you have to service the client. The client is relying on that model to raise capital and to expand their business. The auditors want to know what's going on, my boss wanted to know, the Board wanted to know, so you had to sit in and communicate what was in the model to all these stakeholders and understand their specific perspectives and concerns.

The art of building relationships is a key skill as an investment banker, you must have it. If you look at any investment banker they're charismatic and confident types of people. They must be because that's exactly what they need to do in their jobs. So when I look at finance partnering, where communication and relationship building skills are critical. I was fortunate to have developed those skills in investment banking. As opposed to being an auditor, where you are looking at what happened, as an investment banker you're trying to talk about something that's less tangible because it's looking forward. So, when you're raising capital and doing forward-looking projections, there's a lot more that can go wrong in terms of a model and the set of assumptions in it. You must be great at storytelling and the communications relating to those somewhat intangible forward projections.

On the importance of resilience

A third skill I would say is resilience. The hours that I had to work were pretty insane at times, doing a 24-hour stint once I hope never to be repeated again. You build a huge amount of resilience working under such pressure. At Investec Bank, I regularly finished work at 2 or 3AM, but I was sitting there building models and because I'm so passionate about financial modelling it didn't feel like work. That's when I knew I had found my passion, the thing that drives me, because it didn't feel like work, when I was in investment banking.

On some baby steps to raise your financial modelling skills

I had a team of twenty-six at a major Australian Bank and I observed their month end process. Apart from it being painful, they also didn't enjoy it. There was a lot of copying and pasting, it wasn't automated, the systems weren't there, so what I wanted to do was to help and support them through financial modelling, training and automation. The first baby step is definitely having a look at some financial modelling training.

On the Financial Modelling Institute (FMI)

I'm an approved trainer for the FMI which is the Financial Modelling Institute. Right now, you have your CA, CPA, and CFA as your three main qualifications in accounting and finance that are broadly recognised globally. However, there is no single globally recognised accreditation that has the similar rigor of certification and qualification like those above for financial modelling except the FMI. There are three levels of accreditation the: Advanced Financial Modeler, which is the AFM; then you have the CFM, which is the Chartered Financial Modeler; and then the Master Financial Modeler (MFM). The FMI has not been around for long and was started by the guys who also started Model-Off, the world financial modelling championships.

Modeloff partnered with the Marquee group to deliver the FMI alongside an Advisory Board which includes some global players in Financial Modelling with the likes of PWC, KPMG and EY. I definitely recommend people have a look. It's a very practical exam, where you build a financial model from scratch. You are not allowed to bring your own laptop or do it remotely, you must do it in a formal examination centre or under supervision. Everyone works on a similar spec machine with no add-ins. You get given a set of assumptions and you have to build the 3-way financial model in 4 hours and you get marked not only on accuracy but on your presentation and structure of the model.

On getting out of your comfort zone and taking a growth mindset

I think the rest of the skills you develop are by simply getting out of your comfort zone, that's hard, you can't really learn that, so it can be tough. I was born in South Africa, moved to Australia and have lived in 3 cities. So I think throwing myself into challenges, grappling with it and being resilient is because I take a growth mindset with a lot of things. Being able to navigate through complexity is a skillset that is definitely something that people want to develop. The key thing though is you can't develop it unless you throw yourself at a challenge. It's a catch 22 so people want to build resilience but then they don't want to do that stuff that's difficult. So, you can't have your cake and eat it. If you want to build resilience you have to throw yourself into challenges.

I've thrown myself a huge challenge, after 20 years in corporate life I decided I'm going to start my own business, believe in myself to try and drive some value for people out there and down the track if I do that well and create value for myself then it's worth doing. But ultimately, I think throwing yourself at things that you are not quite sure how it's going to turn out is part of that journey.

On the five building blocks to be a successful Financial Modeller

Financial modelling is not just knowing how to use Excel very well and I think this is the thing that confuses a lot of people. Financial modelling has key five skills.

1. Financial modelling absolutely requires great Excel skills. You need to know how to use Excel better. You need to understand the functions. More importantly you need to understand the formulas and how to construct a 3-way model and understand how the financial statements in the model interrelate to each other.
2. The next part is accounting and finance, you cannot build a 3-way model if you can't build a balance sheet that balances. So understanding accounting and finance is critical.
3. The third aspect is business acumen or commercial insight. Ultimately when you build a model it needs to reflect the core business drivers, and the value chains in that business.
4. The next critical skill is problem solving. You can have the previous skills but if you don't know how to solve problems like mathematical and business problems, then it's going to be difficult for you to build the model logic to calculate the right result. Often in building a model you'll have a problem that nobody saw coming. You often don't know in advance the

necessary logic of how to solve that problem, so you have to rely on a degree of mental flexibility. You can test a possible solution and be agile in refining it until you find the optimal outcome. This is often the biggest challenge.

5. The fifth one is technology. If we sit here today and say that Excel on its own (with no add-ins or other connected tech) is going to help us solve all our problems, then I think that's probably wrong. There are other tools and technologies that you need to embrace in addition to vanilla Excel. I'm an absolute lover of Excel but there are other tools that sit inside and outside of Excel that can help you do your job better. Think of it as the other flavours and different cones at the gelato bar.

On why Excel is not dead despite what some parties are saying

Excel is not dead by any stretch, no matter what anyone else says or what all the marketing and technology firms are saying. An investment bank is not going to build a financial model for project and corporate finance or mergers and acquisitions without anything else other than Excel. Major corporate deals are still being concluded and negotiated for companies on the New York Stock Exchange, London Stock Exchange, Australian Stock Exchange and Johannesburg Stock Exchange, based on Excel spreadsheets. So, anyone that says Excel spreadsheets are gone, is simply deluded. Anyone who says Excel is dead or thinks it is going to die, simply doesn't know how to use it properly and is unaware of how powerful it really is as a software application. ERPs do not replace all Excel spreadsheets they often result in more Excel spreadsheets being created.

On the best bit of advice Lance ever received

My father gave me one piece of advice, he said don't be afraid to try anything even just once. Ultimately, I have applied that in everything that I do. People will say certain things about what you are doing and that it won't work, but you have to try even if other people have failed it. Sometimes if it's really something that you want to do and you've failed the first time, then maybe you have to try harder. So, the first part of his advice was give it a try and see if it's something you enjoy and are good at. If you try you never know but don't just try the first time if it is something you are really passionate about. You have to try again, you're not always going to get it the first time.

With regards to financial modelling skills, when I built my first model, it was it was really hard. I had to constantly go at it time and time again. Fortunately, that was my job and I enjoyed every moment of that struggle. As an investment bank was paying me a salary to build a 3-way model I had the time to develop this skill. That's the challenge for finance professionals today. No one is going to give you weeks on end to go build a model because you've got a whole load of other things to do as part of your finance role.

Recommended Resources

Book: *Mindset – Updated Edition: Changing The Way You think To Fulfil Your Potential (2017)*, by Dr Carol Dweck (link)

Article: The 5 competencies of good Financial Modelling (link)

Video: Developing a growth mindset with Dr Carol Dweck (link)

Website: Financial Modelling Institute (link)

Website: Model Citizn (link)

Website: The Outperformer (link)

"If you shift the thinking from cost to value then everyone's instinctive behaviour towards value is to maximise value. So if we shift accountants from merely doing stuff which is cost-focussed to adding value, then there is no ends to what people will want to use us for."

Dr. Noel Tagoe
LI: noel-tagoe

Tags:

#transformation #value #open-minded #connectivity #disengagement #risk avoidance #failure #communities

DR. NOEL TAGOE is a Professor of Accounting and Management Practice at Nottingham University Business School. He is also the Chief Executive of Noel Tagoe & Company, a start-up firm that provides advisory, research and training services in Finance, Education, Strategy and Technology. Until recently he was the Executive Vice President, Research & Curricula at AICPA-CIMA, the merged operations of the American Institute of Certified Public Accountants (AICPA) and the Chartered Institute of Management Accountants (CIMA).

Noel has advised leading global companies such as Shell, Rolls Royce, GE, Aviva, HSBC, UBS, Unilever and Verizon in the areas of finance transformation, finance talent strategy, digital strategy and managing disruption. Noel held accounting and strategy positions at BP and Elf Aquitaine (now Total Oil), led the financial advisory services unit of KPMG Ghana and taught at leading business schools such as the Michael Smurfit Graduate School of Business (University College Dublin), Manchester Business School (University of Manchester) and Said Business School (University of Oxford). He is a much sought-after conference speaker and executive trainer and has led training programmes in Africa, Asia, Australia, Europe and North America.

Noel was educated at the University of Ghana (undergraduate) and the Universities of Dundee and Oxford (postgraduate). He is also a fellow of CIMA.

On how to make accounting more valuable and relevant to your organisation

If you look at it the accounting function is evaluated more on efficiency and cost, for example, look at the benchmarks that Hackett and CEB produce. If you think about it anytime you mention cost, your strategic and instinctive behaviour towards cost is to reduce cost. So if accountants are regarded as cost the strategic behaviour towards us is to reduce what we do. On the other hand, if you shift the thinking from cost to value then everyone's strategic behaviour and instinctive behaviour towards value is to maximise value. So, if we shift accountants from merely doing stuff which is cost to adding value, then there is no ends to what people will want to use us for.

On how to deliver value

Value is value to somebody; it is not what is value to you. So the first thing you've got to identify is who am I relating to, and to whom am I giving something. That's the first thing, identify who you are creating the value for. The second thing is you find out what is of value to the person, and more directly, ask the people. And once you've done that then engage with them on how to provide that value to those people. Sometimes you have the skills to do that and sometimes you don't. I believe that 95% of the things that are required of us we can do because we either we have the skills currently and if not we can acquire the skills in the course of that time, or we can plug into a network of people who already have the skills and so it will help us to do that.

On an open mind and why it's better than an empty mind

We have to come with an open mind, and by an open mind I don't mean an empty mind. An empty mind is dangerous. What an open mind does is that it takes some things out and it receives some new things. This is what we call in educational language, life-long learning. So you unlearn some of those things when they are less relevant and then you can then learn new things.

On the compounding power of improving just 1% a day

Accountants are very numerically and quantitatively minded so let's do a bit of an experiment. If you decide as an accountant to improve yourself just 1% a day consistently, at the end of the year you'd have improved yourself 3,780%. That is 37 times over. It is consistent discipline, just baby steps, I'll improve myself just 1% today, not 10% today, or 100% today, just 1% and that is doable.

On what to do if we encounter failure

Most people believe that failure and success are not related, they see it as a junction, success goes to the right, failure goes to the left, that is not the case. If you remember Churchill, *"Success is not final, failure is not fatal, what is important is the courage to continue."* So doing an analysis of failure, which enables you to fail fast is the best risk management tool that I have. I don't mind how many times I fail, but I know that the one time I hit the bullseye on the dartboard it will be good. I also don't call it a failure it's just a milestone on my journey to success.

On why being in communities benefits learning

I'd advise people to also get into a community and talk with other kinds of people because that's where learning happens. Learning can never be private, it can be personal, but not private. So I have three communities that intersect. One of them is called a community of *'moaners,'* we moan about every time there is a problem, they are good because they raise the problems. They are saying to you, *"there's a problem here, there's a problem there, and over there."* Without the community of moaners we can't move forward and I say that as an honorary president of that community. Then once you moan there's another community that intersects with the community of moaners, and they're the community of *'solution providers.'* You bring them a problem and they have that knack to solve a problem for you, so we need to tap into them. And then the third group are called the communities of *'practitioners'* where the solutions are now turned into practical things that people can do. As these three communities intersect, people raise the problems, people will solve the problems and problems are then moved into practice and if you are not plugged into any of those communities you find out that it is very difficult for you to improve what you're doing and bring forward any meaningful innovation and development to what you have.

On why connectivity is key

Connectivity is key, in fact now more than ever before individuals and organisations need to connect together and so the whole world of ecosystems has become quite exciting for me. The reason why is simple.

Things are changing too fast for just one person or one organisation to keep up with it. So you need to enter into partnerships, so different people do different things and that's how you can carefully select your ecosystem or the network that you have to help you navigate through these things. And the membership, the interactions and the rules in those networks would have to be dynamic to make sure that it helps you to navigate where you want to go.

On disengagement and why it exists

Often it is the fear of the unknown or the fear of the other. People don't know what is going to happen and the fear paralyses them and so they disengage. So disengagement if you like is a risk management tool, it's risk avoidance. Risk avoidance can help sometimes, it's useful to disengage, to refresh, to have a look at the situation but you cannot disengage completely. At Oxford University I did some work on the interface between theology, philosophy, economics and accounting. and one of the things I came across was what Saint Paul talked about, that in a body you have different parts interacting together. If one part of the body says it doesn't belong to the body, that doesn't make it not belong to the body, unless it cuts itself off, and if it cuts itself off it's likely to die. So sometimes you might be inactive, so the type of disengagement I think of is being inactive for a while, and then coming in. Because sometimes being inactive enables you to reflect, recharge and be of more use. We've got to engage, because the very survival of our organisations and us as human beings depends on that.

On the fundamental rule of NPV and accounting

The rule of accounting is balance, it is proportionality. People study NPV and think about the whole notion of what we do in the organisation. We say you invest something upfront and then you reap from it over a period of time and if you've invested wisely you reap more then you've invested and therefore you get a net present value out of that. And why can't we apply it to our lives, it's the same thing. I want to receive resources; I invest some resources into that upfront. How much of that is uncertain, that's okay, we all deal with uncertainty all the time and we can figure out how to move forward.

On the 6 As of success for accountants and finance professionals

There are 6 As of success. The first one is that you must have an *anchor* of some kind. If you don't have an anchor, you will drift back and forth.

For me an anchor is your purpose and the moral compass that you have. It is the very thing that defines who you are. So spend some time to think about what is it that makes *'me'* what I am? What is it that is my moral foundation? It is often not your work because if you lose your job it would destroy your foundation, so it is other things.

The second A is ***ambition***. I say to people to be completely ambitious and have big dreams. I'm not talking about plans, I'm talking about dreams. If you listen to Martin Luther King, in his address, *"I have a dream ..."* A dream inspires, I mean who do you inspire if you say, *"I have a plan!"* Nobody. Plans have a role in the fulfilment of dreams, but dream big. The third thing is that it must be matched by ***ability***, because otherwise it is just a dream, you will not achieve it. Often if you don't have the ability you might turn to an expert. So your ability is your ability today, the ability of your network, and your ability tomorrow. So you build a coalition of people to help you to realise the dream. Don't do it alone and don't over rely on what you know today.

The fourth A is ***awareness***. Be aware of who you are, self-awareness. My favourite philosopher Socrates said, an unexamined life is not worth living. So spend some time becoming more aware of yourself, but also spend time with others in situations. Because it is in situations with others combined with yourself that opportunities and risks arise. The fifth is your attitude. Someone said that ***attitude*** is a bit like a flat tyre, it will get you nowhere. You've got to have a good attitude. There are three Hs that define attitude. One is honesty, you've got to be brutally honest with yourself and with other people because it attracts good people to you. Once you know your weaknesses you can address them by hard-work. Hard-work never killed anyone and it can be exciting. The third H is your heart or your passion. If your heart is in it you will draw people to you. Passion is infectious and people will help you achieve your dreams. The last A is ***action***. Just do it! Some people are afraid of doing, so if you have to do, it means you have to plan. So that's where it comes in. if you start with planning first it limits your horizon, but planning helps you achieve a big dream and plan for the action.

On the meaning behind the man in the arena speech by Theodore Roosevelt

There was a speech given by Theodore Roosevelt in Paris, in 1930. The relevant passage is called the 'man in the arena.' The whole speech is about twelve pages and it is about the role of a citizen in a republic. He said, he doesn't care about critics who aren't doing anything, but the man who he respects is a man who gets his hands dirty, who does things, who knows sweat and toil and enjoys success in that. But if he fails and knows that he has laid it all out there, then he has no regrets about what has happened. What I say to people in pursuit of their dreams is, just do it!

On the best bits of advice Noel has ever received

The one that sticks with me is, do not accept things as they are, always seek to change. We all have a heritage, but we have to leave a legacy. The legacy you leave becomes somebody's heritage. Now if your heritage is the same as your legacy you've made no improvement, so what is the use of what you've been doing. Instead take your heritage, there will be some things that aren't relevant to your circumstances, so drop them, or improve upon them, so they become more valuable to somebody. Develop it and then it becomes a legacy to somebody else.

The second one that I received, is for a long while I didn't want any restraint and control, I just wanted to run wild. Then an automotive engineer from Detroit said to me, you need to find a balance between some form of control over your life and innovation. He said if you take a car, the accelerator is freedom and the brake is constraint. Then he asked me this question, *"Which car would you drive fast? A car without a brake or a car with a brake?"* And I said, *"Of course I would drive a car with a brake very fast. Because I know if anything happened the brake would stop it. If the car had no brake I would not drive very fast at all."* That's exactly the purpose of a brake in a car is to liberate you, to enable you to drive as fast as you want because you know if you need a brake it is there. The purpose of control systems is to unleash innovation within you. Without controls your innovations would end up nowhere, they would go in every direction, so it has to be channelled.

Recommended Resources
Website: AICPA-CIMA (link)

"If you offer value, and offer that to the community, somebody is definitely going to get in touch and then you also develop your relationship in the long run."

Peter Chisambara
LI: peterchisambara
WS: erpminsights.com

Tags:
#business partnering #cognitive computing #practice #audit #networking #LinkedIn #leadership

PETER CHISAMBARA is an enterprise performance management specialist and the founder of ERPM Insights. He has more than a decade long experience of partnering with business leaders and their teams, helping them implement strategy more effectively, make informed risk decisions and improve enterprise & strategic performance. Peter is passionate about the integration of strategy, risk and performance functions of the organization to drive more effective decision-making. A regular article writer, he has written some thought provoking and original articles on finance transformation, data and analytics, and the potential of cognitive computing to help provide real time insights, among other topics. Peter has also written articles for the Journal of Business Forecasting. In 2018, he was nominated and appeared on two separate lists as one of the Top Finance Leaders to follow.

Peter holds ACMA & CPA designations and is currently based out of Toronto, Canada.

On the main differences Peter experienced between practice and industry
When I was in practice the main focus was making sure that the numbers were correct. It was more a regulatory focus, we have to make sure that we're presenting in-line with the accounting standards. But when I went into industry then you are now trying to interpret the meaning of those numbers, instead of just saying that we accumulated so much in profit. We are asking questions like, what are the drivers behind that profitability? What are the drivers behind our revenues? Where are we going?

Where can we improve? I was also then introduced to the concept of budgeting, forecasting, and instead of having a fixed mind-set that we're only looking for the next 12 months, we start looking beyond the next 12 months.

On how he managed the transition from audit practice to industry

I thought coming from practice what qualities can I bring into industry? Of course, there is the soft skills that are transferable, however if I'm in industry and say I wanted to improve my communication skills, one way is not to sit at my desk. Instead get up and go and talk to your business partners, find out what are their troubles, ask what do they expect from finance? By doing that you're also developing your leadership and partnership skills.

On why LinkedIn is a great place to build relationships

For me relationship skills are important. If you can manage relationships with your prospective clients and deliver value for them then they are going to say it to the next person and the chain continues. At the same time if I want to build relationships, why not do that on LinkedIn, the platform where there are other professionals. If you offer value, and offer that to the community, somebody is definitely going to get in touch and then you also develop your relationship in the long run.

On why quality of connections matters more than the volume of them

When I joined LinkedIn I wanted to develop relationships with key people who I knew were going to be helpful. My strategy is not to have many thousands and millions of followers. I wanted to have a direct relationship for a start. Who knows if the growth will be that massive but always know what you want to expect out of that social media platform? What are you there for? Are you there to engage with people or are you there to spread the noise? And once you're on that platform always look for people with whom you share an interest. When I started for me, because I'm an accounting and finance professional, I wanted to connect with more people who are also in accounting and finance, so I get to learn from them. I don't believe that I'm an expert in everything that I know, so I wanted to learn from them. And then as you progress they're going to refer you to their second connections and you build your network in that way.

On why rotation of experiences is key to developing

Experience is the best teacher in life and I believe the more you embrace yourself, or the more you engage yourself in these other opportunities, you are going to realise at some stage what is it that I love most to do and what is it that I am skilled to do and once you've pinpointed that area, where you're skilled to do it and you're passionate about it, then you are going to grab it and develop around it and work on it and become an expert in that area. So rotation is key.

On the relevance of Good to Great principles for finance professionals

Sometimes we can be comfortable with where we are but being comfortable with where we are is not what we want as finance professionals. There is a saying that finance is always the last to embrace new technology, new systems or new processes. We have to aspire to be greater. And although *Good to Great* (see recommended resources) looks at large companies that have shifted from good to great, I think it also helps at a personal level, in the sense that the principles are applicable. For example it talks about leadership, and what great leadership and discipline looks like.

Great leaders ask questions, they do not have all the answers. I think in this world of big data, of digital transformation, the best professional finance & accounting professionals and best organisations are not going to be the ones that have got all the answers, but are going to be the ones who have inquisitive minds, who are curious about the future, who are always going to be asking questions. What can we do to improve? Where are we going? What are the emerging trends? What are the emerging risks? How can we best prepare for them? What are the emerging technologies? What does the future for finance look like? Answering all those questions would be very helpful for accounting professionals to move from good to great.

On why it's important to continue your professional development

One thing I love about these technologies is that they can augment the human, but we still need that creative thinking. I don't think we're at the stage where these machines can do this creative thinking or have the human and emotional intelligence, the empathy that is provided by humans. So I would say for the next 12 months to accountants and finance professionals, embrace the change in all its forms. Do not be afraid. I know change can be very difficult for everyone but embrace the change. Also focus on professional development. One way I try to help myself to make sure that I remain relevant is that I listen to webinars, I attend workshops, I read white papers, I read books. These events and resources are really enlightening because I get to know the new technologies. I also get to meet and hear from other finance professionals and they share their stories with you. Be focused on your personal development. Don't say that because you qualified, two, three or four years ago, that's it, I'm done. To continue with professional development doesn't mean that you have to go back to school to get another degree, to get another certificate. I love what Warren Buffet says that he spends each day reading. On a typical day he reads about 500 pages and for me that is a useful skill that you can master. You might not be able to read 500 pages a day but maybe start with 2 pages or 3 pages. You learn something, you apply it. Accumulate knowledge and apply it. That's the way you add value.

On the advice Peter would give to his younger self

I would actually advise myself never to be afraid of failure. Never to be afraid to go after an opportunity once it presents itself. These days in your professional career journey I think it's not as linear as we want it to be. It's no longer a straight line where you say that my career starts as an accounts assistant, then the next three years I become a financial accountant, and then three years after I become a management accountant or financial controller and then become CFO of the company. I think in a way with how technology is changing, it's no longer enough to have just technical knowledge. Of course this is very important but you also need to know to borrow from other things. So if you are never afraid you are going to be able to know any opportunity your corporation presents to you to go and get experience in another line of business be it marketing, be it sales, I'd say grab that opportunity with both hands. Unfortunately for me I never got that opportunity to work in another function. I've always worked in finance, but I believe that if I worked in another function such as, marketing, sales, operations or business development, I would be a better finance professional than I'm currently today.

Recommended Resources
Book: *Good To Great (2001),* by Jim Collins (link)

Book: *What Got You Here Won't Get You There: How Successful People Become Even More Successful (2012),* by Marshall Goldsmith (link)

Book: *Prediction Machines: The Simple Economics of Artificial Intelligence (2018),* by Ajay Agrawal (link)

Book: *Human + Machine: Reimagining Work in the Age of AI (2018),* by Paul R. Daugherty and H. James Wilson (link)

Book: *Behind Every Good Decision: How Anyone Can Use Business Analytics to Turn Data into Profitable Insight (2014),* by Piyanka Jain (link)

Magazine: *CIMA Financial Management* (link)

"The greatest gift you can give yourself is really to understand yourself better. When you understand yourself better you become your own biggest supporter, then other people become your biggest supporter."

Talita Ferreira
LI: talitaferreiraacs
WS: authenticityresolved.com

Tags:
#purpose #CFO #transformation #culture #authenticity #change #progression #confrontation #vulnerability #HR

TALITA FERREIRA is the founder and CEO of Authentic Change Solutions which is a Management Consultancy centred on a philosophy of Authenticity and Authentic Change.

Previously Talita began her career at KPMG in South Africa where she qualified as a charted accountant and then moved into Commerce & Industry at Investec before going onto C-suite roles leading Finance and HR teams at BMW in roles in Germany and the UK. An international speaker and author (book in the resources section) Talita still mentors CFOs, CEOs and other leaders. She was also previously a finalist for The South African Chamber of Commerce - Business Leader of the Year 2016 and Rising Star award 2018.

On overcoming a career glass-celling
After joining the role at BMW with a wide-ranging accounting role, I found out that I would reach the glass ceiling there very quickly in South Africa. At that time, I was around about 30, and I always wanted to be a CFO by 30. So I was a little bit behind on my plan, and I also knew that I needed to go to Munich, the heartbeat of the company. BMW is all about having networks in Munich and understanding Munich, and because I'd been in financial services, I then decided to go to BMW

Financial Services in Munich, into their headquarters. I learned German, which is probably the hardest thing I did, I couldn't read even a children's book without a dictionary but was able to master that. Then after three years, I was allowed to enter the CFO world of BMW. I was sent to the UK as the CFO of BMW Financial Services. That started quite a change in my outlook and is one of the most purposeful parts of my career. I was also responsible for Human Resources as a board director; which brought lots of different challenges. I started to see that I enjoyed driving transformational change as well. During that period, we had 3 CEOs, and so I was the one who provided the stability, you could say. We went through the economic crisis, and it was vital to bring more inspirational leadership to the company. I then got promoted again into the CFO of the automotive company in the UK. That position was in the Top 300 leadership group of BMW, which one calls OFK's, and strategy now joined my remit. I was still responsible as CFO and HR board director, but then I also started leading a massive transformational cultural program. This involved bringing two of the companies that I'd worked onto one site and changing their underlying culture. I felt that that's what I was destined to do.

On when Talita uncovered her purpose to leave the big corporate environment

When reaching the Top 300, you have to have a very extensive network within the Company. I had done it, but when I got into the group, I questioned why I worked so hard for more than ten years to be in there. I wondered what was so inspirational about the group, and that was the moment when I then knew that it wasn't my purpose. I then spent the next two years finding what my purpose was while I was doing this transformation project on top of the day job. I realised there was quite a lot of things that I liked and that I enjoyed transforming organisations and helping leaders to grow beyond what they thought they could do themselves. I ended up leaving BMW facing my biggest fear of leaving the large corporate environment after 22 years of safety and setting up my own business to help companies transform culturally and help individual leaders transform.

On an approach on how to deal with confrontations

Whenever you're faced with a confrontation, try and understand where the other person is coming from. Where that person is coming from usually is some place based on their values and it's the same for me. A lot of times when I felt like I was being triggered by someone in the office, it was either a values issue or a limiting belief issue. The greatest gift we can give ourselves is to focus more on knowing ourselves before we go into any of these situations. The moment you understand yourself better, you can relax more, and then you can interact with people from a place where you can go towards them. Otherwise, it's sometimes driven by competitiveness or controlling situations, and you don't want to look bad or look like you don't have the answers, so it becomes very combative. Everyone has meetings or instances where you're walking away from it, and you're not feeling great about the interaction, then there's something to look at and something to try to amend or change about it. I think it starts with ourselves because we can't control other people, so it has to start with ourselves.

On why the route to HR is important to Finance

To make effective changes in our organisations, I think the route to HR is significant, but it doesn't need to mean leading HR necessarily. It could be partnering with HR more effectively. If you're looking at the typical back office, it's typically what finance and HR do. If you're getting that back-office more aligned and aligned in not only servicing and becoming business enablers to the business but also in helping to develop great leaders, then you have got a perfect situation in your back office. You can then drive the organisation by partnering with operations in the front-end or marketing or sales. You are then creating a powerful, cohesive team that can help inform the culture of the organisation. In the end, from what I've seen, organisations are about three things, they are about strategy, purpose, and people.

On a model we can all follow to become more Authentic Leaders

The greatest gift you can give yourself is to really understand yourself better. When you understand yourself better, you become your own biggest supporter, and then other people become your biggest supporter. I think that starts with this awareness piece. The model has two parts, on the left side, it's really about your awareness or your consciousness, and under there it's things like understanding how you feel about change. So for instance, what would your purpose be in that change? What are the behaviours that you need to role model? I like to look at it through the lens of change because we all need to drive change in our lives or the business. Then the other side the connectedness to other people, and in this connectedness, to other people, it's around understanding what our fears are. So in a change process, it's about understanding if there are underlying fears that people are not speaking about? How can we bring those out to get more supporters for the change? To understand more where other people are coming from, having empathy, not being afraid to show vulnerability in our leadership. Because sometimes we don't have all the answers and so having this greater consciousness or awareness as well as this connectedness and purpose-driven collaboration will give us power. POWER is an acronym. So the 'P' is *presence*, because when you understand yourself better, you are much more confident. The 'O' is for *overcoming fears* because we understand those limiting fears come from thinking that you might be caught out or that people might not know that you don't have all the answers. The 'W' is being more *whole* because you're not just working with your mind but you also engaging that empathy, the heart a bit more. The 'E' is for *effortless flow*. I think we spend two-thirds of our lives statistically at work, and if you're regulating who you are in the work environment and not bringing most of who you are into that environment that's pretty sad. The key is this effortless flow. If you understand more about who you are, then you can bring more of yourself into that environment. The last letter 'R' is for *resonance* with yourself, with who you are, with other people because you're connecting from this different place where it's not just based in fear, but it's more based in collaboration, sharing your vulnerabilities and respecting people at a deeper level. It's resonance with yourself, with others and with your core purpose.

On a top tip on how to deal with Fear and Vulnerability in Finance

That's the main thing about looking at yourself first and seeing what those things are that you are mainly afraid of. For me, it was leaving corporate life, and I know that. So whenever I'm now in this new career that I've created for myself, and some of those original fears come out then I'm just thinking, *"Okay, that's just a fear, that's not totally real. Of course, it feels very real but let's just move beyond that and engage a little bit more the analytical mind."* Because that helps when we're dealing with fear. But first, we have to feel those emotions and know that they are there for us to move past them. Once you understand where you're vulnerable, then it becomes easier to share that part. Because if we're not aware of it then what it triggers is more of that ego-based behaviour where you try and hide it and limit your exposure, and that's not really the place if you want to create connected relationships.

On the best bit of advice, Talita has ever received

The first German boss that I had said, *"Set up your own vision of where you want to go."* I think at the time we were talking about other people complaining consistently, and his advice was, just set your own vision of where you want to go and then take steps to get there. Put your head down and do the work, and that's kind of always what I've done. I have set my vision of what it is that I want to achieve. Early days it was that CFO position and then it was CFO of a national sales company, reaching that Top 300. It's always served me very well to go for a goal in mind and quite an audacious goal. Then move towards it, and the pieces fall in place on the way there.

Recommended Resources

Book: *The Authenticity Dilemma Resolved: Unleashing your passion and purpose to live more authentically (2016)*, by Talita Ferreira (link)

Book: *The Management Shift: How to Harness the Power of People and Transform Your Organisation For Sustainable Success (2014)*, by Vlatka Hlupic (link)

Book: *The Expansion Game: A powerful method to transform your fear into brilliance (2017)*, by Gosia Gorna (link)

Website: Authenticity Resolved (link)

AMERICAS

"I think we all need to take a step back and look at lean in its purest form which is customer and revenue focused."

Andrea Jones
LI: andreajones
WS: andreajonesconsulting.com

Tags:
#operations #lean #revenue #customer-oriented #value #six sigma

ANDREA JONES is VP Business Operations at Crosby Hop Farm, a leading grower, merchant, and processor of pelletised hops to the craft brewing industry. Andrea is also founder of Andrea Jones Consulting (AJC) whose staff are experienced professionals with expertise in Project Management and Process Improvement to help companies increase revenue.

Andrea holds an MBA from MIT Sloan Business School as well as an MSc in Chemistry. Andrea is based out of Portland, Oregon, USA

On the important distinction behind what lean really means

I think lean has become what I would describe as a 4-letter word for cost reductions in many organisations. As soon as the floor hears that you're going lean they're all worried that their jobs are going to get cut and that really decreases morale and motivation. If you look back to the original definition of lean from Womack and Jones, back in the 1980s, it was really focused on the customer. It was how do you provide the value that the customer is willing to pay for with the minimum amount of what they would call waste in the system. But again, it focuses on what the customer wants and what the customer is willing to pay for and that is really revenue based. So I think we all need to take a step back and look at lean in its purest form which is customer and revenue focused.

On steps we can take to put the customer (and value) first

Here's an example that I'm actually living through right now. At Crosby Hop Farm we are putting in an online customer portal. We want to be able to allow our customers to go online and purchase hops from us. We already do what we call spot market which is like an off-the-shelf market. Most of our customers have contracts with us and so they've contacted for a certain amount of product every year for the next couple of years. Right now, if they order from us they have to either call us or email us and it goes through this back-and-forth over email or phone on the backend with our customer service team. So we want to put forward a portal on the Internet so they can place those orders and see their positions online. I'm having an interesting discussion between the sales director and the controller right now as to what is more important. Is it a customer focus in making the user experience super smooth? Or, is it automating all of our backend fulfilment and in effect we don't necessarily worry about what the customer wants?

I do think that both of those are valid points, but the controller is saying *"We need to cut costs because if we can get this order fulfilment completely automated then we don't have to have as many people on the backend doing it."* However the sales guy is like, *"I don't really care about that and neither does the customer."* So I do believe that there is a good marriage there and we're really working on articulating when do we focus only on the customer and what the customer sees. Then you know the customer probably is not willing to pay for some of that backend back-and-forth that we currently do, so there is a great opportunity to cut costs but also to optimise our flow and standardise our flow in the backend as well. The finance professional is really approaching it from the ROI only, whereas the sales professional is approaching it from the customers' standpoint. I'm trying to navigate both of those things and also articulate what's both best for the customer, which will generate revenue for the company, and try to maybe save some of the redundant work or the rework in the backend without saying, *"Oh but we're going to have to cut all these people."* If I go to the customer service team and I'm saying to them we're going to automate everything you do and you're going to be out of a job in a year. Well how likely are they going to want to help with this project?

On how Finance can better support operations

I feel like there is such a partnership that may not be as fully utilised as it could be. So just the other day we are working on our budget cycle for this fiscal year and our main produce is hops. They're a product that needs to be processed relatively quickly because they are light sensitive, heat sensitive, moisture sensitive and when you pick them off the vine they really need to get put into this pellet format which is what we sell to 95% of brewers. We put them in an oxygen depleted environment and into mylar bags so they don't see the light. We then stick them in 28 degrees Fahrenheit cold storage so that they're frozen. We need to do that within about 6 months of picking them.

I was talking to our accounting manager the other day about how we were going to run the seasonal shift in the mill which is the production facility for these hops and saying, *"Hey you know instead of running my two crews for two eight-hour shifts, five days a week. I could run two, ten-hour shifts five days a week to get done much faster, about 20% faster and that would finish out this production season earlier than we originally anticipated. However, it would cost me overtime of course to do that so how would that affect the budget and the overall picture?"* He told me that anytime you can get done with the production earlier, that's a positive variance to the budget because of how we account for labor into our inventory COGS. But he told me if we use overtime to be the driver of that, that will eat up all of our positive variance. I thought, gosh! That's a very good piece of information for me to have because it doesn't actually affect the quality, just that 20% I could go 20% longer this season and still have the same quality of our product, but knowing that if I pulled it in, it doesn't actually help the budget if I'm using overtime to do it even though I maybe letting the seasonal workers go a bit earlier. I felt like that was something I'm really glad he told me if I hadn't brought that up to him he probably wouldn't have told me that. So I'd love to see finance professionals be a little more proactive and if they understand what's happening in operations, how operations is being run, what manpower and equipment in capacity and utilisation is being used to drive that production then they can make more informed recommendations to that team.

On where Finance could look first to better understand Ops

A few years ago when I was working with the clients on their strategic plan and I asked a whole bunch of questions around their metrics, around their numbers, around their cash flow, around their inventory turns and their capacity and their utilisation on the floor. I started gathering that information with their controller and she actually didn't know how to calculate inventory turns or what their capacity or utilisation was on the floor. So again to the point of seek first to understand, let's try to gather that data. And the operations manager he knew all those numbers, but it was interesting to me that this information was not being discussed with the accounting professional who's helping workout the budget, and trying to determine whether the company can sustain increased sales and growth without adding capital expense. So we worked on those things together and everybody was happier because of seeking first to understand each other's areas and then making those recommendations.

On the best bit of advice Andrea has ever received

When I was at Sloan I don't remember which professor and why it had not dawned on me to think this way before maybe because I was an engineer, it's that the language of business is money. And if you can't speak conversantly with that language you're not going to be able to move up in an organisation. Maybe it sounds super basic and yeah I was in my 20s at the time so I hadn't thought of it before but that was a very good piece of advice and I think especially in Ops people don't recognise that they need to speak the language of money. And maybe in finance people don't recognise that others don't quite know that language super well. So how can we bridge that gap and that was a really great piece of advice for me that I've taken with me.

Recommended Resources

Book: *Your Brain at Work: Strategies for Overcoming Distraction, Regaining Focus, and Working Smarter All Day Long* (2013), by David Rock (link)

Book: *The Audacious Finance Partner: Reveals The Key Factors and Skills for Business Partnering Success*, by Andrew Codd (link)

Website: CFO University (link)

"Be clear about what it is you want and what you're looking for. It shouldn't be a secret. The more people who know about your goals & aspirations, the more likely you'll be top of mind when there is an opportunity."

Angela Ho
LI: angela-ho-cpa-cgma

Tags:
#audit #public accounting #servicing clients #relationships #goals #top-line #progression #awareness

ANGELA HO is senior vice president and principal accounting officer at OceanFirst Bank. Angela is a successful up and coming female accounting & finance executive within the financial services industry. Angela's career started with a number of public accounting internships before joining KPMG where she provided audit services to global financial services clients.

Angela holds CPA and CGMA designations, an MBA from the Wharton School of the University of Pennsylvania and is based out of New Jersey, USA.

On how to be put forward to high profile assignments
I worked extremely well with the client, I realised that we were in a client service industry, so whilst it is important for us to get the audit done it was just as important, if not more important, to ensure that our clients were happy and not frustrated in dealing with us. I was somehow able to strike this balance of being quite demanding of client deliverables and yet I was quickly recognised to be the person, basically the gopher, if senior people needed something from a particular person, they would send me to go and request it. Sure enough, within hours, we would probably have whatever it was that we were asking for. A lot can be said about relationships and building those relationships. I was quite

fortunate to have invested in my client relationships early on in my career. This is probably atypical of perhaps other's experiences within public accounting in that, I was on the HSBC account from basically my internship until my last days at KPMG.

On an appropriate mindset to take to display confidence in your role

Thinking back to my earlier years in my career I was probably less shy or less impacted by people's titles or position in the hierarchy. I treated everyone as an individual and if I was special enough or if I was important enough to be in the same room as anyone else, I would treat them as an equal. I was confident to be in my role, I think confidence is key especially early on in one's career.

On the importance of taking time to build relationships

So yes business is important and going through the agenda is important, but just as important is getting to know what drives the individual. Is it really their work and their professional career or is it their personal lives or their hobbies? Maybe you're required to work 40% of your time whilst you're awake and during the other 60% of that time maybe you're training for a triathlon or trying to become a celebrity chef or whatever that person's passion may be. And that may drive up some very interesting conversations especially if you have things in common and before you know it maybe you've made a very good friend and maybe someone to share those extracurricular activities with. Just spending time building those relationships is worth it because you never know what might come down the path later on. Not necessarily in their current role, they may start doing something else that's really neat in a field that you might be interested in, and if you're still playing golf together, if you're still doing triathlons together, or if you're cooking together, taking photos or whatever, you maybe their next person to call.

On the importance of remaining chameleon-like to the environment

It's important for us to change with the environment in a chameleon-like way, to change our roles as well in being adaptive to our environment. There's disruption in the finance and accounting industry and how do we prevent ourselves from being eliminated in the equation? Yes, there's robots, machine learning, and all of that. There are efficiencies to be gained, which is always a hot topic for finance and accounting professionals, like being efficient and accurate, but there still needs to be the human component, so it's back to those relationships again. But also providing the analysis helping our revenue drivers to make good business decisions.

On the required mindset shift to contribute more to the top-line

If we are working in a growth mode then the way to grow is not by cutting costs, costs have to be maintained, but the way you are going to grow your business is by increasing revenues. To be a part of that decision making is so critical and very important, especially in any company that wants to improve itself. I would imagine that if you're in business today that's probably a point of focus of yours. It's an empowering mindset to shed the mentality of always being a cost centre and not contributing to the top line. But guess what, we can! If you have really good AI or any kind of technology to help analyse that set of data then we'll be able to arrive at a solution even faster. So there's no reason why we should be afraid of technology or machine learning. We should embrace it so we can become better at our jobs and be a partner in driving revenue.

On guidance for young female executives wishing to progress their careers

There is merit to being hard working, I mean we do have to show that first, being hardworking and being committed to your career. Maybe my path is not similar to all female accounting and finance professionals, but treating yourself as an equal to male, speaking just as loudly, if not louder than the men inside or outside your organisation knowing that you do bring value to the conversation. There are so many articles out there talking about companies with more females on their Board have higher stock returns and how there is a real shortfall of female board members. There is an awareness in the marketplace of, if you want to call it, this issue of shortfalls. So the opportunity is ours to seize and if this is a goal of yours, make it known.

On why it's important to be clear about and share your goals with others

Tell as many people as you can that, *"Hey look, I do want to serve on the Board,"* whether it's a non-profit or for-profit board member. Be clear about what it is you want and what you're looking for. It shouldn't be a secret. The more people who know about your goals & aspirations, the more likely you'll be top of mind when there is an opportunity. So build your brand and really put it out there.

On the best bit of advice Angela has ever received

While my work and career is important to me, I think what I've recently realised is just with spending some time self-reflecting, time outside the office is just as important if not more important. If you're not healthy, mentally or physically, then you cannot be your best-self in the office. It's so important to recharge. I really found it quite helpful to truly separate my time outside the office and my time in the office. Sure there are times when there needs to be some overlap but if you are being fully rejuvenated and recharged when you're not at work, then overall you'll be a better performer when you are in the office. It depends on what works for you. To be unplugged when I'm not here, it really helps me perform at a much higher level when I am sitting at my desk. My personal relationships, friendships, family, a level of a physical health and mental health, are very important to me and when those things start to slide so does my performance at work. I'm not necessarily talking about living a balanced life, because it's not possible to live a balanced life. I think whatever is important to you at a particular point in time. It's really being self-aware and knowing what's critical to you. So if you or someone in your family is sick and more time needs to be devoted there, make that known to your employer, your boss and to your team. People love to help, and people are good human beings, and if that's what you need, people will support you. There are times when that will shift. Someone else on your team may need additional support and I'm sure that you will rise to the occasion if that were to happen.

Recommended Resources

Book: *The First 90 Days, Updated and Expanded: Proven Strategies for Getting Up to Speed Faster and Smarter (2013),* by Michael Watkins (link)

Documentary: *Planet Earth: The Complete Collection: (2006),* starring David Attenborough (link)

"It's important to get other people involved, we can't work in a silo, you might miss something if you do."

Ben Wann
LI: ben-wann-cma-mba-cpa
WS: the-numbers-guys.com

Tags:
#business partnering #lean six sigma #job hopping

BEN WANN is an operational controller at Groupe Savencia, and was recently nominated as a finance professional to watch out for in 2019. He is passionate about finding dynamic solutions to complex problems and Ben just can't stop learning and what's even better he wants to pass his learnings on to you. Ben has created a course on Udemy.com called "Master Business Process Improvement AND Process Mapping" and he frequently shares his point of view in posts on LinkedIn. He also asks the tough questions on where finance and accounting are heading to his network encouraging all of you to learn together with him.

Ben also holds CPA and CMA designations, as well as an MBA from West Chester University of Pennsylvania. He is based out of Cochranville Pennsylvania, USA.

On the hard lessons Ben experienced on corporate politics and leadership not following through on commitments
I learned first-hand about corporate politics. Going into the plant I talked to management about what I wanted to do, they said great, and I got to work. But as we continued to roll this project out some of the plant accountants said, *"Ben you're not telling me what to do, I'm not changing."* That kind of unsettled me, we ran into an obstacle and I went to plant management and to say. *"Okay, can you help me work through this?"* and there's just nothing back, it was sort of, sort it out yourself, which is kind of disheartening not getting leadership support as they didn't wish to create conflict for themselves. So I'm sitting there with a dead project with only half the plants having implemented the improvements.

On how we can practically become that business partner they are looking for

At Savencia, the CFO, who's my boss said to me he hired me for my mindset and I love that. He sees someone who challenges the status quo. They want that person in the room with them, so I'm there, I'm hired to challenge things, improve things, and to do a lot of business partnering. If I could write my own role that's what it would be so I'm really enjoying my time, it's an adventure right now.

On the advantages and benefits of job-hopping in the right culture

I think job hopping is a very good way to earn a ton of experience in a short amount of time to me. I think of it as a consultant without the travel aspect. I've gone to different companies. I've seen how they all handle very similar problems in different ways and to me that's been one the most valuable things too.

The benefits of hiring someone who is a job hopper is they come in with the knowledge and ability to quickly jump into a role and to start adding value very quickly. Someone who is not a job hopper might take a longer time to get up to speed. Or a contractor can do the job but there is no future for them. If it's the right culture, and place for them, a job hopper is going to grow with the company. They're going to want to learn their role and improve it. They're going to want to learn other areas and improve them too. A lot of companies have these same problems and we think they are unique to us, but a job hopper can add a lot more insight than someone who is an employee who's only seen one company.

On the mentality of six sigma and continuous improvement

At DuPont I did a six Sigma training and I thought that was really interesting. What I like about six Sigma is that it gives employees that mentality to think about how they should be doing things differently and to have those discussions. For me continuous improvement is a way of life, so anything along those lines is going to speak to me.

On a walkthrough of what a lean six sigma project looks like

We had this process where it was for intercompany invoice processing. Each week I would receive a file with invoice summaries and the process was to then take that Excel sheet, you manipulate it into a very specific format, then you upload that file to a web-based tool, that web-based tool would export your calculations and you then take these calculations, you copy them into another workbook, and then you complete the Journal entry.

So I wanted to understand how things were now and how to apply it to a specific future state, so that we didn't have any misconceptions. I measured how long the current process took, two hours every week. I also documented a number of things we could improve. For example, there were many steps that are specific to formatting that could throw the process off, or how the calculations were working.

The second thing I did was choose a documentation tool to help me create a visual for this process, a high level process map, to create a diagram to show all the relationships between the inputs and the outputs, the people and systems involved. This diagram was quite cumbersome and showed things looping around.

The next thing I did was I went and asked questions of people who used to do this process, I wanted to know if there was a certain reason as to why we're doing the process this way. Is there a reason why it was overly complicated and the answers I found out were, No. they just had this web tool they liked to use and that's what they did. It's important you ask those questions because if you then created the process it might be missing something. I then wanted to understand how the calculations worked.

I created a diagram of what the efficient future state would be, have all the calculations done in full transparency and kept within one workbook. Since it was a very rules-based process with very defined steps I wanted to use VBA to automate the whole thing, whilst taking it down from ten steps to two at the push of a button.

I also got my co-worker's and manager's input, they said we should do it. It's important to get other people involved, we can't work in a silo, you might miss something if you do.

I then ran the process the new way and then the old way, I produced the same results. So I measured the time of the new process which took five minutes versus five hours.

On how to learn lean six sigma and apply it with finance

My first bit of advice is to take a quick online course or to do what I do and spend a few hours Googling the questions that you have so you understand what six sigma is, what's it for, what it's not for, and what are all the tools that are at your disposal. So the first step I'd advocate for is awareness and then after that I would work with your team to write down some ideas that you want to work towards. Here you'd want to capture the problems that offer you a lot of benefit, so the easier things first and then you work your way up to more complex and difficult issues. Working with your team you identify a few easy projects and then after that you want to review all the tools that six Sigma offers and try to identify three to five that you're going to adopt, understand and know how to use.

You now know what projects you are going to work on, you know what tools you are going to use and then the next thing that I would advocate for is that you would have discussions to understand precisely who was responsible for helping your team with six sigma training. Who is going to review, prove, and validate the project, as well as what this whole process will look like. Now if you don't assign someone to do it, then no one's going to do it. Once you have that in place you can get to work.

Recommended Resources

Book: *The Subtle Art of Not Giving a F*ck: A Counterintuitive Approach to Living a Good Life 2016,* by Mark Manson (link)

Course: *"Master Business Process Improvement AND Process Mapping",* by Ben Wann (link)

Website: The Numbers Guys (link)

"A lot of people will doubt themselves and a lot of the times you'll get caught up in your silos, in your function and say there's no way I can jump over from Finance to operations or from Finance to Sales. There absolutely is a way."

Brett Bourgon
LI: bbourgon
TW: binspiredFG

Tags:
#emotional intelligence #self-awareness #sales #coaching #engagement

BRETT BOURGON after an accomplished career in IT Sales, Operations and Finance co-founded the finance coaching and consulting house B Inspired Finance Group. Brett brings 20+ years of experience and best practices to organisations that need focussed help in three areas: Leadership Development; Finance Transformation Engagements; and Virtual CFO services for Start-ups & SMBs.

Brett is a Registered Corporate Coach with WABC (RCCTM) , holds CPA and CMA designations and lives in Toronto, Canada with his family.

On going from Finance into 'the fire' of leading a Partner Sales Team

Unfortunately we were like a lot of finance organisations that were getting squeezed a bit at the Top. I was one away from the CFO spot here in Canada, and with this squeezing out at the Top, because of course they wanted to do more with less and save money, which happens within Finance organisations sometimes with regards to cost reductions. This meant they were looking for volunteers to rotate to other positions and one came up in the channel world. So they said would you like to go support the IBM strategic outsourcing business and take out there your knowledge of finance and how to structure deals and manage these more complex relationships and organisations. It was a good fit because you were able to take some of the finance skills, those transferable skills, that you want to try to build up overtime.

On the biggest challenge of stepping out of Finance into a sales leadership role

Just the perception that, *"the finance guy is here and he's probably just a mole, and I don't know what he has done to be here, he's probably here to cut the cloth and come into the organisation to be more of a spy than to contribute to the team."* I felt that! I had people who had their guard up and showed their concern. So I had to prove my value and the fact that I was there for real. I was there to help with the business, show them that here are my strengths, and also just to keep an open mind that there was stuff I needed to learn to become a better salesperson and to be more integrated into the sales community.

On how to become more integrated and accepted into the sales community

A lot of it was just relationships. I had already built some good relationships during my time in finance but also because it was part of that role. It's a lot different jumping into the sales organisation and then having to navigate the partner community, the direct sales team, the finance team. because of course I'm on the other side now. So now I need this deal approved and my old finance team are going to you I can't approve it. Then I realised wait up, I've jumped the shark because now I'm starting to talk like I'm one of the salespeople. So really it's just about figuring out how to navigate relationships to take your business knowledge and be able to convert that into success. To be honest, I don't think I would have jumped into the direct sales organisation. I think the nicer fit was the partner sales which was more of a strategic role with long term relationships. It's about strategy between a whole bunch of different pieces, and I was able to take that finance skill set and put it to use in a different role.

On how to get closer to sales teams

Just have the mindset that you will add value. A lot of people will doubt themselves and a lot of the times you'll get caught up in your silos, in your function and say, *"There's no way I can jump over from Finance to operations or from Finance to sales."* And there absolutely is a way, other than the background and experience, you can check off all the other boxes, be strategic, learn how to position your company, understand the business. As a finance professional you've already got these check boxes knocked off if you're doing it properly.

On the main challenge of improving employee engagement

It's just such a crazy environment sometimes. We have clients that are restructuring every three months now, it used to be every five years. So employee engagement is just such a critical thing to make sure we focus in on because there's an axe swinging over everybody's head every three months. And how do you focus on your job when you've got an axe swinging over you and the person besides you gets hit with the axe? Oh, and by the way what is your three to five-year development plan? All you can do is focus on what you can control. When we talk to our clients and we coach people, you can make it worse if you disengage and stop delivering value. So focus on what you can control, focus on delivering that value, and focus on your development. All you can do is make the odds better that you're able to succeed in this kind of restructuring type environment. This is going on across many different industries and many different organisations. It's difficult, we coach people all the time. We get on the call and for the first five minutes they just have to vent because with what's going on in the business, what challenges they've got and how they are having problems focusing on delivering real value because of the environment. The environment today is challenging.

On how we can engage with the business to add value

In finance as you know, you come up the ranks, you've got all your focus on technical training and skill training. Unfortunately, there's no real training on things like business partnering. We've really learned the power of things like self-awareness and working on EQ instead of IQ. Your emotional intelligence today is so much more powerful than we would have ever known but of course in our finance profession no one talks about where they can do it better. They kind of pass it off as hippy-dippy stuff. It's real, just knowing yourself better, having a better self-awareness, managing that self with knowing the environment, being better socially, taking care of these relationships, that just really elevates yourself in your profession and in your career. And it does add value. You build a relationship with a sales leader and have one-on-one strategic conversations that does many things. It protects you, it actually elevates you and it opens up doors to opportunities. I've seen finance leaders go on to be the VP of operations because they have seen the full field of players. They understand the sales, they understand finance, and they can understand the links and the proper connection points between those. I've seen people of course jumping into sales I've seen people rotate across different organisations and all these different things sometimes are built on relationships, sometimes their just built on your mental approach.

On why we shouldn't climb Everest on our own

Our profession is really only focused on people when they get to the Top. It's focussed on executives, it's focussed on leaders, helping and coaching them. However, this is a bit like asking the rest of our finance professionals to figure out how to climb Everest on their own. Maybe they get a check-in every year, *"Hey, here's your annual review, you did great, you didn't miss any reports and you show up to work,"* and you go back to work. That's not coaching, that's not real development, it's not a development plan, that's not mentoring, it's not any of those things. Then we say, well when you get to the Top of Everest then we will actually invest in your real development. On the other hand, if you really want an organisation with strong leaders, you've really got to invest in them as they take that journey. They'll climb Everest faster, they will be stronger when they get up to the Top, and what you've really done is create the next generation of leader. What we are seeing is that this is an underserved part of the market because it's not common practice. Fortunately, there are people out there doing it, kudos to them, if you take that analogy to heart, it's really time to invest in that journey and investing in coaching and helping people along that journey.

The best bit of advice Brett has ever received

I went for a promotion once, way back in the day, and I was all excited because I thought I had built myself a resume of accomplishments. I had all these accomplishments written down and I was ready to talk about these. Then two minutes into the meeting I was basically being laughed at because I was told, *"Listen you could be curing cancer, but nobody knows about it. If you had cured cancer and nobody knows then what's the point if nobody knows about it?"* So I learned very early on that it's difficult for finance professionals to stand up and trumpet that I've done this, this and this. However, it is important to make sure that your accomplishments are known. And also to make sure that your value to the business, and what you've done, and what you've discovered, and what you might add strategically can actually be shared across organisations. I had assumed my manager, because I was junior at the time, was doing that but she wasn't. So when I went for this promotion I was laughed out of the room because no one had any exposure to any of the work that I had done and to them it was kind of comical. It's basically like the Waterboy has come off the bench and he wants to be head coach, it was the perception at the time. So my advice really is about making sure you do some work on your brand. Some of that branding work is done through making sure you get exposure to the right individuals in the business so that they can see your work and they can see your value.

Recommended Resources

Email: coaching@binspiredleadership.com

Website: B Inspired Finance (link)

Video: B Inspired Channel (link)

"Just get the relationship going and demonstrate on a one to one connection basis how you can add value to other people."

David B Horne
LI: david-b-horne
WS: addthenmultiply.com

Tags:
#M&A #private equity #entrepreneur #intensity #connection

DAVID B HORNE is Founder of Add Then Multiply, a consultancy working exclusively with business founders who want to grow fast. David's 30+ year career has included being a CFO of two companies listed on London's AIM where he raised more than £100m in equity and debt funding as well as buying and selling more than 20 companies. David is also the author of the #1 Amazon bestselling "Add Then Multiply – How small businesses can think like big businesses and achieve exponential growth." David also supports UN Global Goal 4 to ensure inclusive and equitable quality education and promote lifelong learning opportunities for all and is a founding trustee of a charity that builds and equips schools in the least developed countries.

David holds Chartered Accountant & Chartered Director designations and is based out of London, England.

On how to overcome inertia as a professional and a leader

There's nothing difficult about it apart from inertia and it's very easy as finance professionals to say, *"we've got these deadlines, we've got these schedules, we've got to get this stuff done, it's nose to the grindstone, let's get on with it."* However if you are a leader in the finance function if you're a leader in any function in an organisation you've got to get out and know the people that you're dealing with. Those who are effectively your customers and I guess having run my own business for a long time it's different because I understand that kind of customer interface. If you've only ever worked in a big company in a finance role perhaps you don't understand that as instinctively. So just put yourself in the perspective of you know, *"Yes, I've got an important job to do as a finance professional and how can I do a better job?"* Well interact with the people who need what I'm providing and find out if I'm providing them with exactly what they need. It could be that actually from a simple conversation with let's say a sales and marketing director all of a sudden they'll say, *"Well actually what I really need is this, and I can never get it."* And then you think, *"that's so easy I could produce that for you every day, every week or whatever."* Just get the relationship going and demonstrate on a one to one connection basis how you can add value to other people and ask them what they want.

On why you don't always need to know all the answers

As you get older and gain more experience you come to realise that it doesn't have to operate that way. If you always go about being the guy who thinks he knows all the answers people can kind of think, here is a bit of a know-it-all git. Now perhaps you wouldn't say in the middle of a board meeting, *"Oh my God I have no idea, I've never thought about it."* However if you're in a one-on-one discussion with someone and they come up with something and you don't know the answer, look at them and say, *"Wow, that's a great question, I don't know the answer but I'll find out."*

On a key insight gained from running his own business

Don't try and be all things to all people. Find something that you're really good at that you're known for and become a specialist in that area. If you think of all of the opportunities that are out there as being in one great big pie. However it doesn't matter if your slice of the pie only takes up one or two degrees of arc out of the whole 360 degrees. Because if you can dominate those one or two degrees of arc, and be known as the expert in that area, and be known as the guy or girl who knows everything to do with that, and who has the contacts. Then you will have more than enough work, you'll get paid better because you'll be much more credible and it seems counterintuitive but it's true. When you actually get approached by someone who asks, *"Oh can you do this?"* And you say, *"Actually, that's not what I do but I know someone who does it."* That gives you huge credibility. I've had a couple of things where I've said that to people and three, six, nine months down the line they've come back to me and said, *"Hey, remember me. I've met someone who needs what you do."* And they've referred me and I've won clients as a result of that.

On how to deal with the demanding intensity of private equity, corporate finance and investment banking

It can be very intense and relentless, so it's very important for you to find *down-time* in a way that works for you as well as for the organisation you're working in. For instance, I've had quite a busy week this week but this afternoon my wife and I are catching a train followed by a ferry over to the Isle of Wight to visit our daughter and son-in-law for a long weekend. That's been put into the diary for a long time. At three o'clock I'm gone, I'm signed off, I'll be back on Monday afternoon. It's just important to have that. Sometimes you can only do that for an evening, or on the weekend. Sometimes you work in organisations and they get very demanding and you need to reach a point where you say, *"I'm willing to do that for a certain amount of time."* I remember years ago one of my early mentors said, *"You know every now and then you've got to ask yourself the question, is my job worth dying for?"* And I've never answered, *"Yes!"*

On the importance and ease nowadays of keeping in contact with your family

In this day and age with communications software and devices it's so easy. You can call anybody for free on WhatsApp, FaceTime or Zoom, all that kind of stuff. It makes it much easier to keep in contact. It's just important that you do.

On the best bit of advice David has ever received

It's from Simon Sinek's TEDx Talk, it's fabulous and his underlying theme is people don't buy what you do, they buy why you do it.

Recommended Resources

Book: *Add Then Multiply: How small businesses can think like big businesses and achieve exponential growth,* by David B. Horne (link)

Book: *Key Person of Influence: The Five-Step Method to Become One of the Most Highly Valued and Highly Paid People in Your Industry,* by Daniel Priestley (link)

Book: *The 7 Habits Of Highly Effective People 25th Anniversary Paperback Book,* by Stephen Covey (link)

Book: *Do What You Love, The Money Will Follow: Discovering Your Right Livelihood Paperback* by Marsha Sinetar (link)

Book: *Secret Life of Trees,* by Colin Tudge (link)

Video: *How Great Leaders Inspire Action*, TEDx, Simon Sinek (link)

Website: Add Then Multiply (link)

"So in reality they're looking for somebody to partner, not to partner in the business, but partner with them on the journey."

Elizabeth Hale
LI: elizabethhalecpa

Tags:
#practice #business partnering #value creation #Millennials #client needs

ELIZABETH HALE is founder and CEO of eeCPA, which is focussed on making a meaningful and positive impact on the business and financial success of their clients, by simplifying the complex and finding creative solutions for the challenges they face.

Elizabeth also holds a CPA designation and lives in Scottsdale, Arizona, USA.

On what business owners are really looking for from their accountants

We train a lot of young people that are just getting into the profession. I really try to impress upon them that the value business owners are looking for is really for someone to listen to them and someone to help them plug the holes in areas that are not their strengths. A lot of times they excel at sales, business development, marketing, vision and ideas and most often accounting, the financials or the numbers are not their strong suits. Although this not the case across the board, I have some clients who are so dialled into their numbers and really enjoy that part of it, but I would say the majority of people that are successful are focused on what their strengths are and for most of them it is sales.

On how we can practically become that business partner they are looking for

So in reality they're looking for somebody to partner, not to partner in the business but partner with them on the journey. To help them make sure that they're overseeing what they need to do to make sure they can find the payroll and that there is a profit at the end of the day. In effect, they're looking for that advice and someone to bounce ideas off of as well as that oversight part. Are they excited about getting their tax return done? No. Are they excited about doing bookkeeping? No. They're really excited though if you can offer something that is going to impact them and impact their business positively. Business Owners are usually looking for some boundaries like, what should I be doing? What is OK? It really depends on that business and that business owner. I mean we can automate a lot of things and there's a lot of great apps out there as well as all these time savers, but it really comes down to human contact and understanding and having someone you know that you respect to put your voice in there.

On the importance of dialling as opposed to contacting clients, great advice for Millennials

Number one, by listening to what they're really saying and what they really want. It's a skill to listen carefully and to pick up on little innuendos and to read into the email. Our team works a lot with emails and text and anything that you can do not to have to personally see someone or talk to someone, obviously it's preferred. However I used to say *"Contact them!"* *"Call them!"* and they would send emails instead. So now I say, *"Dial! Like dial a telephone number in magazines."* You have to call them, because that verbal contact is absolutely critical, and you need to hear what they're saying to you and ask lots of questions. Then I think that you can help them because you can offer solutions or advice that meets with what they're actually looking for. A lot of people ask you questions but those aren't really the questions that they are concerned about. You have to keep digging deeper.

On the importance digging deeper to get at what the client really needed

Yesterday I was in a meeting with a client and he was saying, *"Yeah I have about 11 employees and the highest paid person is paid 58,000."* Now, let's say these 11 employees range from 40,000 to 58,000, so at the high range he should be paying about 600,000 in wages. When you look at his financials and find he's actually paying 780,000 in wages, this means he really doesn't know what he's paying. However you know when you get an idea in your head, it sticks, so you also need to know someone who is there to say well maybe the profit isn't as much because if you're operating with that position, (i.e. you're only meant to be paying 600 but you're actually things are 780) maybe that's why your business isn't netting the 180 difference that it should be because you would have this preconceived notion that that's what you're paying. So bringing people back to reality is part of the value we deliver. People can get ideas into their heads and maybe they were even correct for a time, but things might have shifted or changed in their business since then.

On how to adopt a solution and continually proving your value mindset (as opposed to time and billing)

When I started in public practice everything was pay-by-the-hour. So if it takes you a hundred hours then there are a lot of uncomfortable conversations. So when I started my firm I said we are going to do this differently. We are going to prove our value to our clients, because we have ideas too, and with some of those ideas we might be able to show, *"Hey! Quantitatively maybe you paid us 10,000 but with the ideas that we had we saved you 20,000, so you have actually doubled your money on our fee."* I have always been interested in business and loved working with businesses all the time since I was very young. My dad had his own business it was a restaurant, I love the people and customer service, but I also really enjoy troubleshooting and finding solutions to problems. Almost every time a client walks through the door they have a reason they're here and it's usually because if there's a problem somewhere. They either feel very uneasy, they've been embezzled from or they owe a lot of taxes or they were blindsided by the fact that their line of credit is maxed out. Some problem is initiated so finding a solution to that problem and then maintaining or creating a system to solve the problem and then maintaining that system is really how I approach it. So we really don't tend to do a lot of transactional-only work, we only work with clients where we are actually implementing some meaningful solutions. Otherwise it's very boring.

On why we should "Follow Up & Follow Through"

The best way to succeed in finance and accounting, in the financial world in general, is to follow up and follow through, then you will be successful.

On the best bit of advice Elizabeth has ever received

Do what you love and the money will follow. We have bonus systems here and I just had a conversation recently with one of my team members and I said you can't really focus on how much that client is bringing in. Obviously you have to be aware of it being in business, but you really have to focus on the client first and doing the right thing. Then you will financially benefit from that if you're really doing the right thing. So my advice is doing the right thing first and then focusing on what doing that right thing can bring to you. You can't focus always on the money if you truly want to be successful in business.

Recommended Resources

Book: *Protect Your Profit: Five Accounting Mistakes and How to Avoid Them,* by Elizabeth Hale (link)

Book: *Leadership and Self-Deception: Getting out of the Box,* by The Arbinger Institute (link)

Website: eeCPA (link)

Website: Entrepreneurs' Organisation (link)

"Encourage that curiosity and that's what I look for in the people that I try to hire. It's those people that want to understand the story beyond just the numbers."

Jason Lin
LI: jasoncslin
WS: centage.com

Tags:
#coaching #curiosity #business partnering #decision making #meetings #career advancement #mentoring

JASON LIN is CFO at Centage, a leading provider of cloud financial software that transforms how businesses budget, forecast, analyse and report. Prior to joining Centage Jason held financial leadership positions at Zoominfo, Monster Worldwide, IkaSystems and TripAdvisor – helping to drive profitability, growth and operational efficiency. He boasts nearly 20 years of experience in finance, accounting and administration.

Jason holds an MBA from Fitchburg State University and lives in the Boston, MA area in the United States with his family.

On how we can earn a seat at the decision-making table
The number one thing is accuracy. In this era of big data and all the leading indicators and KPIs that are flying around, being able to bring that financial accuracy to our business partners so that they can make those strategic decisions is important. Then really being their business partner, by that, I mean walking alongside them in their shoes and on their path by stepping outside of the traditional "Office of Finance" where we're so concerned with the general ledger and our financial statements. Stepping outside of that and being true strategic business partners, I think creates a lot of good within any organisation.

On what strategic business partnering means for Jason
It was very early on in my career that I saw that if I approach all my tasks by wearing just my finance and accounting hat it wasn't the best

way to create that kind of cross-functional partnership and collaboration where your business partners in the different functions across an organisation would look to you as a key person to go to for information, for analysis, for strategy. I've always looked at myself as a business and operations professional with a strong financial background. So that's the mentality that I bring to any role and I think that has helped me in my career progression and success. Taking that type of mindset, not losing the financial background that we come from but also trying to make an impact on the business in that way.

On what's involved in his monthly staff meetings

I just encourage that curiosity and that's what I look for in the people that I try to hire. It's those people that want to understand the story beyond just the numbers which is so important to me. I want people to get up out of their desk or their seats and then walk across the company and talk to the development folks, talk to the marketing folks, and the sales folks and understand the impact that your job in front of you has on them and also what they're doing, and the impact that they have on us. In my monthly staff meetings there's a finance piece of it but there's always an operational and business piece of it where we make sure that we're talking about what's going on across the company and cross-functionally. We even talk about competitors and any kind of trends that we're seeing develop. Again a lot of those things we pull from our sales team and our marketing team so it just kind of speaks to the need to communicate to those business partners.

On what tennis and basketball have to do with having a successful career in Finance

The basketball and the tennis analogies for me really encompass how I've approached my career and what I believe to be important in finance professionals' careers. When you think about tennis it's a very individual competition. You're out there by yourself and you're competing against your competitor but you're also playing against yourself. It's a mental and it's a mind game where you're literally on an island and you have to do the work and you have to figure it out yourself. I love that element of tennis, that kind of self-challenge. Absolutely I think in everyone's career you have to be willing to individualise it and put in the hard work to develop yourself as a professional. That falls on yourself as an individual so that's the parallel that I draw from tennis. Then basketball is quite the opposite, it's a team sport where you need that chemistry or else you're just going to have dysfunction. In my analogy you could have a team of the best individual talents, who just don't like each other, who don't enjoy playing with each other, and you can absolutely lose to a team of inferior talent but who has that team camaraderie that plays for each other and that enjoys each other's company. You pick the sport and you see it every single year, where that chemistry trumps talent.

On the mindset we need to bring into Finance

Your business partners are most likely already wanting this faster pace of decision making. Business partners are asking for analysis and for it to be turned around much quicker than in the past. I would implore folks to just don't think about your plan or your budget for this year, but think about your plan and your budget for the next 2 or 3 years. That's the mindset that I always bring when trying to make decisions, It's not only about decisions that make sense for the near term, the next 6 months, but also for the next 2 or 3 years. That's our job as financial leaders, to make those decisions that are going to help our organisations be successful in that longer timeframe.

On the importance of setting aside time to invest in yourself

I really think that finding that personal mentor to sit down with monthly where you're not bringing your laptop or phone and there's no work going on. And all you're talking about is career development and where you have been successful and areas where you need to work on some more. Those kinds of conversations, which as things get busy, when those fire drills pop up, those conversations are the first ones to get pushed out. Let's reschedule that career discussion, let's reschedule that mentoring session, but I just absolutely believe that on a cadence whether it's monthly or quarterly you need to set aside time to reflect on what you're doing well in your career, reflect on where you're strong, and reflect on where to develop.

On a tip on how to get creative to meet with mentors

I absolutely acknowledge that it seems like we're always running from one drill to the next but get creative! I've had times in my careers where I've met my mentor for breakfast on a Saturday morning. You just have to get creative and make sure that you think of it as an investment in yourself, then you have to make sure that you're making that investment.

On the best bit of advice Jason has ever received

Own your own career. I had a mentor say this to me early on and I just feel that when I really understood what that meant, then I really started to make progress as a finance professional. It's all about understanding, at the end of the day that it's not your manager or your organisation's responsibility to push forward your career development, it is your own responsibility and then you have to take accountability for that. So whether that means seeking out professional development training and learning opportunities, or stepping up and proactively taking on projects that are outside of your comfort zone so that you can develop fully. These are the things that I really believe are absolutely the leading indicators to career success and so when I totally understood what it meant to own my own career that was a huge moment for me and I would definitely say that was some of the best advice that I ever received.

Recommended Resources

Article: *"The New CFO Is A Changemaker In The Age Of AI," Forbes Magazine, Nov 29, 2018* (link)

Website: Centage (link)

"Instead of making yourself the hero, make yourself the mentor in the story that you're telling, make your audience the hero. Because that engages the person who makes them want to buy into the story and follow the story."

John Sanchez
LI: fpajohn
WS: thefpagroup.com

Tags:
#communication #FP&A #storytelling #value gap #awareness

JOHN SANCHEZ is a trainer, speaker, performance coach and author who helps people accelerate their careers by improving their communication. With over 20 years of experience in training, public speaking, financial planning and analysis, strategic planning, budgeting, forecasting and financial services, John has specialised in Communication Skills Training, Business Storytelling Training, Public Speaking, and FP&A (Financial Planning & Analysis). His clients include the American Institute of Certified Public Accountants (AICPA) the Association for Financial Professionals (AFP), Accenture Academy, The Ohio Society of Certified Public Accountants (CPAs), and many others.

John holds a BS in Accounting from the Florida State University-College of Business and is based out of Charlotte, North Carolina, USA.

On how to learn and develop the skill of communication

There's a lot of options out there and there's no one correct answer for everyone. The best option for most people is to just get out there and try something. If it doesn't feel like it suits you, let's say for example, you say, *"Okay I want to try this webinar, that so and so is offering."* If it doesn't resonate with you maybe pick up a book on the topic. If that doesn't suit you, for instance books are very challenging for me, I kind of have to force myself to read books which I think is partly why I lean more towards video because it forces me to engage my whole brain as I'm watching as well as listening. For some people and I'm one of those people that's more kinaesthetic I much prefer face-to-face training where I can see people's body language.

On using heroes to improve the impact of your story telling

The whole focus is on using the core concepts of storytelling, those same concepts that entertainers, people that write books or make movies all use. Using those same concepts, breaking something down like Joseph Campbell's hero's journey. Other than people that I've met who are English Lit (Literature) majors in college, most people in accounting and finance have never heard of the ***Hero's journey***. And it's way too complicated and laborious for most people to use in a business setting. However, breaking down a few simple aspects of that, like having a hero in your story can be very effective. Typically, most people are inclined to make the hero themselves. They see themselves as, "*I'm going to be the hero,*" and the champion of, let's say, it's a project that they want to get approved. What I share with people is instead of making yourself the hero, make yourself the mentor in the story that you're telling, make your audience the hero. Because that engages the person who makes them want to buy into the story and follow the story. Then instead of you being the, Luke Skywalker, that's the hero, you can be the Yoda, who is the mentor. Then you're sort of leading them through the story but they're the hero, they're the champion of the project that *maybe* you want to get approved.

On the importance of storytelling

Storytelling engages our brains in very specific ways. It engages people's emotions. I think it's part of the reason that accounting and finance people have resisted it. I have been told many times in my career leave your emotions at the door, this is business, there's no place for emotions here. But the reality is human beings make decisions based on emotions and then they rationalise them with facts and with data. Just because we're accounting and finance professionals doesn't mean that changes how our brains work, they still work the same. So if we choose to ignore that we do so to our detriment, so instead why not understand it and use it to our advantage rather than ignoring it pretending like it's just not the case.

On forget the Golden rule, it's the Platinum rule that's more important in communication

Most people have probably heard of the Golden rule *"Do unto others as you would like done unto yourself."* The Platinum rule simply says *"Everyone doesn't want to be done unto the same way."* To use a simple example like my girlfriend and I, we go out to a restaurant and we ordered the same steak, but she likes hers *well-done* and I like mine *medium.* If we get each other's steak we're not happy. There's nothing wrong with that steak if we just exchange them, she now gets the one that she ordered, it's the one that she wanted and she's happy. That steak is not right or wrong, good or bad, better or worse, it just suits what I want better. Often times what we do in communication is we give what we want to receive. When I was a financial advisor I gave lots of information, I gave lots of details, I spoke from my left brain, I spoke logically, rationally and linearly, but everyone is different. The platinum rule says find out how people want you to communicate with them and then give them the communication in the way they prefer it and not the way you prefer it.

On two things to do to make sure we send the message clearly

It doesn't come naturally for a lot of people so the two biggest things that people can do is #1 ask questions; and then #2 use your awareness, both self-awareness and awareness of other people. For a lot of people that takes time and effort to develop their awareness, to be able to walk into a room and be observant enough to realise that, *"Hey I see that person over there is talking with the person next to them and they reached over and they put their arm on their shoulder they touched them."* That means they're a naturally more kinaesthetic person, they're kind of touchy feely. People who are more kinaesthetic, if you listen to the way they talk, they use kinaesthetic terms. They might say something like, *"that really feels right to me."* The word **feel** is kinaesthetic, so if you're aware of that, you pick up on that. then you respond in kind using terms that resonate with them: *"How does this solution feel to you?" "Do you feel like you could move forward with that strategy that we mapped out for you?"* That awareness of listening to other people and then also having the self-awareness of how am I coming across to other people? Are they picking up the message that I'm intending for them to pick up? Am I being clear with them? Is my voice volume right? Is my rate of speech comfortable for them? Being able to understand where you are in the whole communication exchange and how you're communicating is key.

If you haven't been able to figure it out simply by observation alone, then maybe just ask some simple questions about their preferences, like: *"You know if we're working on a project together what's your preferred medium of communication? Would you rather I sent you a text message through WhatsApp, would you prefer email, face-to-face, or rather I pick up the phone and give you a call? What works better for you?"*

On the best bit of advice John has ever received

I heard a phrase many years ago from a guy that I really admired that said you always have to have a **value gap** if you want to be a leader. People always have to feel like there's some gap between you and them. Where they need to come to you for that value that you have and you can help them in closing that gap.

Recommended Resources

Book: *The 80/20 Principle: The Secret to Achieving More with Less (1999),* by Richard Koch (link)

Book: *Emotional Intelligence: Why It Can Matter More Than IQ (2005),* by Daniel Goleman (link)

Website: FPA Group (link)

"As Finance people we tend to borrow trouble. We worry about everything. We stay awake all night long, worrying about things, but how many of those things, if we really look at it, can be said to have ever really came true?"

Kate Grangard
LI: kate-grangard

Tags:
#self-identification #tools #growth #failure #IT #evolution

KATE GRANGARD is currently the CFO and COO of Gehring Group, Florida. Kate is a regular speaker at events on all things, healthcare legislation, planning & compliance, as well as, developing, authoring and delivering over 30 educational and compliance related webinars.

Kate's commitment to advocating the public sector has been strong and constant, having visited Washington D.C. to advocate for public sector employers by educating Washington leaders and elected officials on the potential impact of proposed or discussed healthcare related legislation on the public sector. Kate has also served on the Council of Insurance Brokers; the Government Finance Officers Association, and the National Association of health Underwriters.

Kate holds both CPA as well as Certified Global Management Accountant designations and is based out of Jupiter, Florida, USA.

On various tools that will help you to successfully grow yourself and work through differences with others

I took this course called *True Colors*. It's a self-identification course, where you actually decide what colours you are. My aha moment during this process, which you do in a group, you break into different tables and you start talking about what it is that frustrates you, what it is that brings you joy, how would you best like to be described, what attributes you bring to success on the team. What I learned during that process is that it is an important tool for team dynamics and communication, because everybody brings something to the plate to be successful and as CPAs, because we do so much remote work and we spend so much time in front of the computer, we don't always work on our interpersonal skills or our EQ. What it allowed me to do was to know that there's other people like me that hate mornings and that was a lightbulb moment. It made me go, *"Oh gosh! Half my team is probably a Gold colour and I need to approach them differently. And, I've got a bunch of Blues I need to approach differently."*

Another tool was the **KIA score** and what that allows you to do is understand whether you're more of an innovator or adaptor. It also helps you to understand that everybody again has an important role on the spectrum but the higher the innovator or adaptor you are the harder it is going to be for you to solve problems together, so you need to change your approach. I think self-identification became a really big trend with me to understand better who I am and how I may be different than other people. Different isn't bad, it just means I need to communicate differently in order to encourage others, give them solace, help them to grow and problem solve.

On the advantages of listening and having data analysts when rolling out new technologies

First of all when we roll out any technology in our organisation we always put together a committee. We have somebody champion it as that leadership role internally and then we also put together a committee because we want to have buy-in across all different ages and generations, and across all different departments within our organisation. We're always making sure we're listening a lot. We do get push back and I would be pretending if I said that everything is all roses over here all the time. We've got a great garden but it's not always blooming. Sometimes we have to still make that decision to go ahead but then we make sure we address what those concerns were so that we can get buy-in.

We also have invested in a data analyst position who really works with the technologies and the implementation process. She is such a facilitator for those people who are the Champions of these products. We've rolled out a number of products, such as the process of a new agency management system. She has been key for us in helping my finance team with recording through things like PowerBI. She's helping us on the operational level with new software that will help our industry. She's got her hands on everything and has become a really important part of our organisation.

On the importance of having a good relationship with IT

Somebody asked the question at a recent conference, *"Hands up who in the room utilises their IT Department on a regular basis with strategy or technologies that they need?"* I was surprised to find that I was one of less than 5 hands in the room that were raised. I think that's a thing as CFOs and accounting people that we have as an opportunity around. We have an opportunity to make sure that we are building the camaraderie and teamwork with IT, data analytics, operations as we go through this process, because they are our best friends. I regularly send my IT Department problems and ask them how we can fix them. I bring them into operations, I bring them into Finance and we have this wonderful relationship where I want them to understand our business, I want them to understand Finance's challenges. They are a crucial and critical part of helping us.

On the importance of not borrowing trouble

One of the things that has helped me through my career, especially in my later years, is recognising that as Finance people we tend to borrow trouble. We worry about everything. We stay awake all night long, worrying about things, but how many of those things, if we really look at it, can be said to have ever really came true? So my mum used to say, *"Kathleen don't borrow trouble."* I think she was 100% right. I've talked to my team about that as well and I think it's helped them to be able to have a better balance, to be able to know that people are going to make mistakes. I think that's another thing that we always fear is mistakes. I've made career mistakes, by not taking time to figure out what I might be better at. So we all make mistakes in our lives. So it's not making a mistake that matters it's how we react to that mistake. It's how we have even repositioned the mistake with people, how do we handle it with them? There are expensive mistakes and likewise we don't want mistakes to happen twice. So we do everything we can to make sure that it doesn't happen again. If you have the right people and they make a mistake, appreciate that it wasn't personal and it wasn't done intentionally.

Also when it comes to problem solving, it doesn't help us when we sit there and expand on the problem. We do have a five step process that we go through for all problems: Are we making sure that we've vetted it thoroughly so that we accept our role in it, our responsibilities, and that we've come to an agreed upon conclusion on how to go forward to make sure things don't happen again.

On the best bit of advice Kate has ever received

It's evolution not revolution. We've got to be careful how we ask for things and have the expectation that things are not going to immediately change. I use it all the time in the workplace because people get frustrated and they want things to be fixed right away. Different people adapt at different times to change. As an organisation, the bigger the ship the harder it is to steer it, reposition it, or to move it. So we've got to figure out a long-term plan and then we need to have steps. We also need to celebrate those steps along the way so people see that it is happening. Some people who appear to want revolutionary things, they really don't, they just want to be heard and they want to know how you are going to work towards changing it. I find people are very patient. Every time you roll around technology it's an evolution. You're not going to go in and have everything tomorrow, there's going to be a process. But when you do it right the reward is well worth it.

Recommended Resources

Book: *Good to Great: Why Some Companies Make the Leap and Others Don't"* by Jim Collins (link)

Book: *Accelerate: The Science of Lean Software and DevOps: Building and Scaling High Performing Technology Organisations,* by Gene Kim and Nicole Forsgren (link)

Book: *16 Things High Performing Organisations Do Differently* by Don Yaeger (link)

Book: *Originals: How Non-Conformists Move the World Book* by Adam Grant (link)

Website: True Colours Test (link)

Website: KAI Test (link)

Website: DISC Test (link)

"So when that alignment happens you end up with just a huge win across the board. Employees win because they're working on the things that they're passionate about. The company gets more out of them. You get a reputation or leadership brand as someone who can develop others and it's just a win-win-win."

Kelly McCleary
LI: kelly-mccleary

Tags:
#influence #impact #leadership #strengths #feedback #global #authentic

KELLY MCCLEARY is currently Global Vice President Finance at AMF Bakery Systems, the global market leader creating best-in-class unit equipment and complete system solutions to help bakeries feed the world. Kelly has previously held a number of senior finance positions at Walmart and Cargill, two of the largest enterprises in the world. As well as her professional successes, Kelly's passion for developing others has seen her have three books published, including one on leadership development co-authored with Christine McLaren and released in September 2017: "You Are Born To Lead: Reflect, Adapt, & Make an Impact Right Now." Kelly has also served as a volunteer board member for Habitat for Humanity Benton County and Wayside House.

Kelly is based out of Richmond, Virginia, holds an MBA from Wichita State and a CMA designation.

On dispelling the myth that individual contributors can't be leaders too
Leadership today is really just about influencing, and so influencing is something that all of us can do from the moment we start our careers, regardless of title or role That's what is the most rewarding to me, I want to make an impact in people's lives as a leader, but I also want to make an impact on the business from being in finance. Everyone wants to have

meaning in their lives, and to have meaning means that you want to have made a difference. To me that's put simply in one of my favourite book titles, which is, *"You don't need a title to be a leader."*

On why it's important to focus on our strengths

We all have different natural abilities and talents, but we also have different passions, and so it's a matter of tapping into that which makes you uniquely you. I view it as we all have the ability to develop a competitive advantage, and that is in leveraging our strengths. It's really important because of the feedback we get we tend to sometimes focus too much on our opportunities or weaknesses instead of on our strengths. Yet it's our strengths that make us unique and have helped us achieve the successes that we've had. We need to not forget to continue to build and develop those strengths as we go through our careers, because it's what got us to where we're at. And that's what's going to make us special, unique, and give us that competitive advantage going forward as a leader.

On the four things people are looking for in a leader

There are really four things people are looking for in a leader, which are: **Trust:** studies show that this is the number one thing people want in their leader. Another is **Vision:** they want to know their leader is going to take them somewhere worth going. The third is **Execution:** it's not much fun having a vision if you never actually get there. Then the last thing is a bit uncommon to think about in leaders, but it is coming to more prominence with concepts like emotional intelligence, and that is **Caring:** people want to know that their leader has their best interests at heart. You can have a lot of different personality styles, but as long as you demonstrate these four things you can be an effective leader.

On how buying souvenirs can help in global finance roles

I'll tell you the advice that I gave everyone who went onto a global team I was on. It was to seize the experience and to take advantage of every opportunity to learn and to experience different things. This may sound a bit humorous, but I actually told all of them to buy all the souvenirs they possibly could. Because you think that you will have a chance to go back and do things, and that's rarely indeed the case. It's the old quote, *"You regret more the things that you don't do than the things that you do."* I feel grateful I took advantage of most of the opportunities I had, and the ones that I chose not to take advantage of are definitely regrets.

On how we can bring our best selves to every interaction

It's so critical to get feedback. The only way to improve as a leader is to understand the impact you're having on others and to develop that self-control that's so important in emotional intelligence. Studies show that it's one of those things that we don't get enough of. Too few people go through their careers getting adequate feedback, and for what it's worth, women get less than men for all kinds of reasons, and so we have to spend our careers actively pursuing feedback. That in itself can be tricky because often people are reluctant to give it, not because they don't care about you as a leader, but it's more uncomfortable, especially if there's any negative feedback to give.

On three practical ways to get accurate feedback from others

So there are ways to get feedback and to more effectively draw it out of folks. One is to really understand that trust relationship that you have or don't have with that person. The more you do, the more likely you already get accurate feedback from them. Another is to be very specific in terms of how you ask for feedback. So if you just ask someone, *"Hey, can you give me some feedback?"* that feels like I'm asking you to pass judgment on me as a person and that's very intimidating. It's far less likely to get you what you're after rather than if you just say, *"Hey, I feel like I didn't hit my stride in that last meeting, do you have any feedback for how I could have done it better?"* Be very specific and then it's much safer for people to provide you feedback. The other type of feedback I encourage people to practice is informal feedback. That is the body language that you get or the reactions you get, whether positive or negative. And just taking time, not a lot, but just a little bit of time after a meeting or interaction to process and reflect on how did that go? What can I learn from it? And develop that habit, and even then we still won't have enough feedback, but at least if we're being very deliberate about collecting it and asking, then we will at least have a better shot of knowing what our blind spots are and then adapting over time to that, whilst staying true to yourself.

On why not all feedback should be reacted to

Not all feedback should be reacted to. Whether it's because you're not sure that you trust that the giver has your best interest at heart or that it's just a part of who you are. You've got to stay authentic: there are impacts to your health if you're not, and people can always tell if you're not. So you have to know when to react and when not to. Although I do encourage people that if you ever choose not to react to feedback, to do so extremely thoughtfully and deliberately. Because the reality of what I have learned the hard way is that if someone actually says something about me that I'm not sure that I agree with or that I don't want to change, then I need to recognise that just because one person felt that way, then it's highly likely that others will feel that way as well. So if I ignore it, I just need to be really mindful of the potential impact of that.

On Kelly's best advice for our future

I think it's really developing a focus on your team. Organisations never have enough strong, good leaders and we have an obligation to help develop those on our teams to meet the needs of the future. There are too few leaders who've had good role models and know how to develop others, but it's a skill that no one taught me. Just simply by practicing it it's something that can be self-taught. So I would just encourage people to begin focusing pretty immediately on ensuring that your team members have good strong development plans. That you're drawing out what it is that they want to do and drawing out their passions. Helping align their interests with the work that needs doing. I always tell folks that came onto my team for the first time that you were going to spend a fair amount of time on your development plan and it's purely selfish, because I will get more work out of you. People always work harder for themselves than they ever will for anybody else. So when that alignment happens, you end up with just a huge win across the board. Employees win because they're working on the things that they're passionate about. The company gets more out of them. You get a reputation or leadership brand as someone who can develop others, and it's just a win-win-win.

Recommended Resources

Book: *You Are Born to Lead: Reflect, Adapt, & Make an Impact Right Now (2017),* by Christine McLaren and Kelly McCleary (link)

Book: *StrengthsFinder 2.0: A New Upgraded Edition of the Online Test from Gallup's Now Discover Your Strengths (2007),* by Tom Rath (link)

Book: *Managing Transitions: Making the Most of Change (2009),* by William Bridges and Susan Bridges (link)

"We need to come to a point where we have to be comfortable with the fuzziness and help to make or support logical decisions in the right direction."

Tags:
#FP&A #continuous accounting #ambiguity #opportunity #expert #communication

KEN FICK is an FP&A thought leader & the founder of fpaexperts.com a digital media platform for the corporate finance market providing tips and ideas to accelerate a career in finance, improve lifestyles, and enhance businesses. Ken is a Director, Strategy & Transformation at MorganFranklin Consulting, Inc. Ken brings 20+ years of experience in various positions in industry and consulting where he has led critical accounting, forensic, business planning, forecasting, analytic and strategy initiatives.

Ken holds an MBA in Finance, CPA and CGMA designations and is currently based out of Washington DC in the United States.

On the usefulness of the "but-for" test
Laurence J. Peters published his now infamous book, *The Peter Principle* in 1968. Within it he states:

> *"In a Hierarchy Every Employee Tends to Rise to His Level of Incompetence."*

It is questionable as to how much of the book was meant to be a joke and how much was meant to be practical advice, which has probably led to its continued popularity. Assuming that there is at least some truth to the above statement, then we are all operating in an environment by which the person that you're advising (assuming you are a consultant), or the Senior Leadership of those organisations you are employed by (assuming you are a corporate employee) has reached some point of incompetence of their assigned duties.

Thinking about that further, I'm not saying everybody has attained such a perch to the same level, but your boss or the people you are advising, probably have to some degree or another, a sense of impostor syndrome. Imposter syndrome is quite common and entails a collection of feelings of inadequacy that persist despite evident success. Therefore, most people are faced with some degree of paranoia in everyday life and are just waiting for somebody to find out that they are fraud. This state of heightened awareness is more common than most people may think.

As a Finance professional you must work to effectively convey your message regardless of the audience's mood, character or any other qualitative measure. The best way to do this is to address the key issues on the basis of pure finance, analytics and data science in order to minimize the emotional component. One way to do this is to use the *'but-for'* argument. In forensic & litigation consulting it's very common to ask "but-for" questions. But-for this or that, what would have occurred? Would the business have continued? Increased in value? Decreased in value? What would (or will) have happen(ed)? Similarly, you can use the *'if-then'* argument. The if-then argument works best when a variety of scenarios are available that can lead to vastly different outcomes. Ultimately, there is almost never one right answer, it is all probabilistic, and as Finance Professionals we have to work to advise senior leaders regarding the scenarios available to figure out the best course of action.

On the advantage of FP&A and continuous accounting into the future

FP&A has been around in different shapes and forms for decades, but in regard to its development as a separate department within the office of the CFO, it is relatively new. I believe in continuous accounting and that within the next 10 to 15 years the accounting close process will be eliminated because of automation, use of the cloud and other digital technologies. This may present some difficulties but it's critical for us to evolve as a profession. There's too much data being created every day to process manually let alone analyse. Regardless of how many accountants & finance people are minted each year, there is physically not enough of us to manage and analyse the volumes of data available.

To address this, new professions such as data scientists & data analysts have been created. But the finance function is really the one that still takes everything and looks at it through the lens of profit and loss (dollars and cents) which is important to optimize organizational performance.

Finance applies the results of data analysis to the outcomes of an organization. Outcomes are determined based on the organizational objectives such as profit or mission. The future of finance will become less operational accounting and more FP&A. It's kind of a tough thing to say because as a profession we don't like to change. For Finance to progress we need to evolve our skillset into being more FP&A, there will be more people in FP&A than accounting in the future.

On why we need to get comfortable with ambiguity & fuzziness

If we're accountants, then we love to make sure things are reconciled, put into the right categories and balanced. That's our nature and it has served us well for generations. Arguably, the genius of double-entry accounting, invented by an Italian Monk in the 14th century, is its simplicity and symmetry.

There is a need for the Finance Professionals of today to gain comfort in ambiguity (or fuzziness). A forecast is never right, but it's incredibly valuable. You don't want it or intend for it to be always right, it's probabilistic, you have a picture with different scenarios of how things are going to look. Iterative scenario analysis should be able to tell a story. Sometimes the story is hard to decipher but we must still strive to find it and compel others to act upon it. Frequently, the finance profession leans toward becoming masters of Excel and data analytics but lack storytelling abilities to drive action from their results.

In my previous life as a forensic account I used to work with absolutely brilliant mathematicians, economists and experts in a variety of fields and I'd have to sit there and have to listen to them. Dissect and digest all this amazing information which was highly quantitative and then translate that into usable information in smaller chunks to juries and lawyers. Those are smart people too, but they're a different intelligence or a different smart. These experts were wonderful in picking up theories and thinking up new ideas or concepts but they weren't necessarily the best at communicating how to use them. The hardest part was getting to the point of a reasonable conclusion. Many of the experts looked for solutions in a mathematical way, needing to get to as close to 100% right and kept saying but this, but this, but this, … . So you'd have to say, *"Okay, if this works the vast majority of the time, let's put down every single caveat there, even if it 5 pages long that is OK."* I'm okay with caveats but people don't read through 5 pages of caveat. We don't have the time to do this. Business moves too fast and if we wait for *perfect*, we will miss *good enough*. We need to come to a point where we have to be comfortable with the fuzziness and help to make or support logical decisions in the right direction.

On the best bit of advice Ken ever received

"Run towards the gunshots." I'm by far no warrior I'm more a lover, they don't what me in war. For example, many years ago I remember that derivatives were a hot topic. There were things called mortgage backed securities or REMICS, and a variety of different structures being created. This was fascinating, so I started to learn more about it. I bought a textbook on it, put it on my desk, started reading about it in my spare time, started talking about it with people, I even did a couple of presentations on it. What I found is that was where the gunfire was. That's where all the fun, the hot stuff, like stock options, or litigation, or whatever in my industry was going on. Because I had that interest and expressed it through writing and speaking, people gravitated towards me as an expert. Now I didn't consider myself as an expert by any means, but they started coming to me with questions and being a naturally curious person who loves solving problems, I wanted to answer them. It grew from there to writing for the Journal of Accountancy, CPA Journal, and a variety of other opportunities, by which over time I actually became one of the leading experts in the accounting and analysis of complex securities. On several occasions, I was called upon not only in my firm but externally to pontificate and write reports on the topic.

Run towards the gunshots is another way of saying that you should look to do what nobody else wants to do. Look to the hard, complex, esoteric, unproven, maybe even naïve concepts and ideas. I am not saying that if you see a guy who is picking up dog poop for a living and no one wants to do that then you should learn more about it, but there's obviously opportunities where things are just a little bit harder. Just by taking a little bit of time, a little bit of interest you can help yourself personally and professionally by running towards that, learning about it, going and being a part of that. That's some great advice that I received from my father but didn't believe him because it was from my parents, but they were right about a lot of things.

Recommended Resources

Book: *The Peter Principle: Why Things Always Go Wrong*, by Laurence J Peter and Raymond Hull (link)

Book: *A Rogue Economist Explores the Hidden Side of Everything*, by Steven D. Levitt, Stephen J. Dubner (link)

Book: *Growth in the Age of Complexity: Steering Your Company to Innovation, Productivity, and Profits in the New Era of Competition*, by Andrei Perumal and Stephen A Wilson (link)

Website: FP&A Experts Website (link)

"We have these competitive advantages that come to us because we learn as mothers, that oftentimes we fail to leverage in the workplace."

Lindsay Stevenson
LI: lindsaystevensoncpa

Tags:
#moms #dads #competitive advantage #prioritisation

LINDSAY STEVENSON is the VP of Finance at 1st Financial Bank USA, having eight years of experience in the tax field of public accounting as well as six years of experience in the audit field of public accounting. Lindsay is specialised in governmental audits, single audits, for-profit audits, partnership and corporation tax returns, financial statement drafting and analysis. She is dedicated to developing her skills to promote the transition of the CPA profession into the future in the banking and finance industry.

Lindsay holds CPA and CGMA designations and is based out of South Dakota, USA.

On why some mother's feel it's hard to be a great finance professional
There was a time in my own life when I was saying, *"Gosh you know! There's all these things going on, I'm feeling overwhelmed, like I can't be a great mom and be a great professional. I was feeling like, I have to choose."* Then talking to other women who were also moms and feeling that way too. So I looked at it again and asked the questions, *"Well as moms, if we're finding it so hard, then, 1. Why is it hard? What is the psychology behind that? and 2. Is there something that we're missing? Is there something that we could do better or do differently that would help alleviate the way we feel?"* What I discovered through some research around the psychology of what happens in motherhood, in addition to doing some polling of CPA moms whom I asked to respond to a few questions, is that we have these competitive advantages that come because we learn as mothers that oftentimes we fail to leverage in

the workplace. As a mom you are forced to develop a significant amount of patience in a very short amount of time. If I'm being honest, I was not as patient before my children were born. I had to develop that skill set but had then not necessarily translated that into a competitive advantage in the workplace. I want to be clear that dads can also have these skills. This is not a male-female thing. It's just the way from a societal standpoint in general that mothers, in the first few years, are going to spend much more time with their children than fathers do. Some of that is changing which is a very good thing. I don't necessarily think that it's just a female thing. I just think that because the way society works we have the opportunity to develop those skillsets much earlier on in our parenting life than the dads do, we don't bring that enough to the office.

On how in finance we can slip into prioritising the business

People throw out a word like balance, or integration, and those words are nice, but if you're taking care of aging parents, or you have multiple jobs, or anyone that has more than just one thing going on, you recognise that work and life is about prioritisation. At one moment it can be all about a client or all about a project that you absolutely have to get done and it's vital that you do it. I recognise that. In the next moment it may be that you have to leave early because you need to get to a meeting with your son's teacher, or you need to get your daughter to a soccer game, or whatever that might be. So for us, I think especially in finance, there are so many demands on us that to be at 100% in every role all at once is going to be tough. We're that trusted advisor, we're the one that everyone in our business depends on, we're supposed to always have the answers, we're supposed to be able to guide them in the way that makes the best sense. I can appreciate that; I think that's a great thing for us and a great position for us to be in. However, the downside is we convince ourselves that we have to be that all the time. That is, 100% of our time is prioritised for the business and I don't think anyone realistically expects that of us but we do it to ourselves.

On micro-prioritisation and easily switching to more important issues

I think as a parent you learn to micro prioritise very quickly and you get to become very good at it. When I say micro-prioritise, it's the little things that you don't even realise that you're doing, that are competitive advantages you can also do in the workplace. At home when you have let's say, your toddlers running around, whilst you're in the middle of making some macaroni and cheese in the kitchen, and you hear the water turning on in the bathroom. Your brain immediately recognises it's probably your two-year old and that you should turn off the burner and run to the bathroom. There's no thought process related to that what-so-ever. You are instinctively driven and the magic of that is in the workplace we don't even recognise this as something that we can leverage. But think about the impact that has for you as a professional when you're in the workplace and you're working on something. Another project comes up, or another issue, or crisis, or whatever it might be, and your ability to recognise that while your project is important and there's a deadline, and you're going to have to make some calls that may be uncomfortable since this other thing takes priority, you can switch to it easily. That's typically difficult for accountants and finance professionals because we like to just get things done. We like to do it in this linear fashion and we like to really focus on something all at once versus to think about it with other things over time. However the reality is we don't live in that workplace anymore. Fifty years ago when there was no access to the Internet and people weren't sending you emails every second of every day, maybe that was a possibility, because you didn't know the other project was a priority until three days later. But now in this real time world that we live in, there is such an expectation for us to be able to manage all these things. And the reality is we have the tools to do it. Those of us that are parents are already doing it at home, we just need to figure out how we can also do it at work.

On four ways to find success and happiness

I was introduced to this idea of a 21-day vision quest and we do it at Thanksgiving every year. All you do is starting on Thanksgiving Day, is to begin journaling things everyday. Start with what you're grateful for, what you're thankful for and then you just vision out what life looks like. It doesn't have any framework around it. So it's really hard to do. I will tell you as a CPA, when I started this, my journal had bullet points in it because that was all I could vision out. Sometimes it's related to finance and accounting, sometimes it's about my kids, sometimes it's about me as a person, and sometimes it's about my financial wellbeing, as well as what I see myself doing in the years to come and that has helped me set a better course. It has helped me be able to take a step back and say, *"Okay, how can I be more effective when I'm at work?"* And the way that I do that is by saying, *"Is this in alignment with what*

I see as success?" It's always changing, but it's the journey of just being able to say what makes you happy and then making sure that you align your choices with those things.

On why spending time on yourself is just as vital as having the technical skills

We as finance professionals are really the go-to people when it's anything business-related. In order for us to be effective at that we have to be great at relationships, communication and all the things that we aren't taught when we go to school. And yes, these may not be on the curriculum, so it's a hard lesson to learn when we make mistakes along the way. However, it's just as important as the technical aspects of what we do. I believe the profession is moving more in this direction because of technology as we're in the digital age right now. We have bots and AI and those things are going to do a lot of our compliance related tasks which shouldn't be scary to us. It should be a relief, because it allows us to actually be better at advising, guiding and giving insights. Because I think that's what the majority of us actually love to do. So develop yourself further by continually investing in yourself, that's the best advice I can give someone.

On the best bit of advice Lindsay has ever received

I was given advice to love myself more and to allow myself to recognise that I'm not perfect, even though I really want to be because that's what CPAs and accountants just desire more than anything else, is to always have the right answer and to always be perfect. Now when I make a mistake I just ask, how do I move forward? How can I take accountability for it and be transparent and authentic? Those words have a lot of meaning to me and every day I try to live true to that.

Recommended Resources

Book: *The Big Leap: Conquer Your Hidden Fear and Take Life to the Next Level* by Gay Hendricks (link)

Book: *Rising Strong (2015)* by Brené Brown (link)

"The exciting thing at the moment is the proliferation of agile, it's just at the cusp in the finance world."

Mike Huthwaite
LI: huthwaite
WS: financeseer.com

Tags:
#agile #influencing #strategy #integrative planning #systems #j-curve #artificial intelligence

MIKE HUTHWAITE started his finance and accounting career as a consultant 20 years ago and is now founder and CEO of FinanceSeer LLC, which won Gartner's cool vendor award and counts global multinationals such as Chrysler and British Airways amongst its customers. Mike is a passionate advisor and thought leader in helping organisations enhance their strategic planning capabilities. Mike is a regular speaker and blogger on the topics of uncertainty, Real Options (advanced scenario analysis) and various financial modelling technologies as well as an advocate for Cash Flow and Discounted Cash Flow (DCF) analytics. Mike has an MBA from Northwestern University's Kellogg School of Management and is based out of Chicago, Illinois in the USA.

On the importance of a systems wide view

A lot of companies will be given a certain directive, something like, we need to grow market share, or we need to increase net income. And these are just really local efficiencies. Most companies do quite well when they focus on some of those leading indicators or obvious areas for improvement, but some companies literally go out of business or struggle to actually sustain that growth. So you can try to increase your market share only to find out that the cost of acquisition to get into that market is actually greater than the incremental revenue. Or you find out that it's just not sustainable. Both of those cases are really examples of not looking at the financials as a whole system, where sustainable growth is the ultimate output. It's just having that broader view. The best thing we can do as finance people is really to educate the company on that message. We don't need them to be experts in finance nor do we want them to be, but understanding that whole operational system, if you will, in a finance sense. It's well worth getting the rest of the business to understand that.

On the J-curve and why growth is not linear

We all have in our mind this different vision or view of what growth will look like. But what growth looks like is definitely not going to be that straight line, it's not linear, it's not flat. Usually what it is for organisations is what we would call the J-curve. So it starts off as you invest in our product, you're investing so it's going down and then it eventually swings up, hits a plateau at the top, that's when you're investing in the business but your growth is sustaining, then eventually it falls back down a little bit. The key is, without going into too much detail, is to break your business down into different subunits and figure out where your strategy really lives (i.e. where are you really sustaining growth and what stage are you in?) Are you in an investment stage, or even the growth stage, the plateau, the decline or steady state? For anyone looking to get into strategy analytics it's about the big picture. It is not about individual revenues or individual costs but the big picture, how it interacts, and then understanding where your business is and at what stage it's in so that you can optimize it. For instance, staying in plateau is not a bad thing, you're still creating value but obviously you want to get out of the investment stage pretty early on. I think that's the best visual I've ever used when it comes to analytics and strategy is that J-curve idea.

On what type of agile works best in Finance

The agile framework we tend to hear about comes from the IT development space. The idea that a waterfall approach to addressing how to build a solution or answer a problem is really not going to work in the strategy world. We need to start with a prototype, have one person spearing that initiative and then inviting other people to come into that process and to make suggestions and offer alternatives. The challenge in today's world is, if you took a business environment and you allow everyone to make suggestions and alternatives you'd end up with a major version control issue. And so how do you avoid that issue? How do you capture those different ideas so that they're easy to piece together and arrive at the optimal strategy? Then you can take that strategy and send that down to tactical planning, which is more commonly known as, budgeting and forecasting.

On the proliferation of agile in Finance

The exciting thing at the moment is the proliferation of agile, it's just at the cusp in the finance world. I think as we look around people have a great understanding of agile, of agile tools, and team-based tools. We're not talking about enterprise tools here, we're talking about team-based tools, for teams to get things done and there's a whole host, not necessarily in the finance world per se, but there's Slack and Microsoft Teams. All of these solutions are out there in general usage and are really bringing out team-based collaboration and agile approaches.

On why it is unlikely that the strategy space will benefit from AI

I do think technology is really shaping the way we are going to do things in the future. I think you're seeing that a lot both on the tactical side of planning, so the budgeting and forecasting side, as well as on the strategic side. On the tactical side it is all about building efficiency and mitigating risk. You're seeing a lot of that with even things like AI (Artificial Intelligence). I know that's a pretty popular buzzword, but I think AI is pushing that boundary quite well. Prescriptive analytics, getting the idea that the computer is going to make suggestions for us, I think that's coming along. I'm more on the other side, the strategic side, which I don't believe will benefit from AI at all. I say that because in the strategy world you're beyond very strong levels of probability. You're in the space of, *"I need to influence the world because if you can't measure it, we can't manage it."* So in those instances you really should be influencing the direction of things. That's what strategy is all about.

On an analogy for a strategic finance function

Let's say you're walking down the street, it's dark at night and you have a flashlight or a torch in your hand. You kind of know where you're going, so you're walking straight down the path, although you're using your flashlight or torch to figure out whether to go to the left or the right a little bit. You're looking for a different path that's perhaps a little less rocky, or maybe avoid a critter jumping out at you or something. So that's in effect identifying your opportunities and threats. You're moving your flashlight back and forth; in effect you're really screening for opportunity. You're doing that the whole time you're walking. And obviously at certain points you might be in a darker area so you might flash the light around a little bit more or a little bit faster. Other times maybe not so much, but at the same time you're not walking that same path. I mean your feet are still firmly on the path, you're still going forward and you're keeping your eye out for alternatives. That's really the best analogy I can come up with for a strategic finance function. It's just a constant screening process looking for opportunities. Now, you won't take advantage of most things find you but it's the need to continuously do that because that's really where the value is. For example, let's examine the budgeting process, how many of us say that it takes too long and also want to compact that process? Generally, we do, but on the strategy side it doesn't involve everyone. It involves less people, less time, less effort but it's something you want to do more of. Because the more you can evaluate alternative ideas and opportunities, to catch the market on the early side and find where the disruption is coming from, that's a good thing and we should be doing more of that.

On the best bit of advice Mike has ever received

I would say it's to have persistence and grit. They sort of mean the same thing but having persistence or building up persistence is really the key to success. You could be very intelligent, super smart, or even the subject matter expert on something, but the key in long term success is to be able to be consistently persistent. Don't give up, keep moving forward, grind it out, put the hours in, do the reps. That's the one thing that has helped me out the most over the years.

Recommended Resources

Book: *A Curious Mind: The Secret to a Bigger Life (2015)*, by Brian Grazer and Charles Fishman (link)

Definition: *Definition of the J-curve* (link)

Website: Financeseer (link)

"It's not outside of the realm of finance to be creative and to innovate."

Nevine White
LI: nevinewhite

Tags:
#transformation #beyond budgeting #innovation #adding value

NEVINE WHITE is currently the VP Accounting at Hargray Communications, however has over 20+ years in building and directing highly-skilled financial management teams to support achievement of overall corporate goals and objectives. Nevine has achieved this by providing reliable and useful information to decision-makers, reducing bureaucracy, and increasing agility. While most of Nevine's tenure has been in telecommunications, she has also had the opportunity to work on improvement initiatives in several industries, including healthcare, logistics, and manufacturing. A strong leader with experience in setting up high-value processes, Nevine holds an MBA in Accounting & Finance and is based out of South Carolina, USA.

On the first impacts of embarking on finance transformation
When you are doing transformations you don't always know what you don't know - and there was an awful lot of stuff I didn't know. I definitely didn't know that as we started to dismantle our budgeting process, it would be like pulling on a loose thread of a sweater, because you end up unravelling all kinds of other things as you go. It impacts how you handle rewards & compensation; it impacts how you target set; it impacts how you allocate your resources; it impacts the management style of people and what they are required to do. The implications are far-reaching and I really didn't understand that when I first started this transformation. However, having the support of a strong leader behind me and him saying, we have to do something different, because we have to be more responsive to be able to compete against the other huge telecoms, since we're not big enough to leverage sheer market power. So, we wanted to be more responsive and provide better customer

service, but you can't do that if you're stuck in this paradigm where you can't move because you're anchored to an outdated budget.

On the adverse impacts of traditional budgets

You don't ever want to have a salesperson sitting in front of the customer saying well we can't do that because it's not in our budget. Besides being just embarrassing that's just such a wrong way to run a business. You don't need to be airing that externally, that you're in this mode of constantly being hamstrung by this artificial construct that you've put in place. Budgets not only create this perceived ceiling on your spending but they also create a floor, because we know one of the behaviours it drives is that people will spend every red cent of that budget. They know that if they don't spend it, the following year they're not going to get that money back. It drives really bad behaviour throughout the process, throughout the organisation and so the CFO that I was working for had the vision to see where this was the problem. He really didn't have a solution, rather it was like, *"I know this current way isn't going to work for us long term."*

We moved to a quarterly planning process that was really agile, nimble, really downscaled in the sense that we were only looking at a few lines. This wasn't your traditional approach of taking all your G/L accounts and running the budget for 12 to 15 months out there at that extraordinary level of detail. Frankly nobody can predict numbers with that level of precision anyway and for the most part it's completely irrelevant. We really focused on the things we needed to understand about the business and so we just started running a very routine quarterly process, only having people project out what they could see. We figured out that our sales organisation had about two quarters worth of visibility so that's all we asked them to forecast. We just decided that beyond those first two quarters we'll add four more quarters but do it from a much more mathematical and top-side approach in terms of truly understanding trendlines, from doing some regression analysis and understanding what drives the business beyond that.

It took us a while to get there I mean this isn't like turning the switch and everyone got it the first time out. When you're doing this kind of transformation you really have to talk to people – over and over again. There's a lot of training, a lot of hand holding, a lot of acknowledging that I don't know the answer to this question I'll have to get back to you, because you don't know everything you're going to break as part of something that significant. It's going to be a different experience for anybody who goes down this path because it's very much integrated with your organisational culture.

On the importance of culture in selecting the right transformation approach
Culturally we're an organisation that will jump off the cliff and when we hit the water, we'll figure out how to start swimming, as opposed to trying to make everything perfect. That was probably a good thing because I think it's like trying to take that first dive from a 3-metre platform. When you first stand up there you're like, *'I hate this.'* Then when you start looking at how far the water is below you, the longer you stand there the more terrifying it becomes. I think for us being able to take that kind of jump was the only way we're going to do this because if we had thought about this much longer, we wouldn't have done it. It's crazy but it worked, it really made us a much better company with a much more value-add, focused finance organisation that really started to drive a different conversation. We moved from being that 'revenue prevention police' to being business partners with our frontline.

On the focus that the finance group provided on the frontline
We also embedded about half the finance organisation on the frontline because we figured out that the issue wasn't so much the budget. The issue was any process that was just overly onerous in terms of getting things done. This included the approval processes, it included all those different things, how we paid people, how we looked at performance, all that had to change. By embedding my team on the frontline, what we were able to do is really get them much closer to the source of the issues and really understand much better how the organisation functioned as it met the customer. So, by having my team a lot physically and operationally closer, they were then able to see some things first-hand. They became significant advocates for the field back at corporate, in terms of helping people understand what processes were breaking down, as well as those that were just overly bureaucratic and then coming up with solutions to help. I mean they paid for themselves over and over again just in the cost savings they generated by fixing processes that were just too cumbersome.

Things like capital approvals were emailed around the company and it wouldn't be all that shocking just to see an email that had 25 people on it with everybody putting *"Yes I approve."* Do we really need 25 people looking at a $25,000 purchase in a company? This took time and we really had to research what is it that people really must approve? What clears about 90% of the stuff off their desks? What level of risk are we willing to take versus delaying the process? In other words, if we're talking about buying a tool kit for a newly hired technician, why can't the operations manager approve it? We've already agreed that we're going to hire a technician, it's not like we're not going to buy them tools. Why does it have to go any further than the guy's boss? It involved letting good judgment and common sense prevail over onerous policies.

On being brave enough to try something different

Be brave and don't be afraid of trying something. Even if you can't convince yourself that doing this for your whole organisation is going to get traction, then why not try it in one area. Find a friendly leader in a business unit or department who wants to change their functional area. See if you can make it work and get some ways to improve the process to make it more humane, make it more productive and really focus in on the things that are critical to the business. Just don't be afraid to try some things because that's how you learn - that's how you figure out what will work and what is not a cultural fit. It's not outside of the realm of finance to be creative and to innovate.

On the best bit of advice Nevine has ever received

"If nothing changes, nothing changes." It's so simple but it's really very profound when you think about it. If you're not willing to change something, it's going to remain as the status quo. So change is a good thing, you just have to approach it with some thoughtfulness. I strongly recommend anybody doing something transformational to learn about change management methodologies and engage in making that a foundation to bringing the rest of the organization along on the journey.

Recommended Resources

Book: *Beyond Budgeting: How Managers Can Break Free from the Annual Performance Trap,* by Jeremy Hope and Robin Fraser (link)

Book: *The Leader's Dilemma: How to Build an Empowered and Adaptive Organisation Without Losing Control,* by Franz Röösli, Jeremy Hope, and Peter Bunce (link)

Book: *Future Ready: How to Master Business Forecasting,* by Steve Morlidge and Steve Player (link)

Book: *Implementing Beyond Budgeting: Unlocking the Performance Potential,* by Bjarte Bogsnes (link)

"If you want motivated people, you must be motivated. If you want committed people, then you must be committed. If you want people to embrace work life effectiveness to thrive and avoid burn out, you must show them the way by endeavouring to be your best self, and live your best life."

Nigel Franklyn
LI: nigel-franklyn

Tags:
#innovation #motivation #mindset #best-self #health #relevance #self-care #self-leadership #Me Inc

NIGEL FRANKLYN is a Vice President of Financial Reporting in the controllership function of Prudential's Financial Inc. and has an 18-year career in and around the Financial Services Industry. Nigel is a speaker and thought leader as well as the creator of Me Inc. which is about being our best selves and making better use of our energy in Accounting & Finance. Nigel holds CPA and CGMA designations and is based in New Jersey, USA.

On his Me Inc. concept that he delivered to an AICPA Controllers Conference
Me Inc. is a conversation in self-leadership, maximising my own or the participants current potential and understanding how self-care, is very important to ensuring that you show up as your best-self every day. Essentially, wellness is a conscious, self -directed, and evolving process to achieving one's full potential. We often make the worst of situations but the one thing that's with us through every experience is ourselves. So you are unhappy in one place and you get up and you go to someplace else figuring you'll be happier, but if you haven't changed and you are the same person who's going along you're going to be just as unhappy. The Me Inc. conversation is how I have successfully approached my daily walk over the last couple of years. Through new experiences, inter-

actions with different people, an introduction to emotional intelligence, finding out what motivates me and I landed on three segments: Mind (Engine), Body (Vehicle), and Spirit (Fuel). Everything starts in the **mind**, so in the pursuit of the *"best you"*, you must be intellectually curious and embrace a mindset that anything is possible. Your **body** is the vehicle which carries you through this experience called life. Your **spirit** is your purpose and the joy in your daily activities which excites you from day to day. You have to invest some effort on a daily basis to feed these areas to ensure that you are making progress to be the best version, or a better version of yourself.

On the observer theory and why it's important for finance professionals

The mind is a muscle, so like any other muscle it needs to be exercised, it should be challenged and stretched. What happens if you don't care for your muscles? I recently learned of the observer theory, which is basically that your mind creates your reality. Reality will morph based on who is observing it. So if I go to work thinking I hate my job, then I am going to make the experiences that follow me through the day confirm my outlook that I hate my job. Your perspective matters.

On how a shift in mindset can shift how you approach your day

If you just smile now, it makes you feel better, right. If you smile at someone else, their brain is wired to smile back. It is very important to have a positive mindset and exhibit behaviours that reflect your positive mental state. With awareness and small changes to your mindset it becomes so much easier for us to align our behaviours with the goals we want to achieve. For example, think of sleep as how you start the day as opposed to ending the day. Actually flipping it around this way will help you go to bed on time which will allow you to go into everyday fully rested and with the energy required to tackle the demands of that day.

On your boss's amazing superpower

We often don't have time to do the things that will be most beneficial to us. Have you ever had that situation where all day your staff want to meet with you, your peers want to meet with you and you don't have time, you're busy? Then all of a sudden, your boss calls and then just amazingly time is created. And on that same theme of how your boss calling creates time, it also creates commitment, it creates motivation, you're able to work late, you're able to postpone things with the people you love, you're able to miss your kids' games, it's amazing how much power your supervisors can have. We all struggle with it. In the Me Inc. construct you should make time every day to invest in those things that will help make progress in accomplishing your goals, whatever they are. I am not saying you should ignore your boss's requests. I am saying you should respectfully prioritise your needs.

On how to stay relevant

I may get into trouble for saying this, but there is a huge leadership vacuum in our profession. I feel that many of our leaders don't exhibit behaviours that younger professionals should emulate. We often solely focus on the tasks on hand. However, to remain relevant we have to lead from the front which requires so much more. If you're trying to improve engagement you have to care about people, you have to be able to inspire people. Therefore, we have to develop intellectual, emotional and social intelligence, and work to create a collaborative and inclusive work environment. There are so many opportunities for us to lead from the front as the accounting and finance profession continues to evolve. If you want motivated people, you must be motivated. If you want committed people, then you must be committed. If you want people to embrace work life effectiveness to thrive and avoid burn out, you must show them the way by endeavouring to be your best self, and live your best life.

On treating lunch as a midday vacation

In busy times the conventional thinking is that if I sit at my desk for as long as I can with minimal breaks, I will get all my work done faster. However there is research that supports the opposite. Your productivity will actually improve with taking periodic breaks and time to refocus, throughout the day. So treat lunch as your mid-day vacation, a time for you to rest, and refocus the mind, to improve your effectiveness in the second half of the day.

On the best bit of advice Nigel ever received

I asked my granddad what advice he would give his 36-year-old self and he said to me, *"you can gain everything in the world Nigel, but if you lose your health it was all for nothing."* It floored me, because our health and selfcare is often a secondary consideration as we pursue goals. Me Inc. embodies my reflections after that conversation, and any efforts since to be healthy, happy, and productive.

Recommended Resources

<u>Book:</u> *Who Moved My Cheese?: An Amazing Way to Deal with Change in Your Work and in Your Life (1998)*, by Spencer Johnson and Kenneth Blanchard (<u>link</u>)

<u>Book:</u> *Kiss Your BUT Good-Bye: How to Get Beyond the One Word That Stands Between You and Success (2013)*, by Joseph Azelby and Robert Azelby (<u>link</u>)

<u>Book:</u> *Search Inside Yourself: The Unexpected Path to Achieving Success, Happiness (and World Peace) (2014)*, by Chade-Meng Tan and Daniel Goleman (<u>link</u>)

<u>Book:</u> *Triggers: Creating Behaviour That Lasts–Becoming the Person You Want to Be (2015),* by Marshall Goldsmith and Mark Reiter (<u>link</u>)

<u>Book:</u> *Resilience: Hard-Won Wisdom for Living a Better Life (2016),* by Eric Greitens Navy SEAL (<u>link</u>)

<u>Website:</u> Project Aristotle @ Google (<u>link</u>)

"Where I see it working well is when the finance group is less focused on the transactions and more focused on creating value from what the transactions are showing."

Paul Sweeney
LI: sweeneypaul
WS: flexxus.biz

Tags:
#software #value #sales #storytelling #generations #Toastmasters

PAUL SWEENEY is a director at Flexxus Business Solutions and has leveraged his finance training to help small and medium-sized enterprises gain maximum value from their ERP systems, whether this is via consulting, implementation or support with his hands on experience in financial and operations system development.

Paul is a Certified Business Consultant and is based out of Vancouver, Canada.

On how to avoid over-buying finance software capabilities

From what I've seen a lot of this comes back to how well do you really understand your business and how well do you really understand what tools are going to help you move your business forward. The analogy I like to make is we'd all like to have a Ferrari. And buying the Ferrari is quite possible but keeping it on the road is something completely different. So when you go out to buy software it's a similar thing. Buying it is one thing, installing it and getting it running is another thing. But then what's your plan for keeping it running and continuing to get value out of it? Because the piece that I see fairly often, is when you put the piece of software in, I teach you the capabilities to get it running, and then if we don't continue to be engaged that's where your learning stops. And that's from a lack of curiosity, which to me is a very big thing that impacts the value you can achieve from anything you bring into your business.

On how to remain relevant in finance

Where I see it working well is when the finance group is less focused on the transactions and more focused on creating value from what the transactions are showing. So let's not focus on the mundane and put your head down to do this reconciliation, or create this report, because that's just busy work. It is really not creating value. And with machine learning on the horizon, that transaction processing stuff is going to disappear. So to me if you want a solid future in the finance profession you need to do more than transactional work. I heard a great clip from a guy and the way he described it is, *"What's your extra?"* Anybody can do a journal entry, anybody can create financial statements, what are you going to do that's extra value, that's different from what somebody else could do?

On why finance can also be in sales

Your title might say finance, but you're in sales too because if you want your organisation to change, like for example, this software is not working for us we need to buy something new. Well guess what? You're in sales, because you have to convince a whole bunch of other people to agree with you. That's sales. If you want to get a raise. You're in sales.

There are so many things that influence a business's success or failure and some of them are a train wreck that you're just watching and can't do anything about. Other ones are a complete surprise, and other ones are thoroughly preventable, but sometimes a person that sees the beginnings of it doesn't have the salesmanship to convince the rest that this is an issue.

On what Toastmasters has to do with good salesmanship

Good salesmanship is just good storytelling. So I decided, you know what, I need to improve my ability to tell the story so I'm going to join toastmasters to work on it. I just started two weeks ago. The piece that I've seen right off the top is that they're very focused on giving everybody the opportunity to stand up and speak in various different ways so that you become comfortable with it. I see a lot of people are very nervous whilst standing up and talking. And the biggest part of that nervousness is you don't have the experience to realise that it's actually not that bad.

On why there needs to be a meeting of minds between generations in Finance

This is something that people latch onto in conversation, but I think what they fail to recognise is that a similar conversation has occurred with every generation. The words are different, the specifics might be different, but every generation that comes along is different. And the older generation and the younger generation need to have a meeting of minds of how we're going to work together because there is no other option. One of the things that I encourage businesses to do is to find the younger people who are going to pick this stuff up really quickly and easily. And have them teach the older ones, be the on-site resources for the ongoing education and encouragement because that process of teaching and learning also creates that interpersonal understanding between the generations.

On the best bit of advice Paul ever received

The best piece of advice I ever received was from my father. At the end of every day you should be able to be proud of what you've achieved. Look yourself in the mirror and ask, *"Am I proud of what I've done?"* Because one of the things I see is that there's so many people that need external affirmation of their value. Why does it need to be external? Can you not value yourself? Be proud of what you've done and say well somebody else might not like it but I feel it was the right thing to do here and what I did was in alignment with my core values. You can use this frame of mind to draw upon to move forward no matter what happens around you.

Recommended Resources

Website: Flexxus (link)

"Value has to come first, we have to put the value up before we can ever hope to put the price up."

Rhondalynn Korolak
LI: imagineering
WS: businest.com

Tags:
#practice #pricing #value creation #influencing #storytelling

RHONDALYNN KOROLAK is founder and Managing Director of Businest® and award-winning Business App which teaches accountants to master the specific skills required to build & scale a thriving advisory practice. Rhondalynn has worked across two continents, articled as a tax lawyer, and served in general management and as a business coach.

Rhondalynn has also written four books (see recommended resources), holds a CPA designation and lives in Melbourne, Australia.

On why financial illiteracy in SMEs is a big problem for us accountants

If you're going to run a business you'd think that you'd have taken some time to learn about finance, because you're going to need that to run your business successfully, but I was wrong. I discovered that 95% of small business owners are financially illiterate. That's a huge problem for us as accountants and finance professionals. This means for those of us who deal with small business clients we've got a huge block of clients that are financially illiterate and they also, for the most part about 87% or 90% of those, have severe cash flow and working capital problems. Why? Because they can't get loans traditionally from banks, either the banks aren't lending to them or they don't qualify.

On why accountants don't have a sales problem but an influencing problem

So we've got all these business owners crying out for cash to survive, let alone thrive and grow, and we've got a whole bunch of accountants like me who went to school and we're taught accrual accounting which obfuscates financial performance. We're not in the business of making it simple for people and that is a huge dilemma and a huge opportunity for us. I believe that the biggest opportunity doesn't lie in any of this technology, the apps, any of the stuff that we've already got to hand. I believe it lies in us unlocking within ourselves better communication styles that actually speak to a layperson. As well as learning what we need to gain leverage on our clients to influence them to take action and I think that is the future of our profession.

On the reason why business owners don't go their accountants first

I used to be the national speaker for MYOB, which was before cloud accounting, and it was pretty much the main accounting package that was used in Australia. I went on this huge speaking tour with them back in 2010 and in one month I presented to 5,000 accountants and small business owners. While we were doing the tour and I was talking about improving cash flow and helping businesses, they did some surveys and one of the survey questions asked was, *"If we, MYOB, did one thing to help you with your business, that one thing that would make all the difference in the world and fix your number one problem what could we do that would help you the most?"* Do you want to take a guess at what 96% of the survey recipients said? *"I need more customers!"*

So the average financially illiterate SME out there has it in their heads that they need more customers to fix their cashflow. That is technically incorrect, but let's just say that they are right and they actually do need more customers do you think that they're going to go to their accountant as their first person to get help on how to get sales and marketing advice? Even Shakespeare couldn't even write comedy like that.

A story on getting clients' attention

I was out coaching this electrical contracting firm in Melbourne, they had 189 full time electricians, so this was not a small business. At the very beginning they were carrying 2 million dollars of receivables every month at 92 days to collect. I kept telling them they had to collect the debt, this is really serious, 92 days, I had graphs, all the whole rigamarole. However it wasn't until I went away and thought about it and came back with a simple calculation:

I said, *"Hey boys explain something to me, you guys both have mortgages on your homes?"*

"Yes!" they both nodded.

"And I notice that you guys both bought boats this year?"

"Yes!" they both nodded.

"And you have young families, you know your kids are still in school?"

"Yes!" they both nodded.

I said, *"Do you realise that if you just took action and worked with me for the next 60 to 90 days to clean up this receivables mess that you would actually stop wasting, flushing down the toilet $234,000 worth of money?"*

I had their attention then as everything else I had said up until that point didn't mean anything, but they understood wasting $234,000 dollars. How I calculated it was I said *"If you are carrying the cost of all these debt factoring facilities that you've got going, what happens when you don't pay your credit cards on time? How much interest are you paying on that?"* So I just started adding everything up you know how much does it cost to have the receivables person chasing all this debt? The emails, faxes, going back into files and rehashing stuff. I just totalled it all up and I got their attention.

Similarly, I'm passionate about teaching accountants how to quantify the ***cost of doing nothing***, that's how you get leverage.

On why the future of our profession involves storytelling

In addition to doing law and accounting I spent some time learning about how the brain works so I became a clinical hypnotherapist. I studied neuroscience trying to delve deep into understanding how our brain actually functions. I was really shocked to discover that the part of the brain that decides can't read numbers or words. Just think about that for a moment, because if this oldest part of your brain is survival based and instinct driven, and it cannot read numbers or words, what business do you or I have trying to sell a dashboard?

We need to be in the business of storytelling. We need to be in the business of creating really compelling visual pictures. By that I don't mean graphs. It has nothing to do with technical skills or financial skills, or even financial modelling. Financial modelling is already too complex for the part of the brain that decides it can't read that stuff.

The importance of Pricing Value as opposed to Value-based Pricing

If there are two words in a phrase, value and pricing, and pricing is the action word in that phrase, then what's going to instinctively happen? People are going to naturally gravitate to spend all of their time and energy on pricing. How it plays out is that people will then ask a whole bunch of really stupid questions because they're focusing on pricing instead of value. For instance, they say things like: "How am I going to get my clients to pay more? What happens if my clients don't pay more? How do I double my prices and not lose clients?" Everything becomes about YOU, the price YOU need to get, the price that YOU deserve, the price that YOU want. And so there is no time and energy whatsoever spent on the most important word in the phrase which is value.

So I decided I was going to switch them back-to-front. What I like about this concept of pricing value is that when you say pricing value what we're basically saying in essence is that we're going to put a price on the value that we bring to the table. So we never now talk about repricing the clients, we revalue them. Value has to come first, we have to put the value up before we can ever hope to put the price up.

On why Pricing Value is not linear

There is no course, there is no examination, there's no formal linear ascension to pricing value, you just face your fears, make a decision that you're going to do it and you start having conversations with people and really understanding what they value and what the cost to them of the solution is before you ever open your mouth and quote the price. If I could give one piece of advice to an accountant it would be stop premature quoting, it's like premature ejaculation, it's not good. We shouldn't be quoting a price when we don't fundamentally understand the value proposition.

On the best bit of advice Rhondalynn has ever received

People don't really care what you know, they care that you can help them to achieve what they need. We've got all this knowledge and yeah it's great, it can help people to do a lot of things, but how do we take that knowledge and really understand what people require of us. What big hairy audacious goals do they have? What pain points are keeping them up at night? And how can we take all that knowledge and turn it into something that changes people's lives for the better. Businesses, they're not real entities, they are legal entities. Businesses don't exist except for the people that run them, so we're not in a transactional business we're in a relationship business and we need to get serious as practitioners about actually becoming better at developing relationships.

Recommended Resources

Book: *On The Shoulders of Giants: 33 New Ways To Guide Yourself To Greatness 2008,* by Rhondalynn Korolak (link)

Book: *Financial Foreplay, Whip Your Business Into Shape 2010,* by Rhondalynn Korolak (link)

Book: *Sales Seduction: Why Do You Say Yes? 2012*, by Rhondalynn Korolak (link)

Book: *Pricing Value: The art of pricing what your accounting clients value most 2019*, by Rhondalynn Korolak (link)

Website: Businest® (link)

Website: Make the SHIFT™ (link)

"Ultimately, I see FP&A as a valuation exercise because the concept behind it is truly in assessing and creating value."

Rob Trippe
LI: rob-trippe

Tags:
#FP&A #corporate finance #modelling #value creation #operating leverage

ROB TRIPPE is a corporate finance executive, lecturer and writer. Rob started his career in investment banking as well as holding senior finance roles at large blue chips like Hertz and GE Capital. During his career Rob has developed financial models and managed projects spanning every balance sheet asset and capitalisation class, numerous industries and for a variety of decision-making and regulatory purposes and applications. He is even the former MD of a private equity group which purchased a coveted professional minor league sports team.

Rob also holds an MBA in Finance from Boston College and lives in the greater New York City area.

On the fundamental equation of FP&A and value creation
Ultimately, I see FP&A as a valuation exercise because the concept behind it is truly in assessing and creating value. The fundamental equation in value creation is really price equals cash flow divided by a certain discount rate. So we need to look at each individual piece. We need to thoroughly vet our cash flow, where is our cash flow coming from, what are the sources of cash flow? Are they financing-oriented, investment-oriented, or are they operationally-oriented, which ultimately is our goal? At what discount rate, the denominator, will the market employ in assessing our potential future risk and reward and that's cash flow divided by 'r' and that equals 'P', Price, which really is the concept of value. And FP&A to me is all about creating corporate value. Now we might not be employing that valuation formula in what we do. Let's

say we're simply constructing a pivot table so we can look at how many scarves and hats and mittens and boots we've sold. I'm not trying to knock any particular Excel formula or capability, but we're simply looking at it as a pivot table. Well Okay, so we're not at that end value result yet, but we're starting to get there. We're looking at sources of value when we do things like sort data and manage data, when we create tables and so on and so forth. That type of analysis ultimately is leading us to the bread and butter question of how do we create value, where is it coming from and where can we create it in the future?

On how to ensure we're solving for the right answer

Number one, we can go back and open our textbooks. I handwrite my basic valuation formulas every year, all the ones that we learned in college and in grad school. Number two is open our textbooks and make sure that conceptually we are going down the right path. I'll give you an example and I've seen this in large corporate environments. You don't divide net income which is an equity concept by total invested capital, which is all sources of financing, debt plus, preferred, plus equity. You've mixed apples and oranges and I see all the hard work of calling data, taking it through the calculation process, coming up with a final answer (i.e. useful business information), but unfortunately, it's the wrong concept. I see this time and again, and it's somewhat frustrating that we can dedicate so much resource and still somehow be off the mark in our final answer.

On why we may be dedicating time to non-value adding activities

Human nature! Do we really trust the finance theory that we learned? Quite frankly a lot of functional areas are pretty happy to dismiss corporate finance theory because maybe that's not what they learned and we need a little more trust around the table I think at times. And also mankind's instinct to go for the busy work. The way around this is starting at the end result and working backwards.

On the importance of starting at the end result and working backwards

Let's start at the end result and work backwards. Let's take the time to start at our final model output and let's start working backwards. Okay, as we move through our calculation processes and then ultimately back into our underlying data. That's a great way to build financial models, for example in Excel. Start at the end result, make sure you nail that down and then move into your data fields.

On the concept of operating leverage that's used by the best financial models

Models operate on the concept of quote unquote *operating leverage*. All of us in FP&A, we've all been run over by updating our models through the week. We never quite get to those little tweaks we've been dying to make for weeks, or months. We've all been caught at 4:00PM or 5:00PM on a Friday, jamming stuff into our models to get a product out the door. We've all been there and we never quite get to the model we've always dreamed of. Financial models, and let's talk specifically about Excel because half a billion people use it, operate under the concept of operating leverage. That means let's take the upfront fixed time to get our model to where we really want it to be before we start with the variable expense elements of let's say populating the model. Let's take the upfront time, let's nail down the right answer, that end product that we really truly desire, and then we'll start investing in the updates, what I call the variable expenses, populating your model, the repeated updates so on and so forth. I think that's what the industry historically has not done. We've kind of worked the other way. So as financial modelling becomes increasingly accepted I do believe that people and organisations will be far more open to the idea of FP&A analysts investing heavy upfront time to make sure their model is nailed down correctly.

On a tip we can all do to improve our financial models

One way where we can improve our models is we can sit down and start writing about them. I don't mean here's how you operate my financial model that I built, this is the SOP, the operating procedure, that's great. But let's sit down and start writing about the concepts behind our models and our analysis. Let's sit down and explain what the model is truly solving for and how it gets there. Let's focus on the three core components of any financial model, that's: data, calculation processes, and that end result of useful business information. I've found that when I sit and write about financial models either that I've created or that I'm reviewing I uncover all kinds of questions that I wouldn't have either asked or answered if I was simply staring at Excel.

On the best bit of advice Rob has ever received

Don't give up, just keep going! Hey it's 8:00PM on a Friday night and you're trying to get something out the door, or maybe preparing for the weekend or a Monday morning meeting. If there's a corner you need to cut, because of resources, state that up front, be honest and hopefully in the future you will be able to really nail down and address all the elements you intended to. But really don't give up, just keep going. All of our models could be better and we all know it. And don't just solve for half the answer. That's one of the most frustrating things, but it happens all the time. We all operate under resource constraints, but be dogged and don't give up.

Recommended Resources

Website: *FP&A Trends* (link)

"In fact, when we think we know what the answer already is, that limits possibilities, because all we see is the answer we think we know. Creating new things, new solutions, new ideas, innovating that happens outside of what we think we know."

Sarah Elliott
LI: sarahelliottcpaacc
WS: intend2lead.com

Tags:
#coaching #mastermind #culture #questions #innovating

SARAH ELLIOTT is co-founder of leadership development firm Intend2Lead that coaches accountants to access the Dimension of Possible: an elevated place where fear is no longer the enemy, and love reigns. Sarah is also founder of Ellivate Alliance, which connects people, ideas and resources in a way that creates powerful new opportunities to elevate women entrepreneurs. Sarah is a CPA, a Professional Certified Coach and lives in the Austin Texas area in the United States with her family.

On turning down an equity partnership to run her own business

It was exhilarating, it was exciting, and it was also terrifying. I laugh, looking back, because I actually thought it would be a little easier. I think I was over-confident, and I'm really grateful that I was, or I might not have done it!

I have a lot of people in my life who believe in me, and that really helped me. When I took that leap of faith, I was the primary earner in my marriage at the time, so, I was walking away from two-thirds of our household income. My husband and I made that decision together. When I left my old firm, I was 5 months pregnant with our first and only child, and I also went back to school for a year to get certified as a professional coach. We actually went negative from a cash flow perspective for the first couple of years because I was investing in a business and bringing a new life into the world. At times, I wondered, *"Have I lost my mind?"* At the same time, it was incredible, because I was recreating my life on my own terms - as a mom, a coach, and a business owner. It was a lot of fun, and scary too!

On going from surviving to thriving, running her own business
There were a lot of things that supported me. First off, I have an incredible support network in my life - my husband, parents, sister, family and friends who truly believe in me. There's nothing else like it!

I also tapped into the power of a mastermind. A mastermind is when people come together to support one another in a safe, confidential space. There were two women in my life who were starting up their own businesses at the same time as me, so the three of us would connect once a week. We shared our journeys with one another. We set intentions for the week ahead. We shared what's most important to us in our business and our life (because we're all just one human being - we can't compartmentalise ourselves).

We had this amazing space to share how it really was - to share the tears, the disappointments and the struggles. I was able to share those moments when I was on the bathroom floor crying because this wasn't working out the way I thought it would and wondered what to do next. These women were there to remind me what mattered most to me when things got hard.

Many of us wear masks, as though we have it all together and know what's going on, and we're afraid to show vulnerability. Yet, it is so powerful when we share our vulnerabilities with another human being. We are reminded, "I'm not the only one going through this." In reality, what I was going through is a common challenge in starting a business - it's hard! So, let's talk about it, so we can learn faster and better together.

On a definition for coaching
Coaching, at its heart, is helping another human being discover their potential so they can step into it. We do that by providing a safe space for that person to explore. We sit back, and instead of telling, we listen and ask curious questions. We try to understand this other person's world and how they make meaning in it. When we can do that for another human being, they start to understand themselves better – what

they want, what they want to create and contribute in the world, what lights them up - and then, they can explore ways to bring that into the world using baby steps by experimenting and trying new things. Coaching provides the space to do that.

On where to start with creating a coaching culture in our finance teams
There are many ways to start a coaching culture at an organization. There's no one right answer. You need to discover your own answer.

If you want to create a coaching culture in your organisation, step one is to understand and embrace the coaching mindset. I believe the best way to truly understand what coaching is and become a believer in it is to receive coaching yourself! Be open to that, and focus on your own personal growth. This creates space for you to help those around you.

Coaching skills help us figure out how we can help our people become more resourceful. They help us connect with one another and collaborate.

To be a good leader, you have to be a good human being first! We must take care of ourselves first and help others from a place of strength. We must work on ourselves, so we have the potential and capacity to help others.

In accounting and finance, we like to see hard dollars and ROI in coaching and come up with an equation for this. But, sometimes, you just have to experience coaching to see its benefits. You will realize all the results you and others receive through the coaching when you experience them.

One of the most expensive costs of doing business is people-related, and coaching helps with hiring, retaining, and engaging your people. It helps you tap into your people's potential and helps them better understand how they can contribute as a unique human being to your organization.

Everyone can benefit from a coaching culture. Maybe you don't have the budget for every single person in your organisation to receive professional coaching, but there are other things you can do. You can teach coaching skills through group learning and invest in coaching programs to support specific groups, such as high potentials and emerging leaders, in the organization.

On how finance professionals can ask more creative questions

In accounting and finance, we are usually seen as experts. That is incredible and powerful – it's what people pay us for! I don't want to diminish that, but I do want to encourage you to also be open to the idea that there is a lot of power in a question as well. In fact, when we think we know what the answer already is, that limits possibilities, because all we see is the answer we think we know. Creating new things, new solutions, new ideas, innovating – that happens outside of what we think we know.

We have a natural temptation to give an answer when someone asks. I do it, too! When someone asks me a question, I really just want to jump in and answer. Step one in making a change is to first notice that automatic response to answer. If I notice that, then I can separate myself from that habitual response. I can create a little space. I can take a deep breath and think, *"What might be another response?"* Maybe you can even pause and ask yourself, *"What's a good question I can ask?"*

Just like anything else in our lives, this can be a habit. It's something we have to learn, practice and give ourselves space for. We're not going to be perfect every time, but just noticing our desire to jump in and answer is a very powerful step, as it creates awareness.

On how coaching helps with resourcefulness

When we give someone the answers right away - when we give into that temptation to just tell someone else what to do - we're creating a dependence between the two of us. Because, if you asked me questions, and I always answer them, what's going to happen the next time you have a problem? You're going to come right to me again! If, instead, I create some space and ask you question such as, *"What's really going on here? What are you thinking about this situation? What do you think is really at the heart of the challenge?"* We can peel back the layers together. I've helped you extend your capacity to understand what the true problem is. I've helped you explore opportunities, ideas and resources. I can ask you, *"Where might you look for that answer? Where could you research? Where could you explore to uncover what you need?"*

I get it! Sometimes, it's faster and easier to just tell you the answer. But that's not a sustainable long-term approach for your career. I'm not doing you any favours. I want you to be successful. How can I help you figure out your own answer? Because when you figure out your own answer, that's yours - you own it, you're going to be accountable for it, and you're probably a lot more likely to follow through and own the results. On the other hand, if I told you the answer, but it didn't work out, you could shirk that responsibility.

It's really empowering for another person when you take a coaching approach. You create a resourcefulness in the other person, and they can do even more going forward! This enhances their leadership capacity forever. They get to carry the learning forward.

On the best bit of advice Sarah has ever received

Let's not take things so seriously! Sometimes we take life so seriously – in our job, in our business, in life. We limit ourselves and our possibilities. We forget why we do what we do, and it's no fun anymore. Let's have more fun!

Recommended Resources

Book: *The Big Leap: Conquer Your Hidden Fear and Take Life to the Next Level,* by Gay Hendricks (link)

Article: *Top 10 leadership books for accountants* (link)

Article: *A toolkit for possibility: Creating a coaching culture at your organization* (link)

Website: Intend to Lead (link)

"It's so critical, you have people in finance who are not focused on today or yesterday, backwards looking. We have to be focused on where do we think opportunities lie, where do we think we have problems, areas that we could explore if we didn't have so much on our plate."

Scott Hirsch
LI: scott-hirsch

Tags:
#business partnering #data-driven #data intimacy #Google Time #creativity

SCOTT HIRSCH is Finance Director Customer Service Pricing & Recurring Revenue Generation at Dell EMC the third largest privately controlled company on the planet following the acquisition of EMC in 2016. Scott's team is tasked with protecting and growing $5bn of prepaid and renewal maintenance revenue and is a big user of cognitive computing technologies to combine data in legacy Oracle & SAP systems with business partnering to provide insights into optimising pricing of customer lifetime value and delivering benefits for end user customers and Dell EMC. Scott was previously a management consultant at Accenture in their Operations Consulting Practice and has also participated in a number of entrepreneurial adventures.

Scott holds an MBA from Babson and is based out of Boston, MA, USA.

On how you know when you have a data-driven understanding of the business
We spent a lot of time getting to that point to be able to express it in a simple financial model where we really understand the point of leverage and where we make money and also where we don't. Then you have a real solid data-driven understanding of the business and you can say, *"Okay, let's make this trade-off now in terms of cash to get customers locked in. We know how long our customers typically own our products, how many times they upgrade, how much software they use, and what*

our pricing is." And so, you can then adapt that and create new models that makes you much more confident in terms of the ability to take calculated risks and do something different. Whereas if you don't have that intimacy with the data you then don't fully understand the customer journey, you're not tracking this type of information, and so not supremely confident in how this works at scale.

On three baby steps to take to get more intimate with the data

It doesn't come naturally to a lot of finance people because their specialty is in financial analysis, not in getting information. Some of the baby steps certainly are upskilling and learning about how to be self-sufficient. Finance professionals are excellent at asking the right questions: *"Hey, what if I could get this? And, I want to see it this way. Or, let's cut it that way."* Where I think maybe more experienced financial professionals, who haven't really grown up with this digital revolution and who are hungry to get information but don't have the right skills to get it themselves or don't want to rely on the IT department who are always bogged down, they will have to be more self-sufficient. So further baby steps, experimenting and learning with SQL, getting exposure so you know how data works. If you were starting from zero then one of the best places to start with is mapping the customer journey.

On getting intimate with data by mapping the customer journey

By understanding how we market to customers, quote, sell, ship, service and if you can trace that through, even in Excel, you can go into all the systems and say, *"Let me just see what happens to an order overtime."* You can start to build things without knowing SQL. Then you start to say to yourself, *"I really want to automate this,"* and then you can go into the systems and you can start pulling this data in an automated way and start bridging it together.

On leveraging Google Time to be more creative

Start with things that are low risk and build your knowledge base from there. I've always come to work and encourage people on my team to do two things. One is, I love the idea of ***Google Time***, so spend 20% of your time on stuff that you're interested in or got hunches around where there might be value. I don't think we allocate enough time in finance to being creative and exploring. I'm not knocking finance but I think we have so much responsibility in running the business that we don't allocate enough time to exploration. So a big thank you to some important people in my life for sharing the vision to say, you know, we're going to carve out a specialty finance team that's not working on quarter close and is not working on just reporting but is more of a Skunkworks or Ninja team that is focused on the future. It's so critical that you have people in finance who are not focused on today or yesterday, backwards looking. We have to be focused on where do we think opportunities lie, where do we think we have problems, areas that we could explore if we didn't have so much on our plate. That's to say we're not busy, it's to say it's a different focus. Spending 20% of your time, literally 20% of your time doing things that are, *"off-the-grid"* or different because those are always the greatest sources for inspiration.

On one thing you can start doing to make an impact faster

In addition to trying things that are low risk and experimenting and the third thing is come into work every day and do something better and improve something. If it's the way you organise yourself, if it's the way that you run a certain data set, if it's a certain process, automate it, get it off your plate, make it better, improve it and then move on. I think that's so important. I always tell the people that I work with, is if you don't come in every day with the attitude of I'm going to fix something and make it better or innovate, then I think you're losing out on many opportunities to drive results faster.

On the shoemaker's son mentality that's damaging the finance community

What I really don't like about finance is the shoemaker's son mentality. It's that we have to live without any means, we have to lead by example, not spend any money and then not travel to be with other colleagues and that we're an overhead function. No! that's not how we should operate as finance professionals. We need to invest in tools, we need to invest in our own productivity potential, because if we don't do these things, if we don't spend more time being creative and giving our business partners creative solutions, how irrelevant are we going to be in the future. That's very entrepreneurial thinking but I don't think of finance as being black-and-white and so defined. I think finance has tremendous power when you've got people in leadership positions in the finance world who really get it and can help the business. It can be an incredibly useful and valuable role within the company, because it is the one place really next to corporate strategy that has an understanding of how the overall business works.

On the hard lessons when moving from consulting into finance

I was not prepared for a finance career when coming in from consulting. I had to learn a lot of very hard lessons. I really didn't understand what finance did and I would say the biggest challenge that I had was figuring out how finance adds value and what our role is in finance. If you're coming from consulting or outside into finance, the biggest question is how can you really get people's attention in finance? It maybe because it's related to, 'big company' syndrome but sometimes in finance you see something that needs to be addressed, something so obvious, but the company is not interested in solving it. I know sometimes we operate in such a political environment, but as an operation's professional I would want to just go fix it, explain it to stakeholders, get them to understand and in some cases educating them along the way. It seems much harder to do this from finance, perhaps because sometimes it's difficult to explain and for others to understand some of the finance concepts. You're staring at a spreadsheet all day; you get it to make sense when you're doing the work, but then try and bring that ten levels up to its bare bones, it's not easy. Just because the company may not be interested in something you think may be important today doesn't mean that you shouldn't do your job and write up a business case and document what you've seen, you're analysis and approaches, and put it in a desk drawer. Because it may not be the right time, today something else might be more important, but next month it might be what's needed then. In finance you have the unique position to have an arsenal of things and there's never a shortage of things you want to do. So don't get discouraged if you're coming from outside the finance world.

The similarities between good finance people and good salespeople

I think good finance people are like good salespeople. If there's trouble, you should be able to know where the change is hidden under the couch cushion. That was a great learning experience for me was take your great ideas, file them away, lobby, continue to educate people, but it takes time, you've got to be patient.

On Scott's best bit of advice to his younger self

"Hey Scott, you really have a lot to learn!" You've got a great education but it's not even half of what you need to know. So your job for the next 5 to 7 years should be to consider yourself an apprentice and be patient about your career path. And learn and experience as much as possible. Travel, meet as many people as possible, build your network and that

should be your focus as opposed to, and I think a lot of recent graduates think like this, *"Oh I think I'm going to be the CEO as soon as I graduate."* That's unlikely to happen and so I think it's key to have some patience and perspective. I don't know if it would have served me better, but I think I maybe would have captured some opportunities that I wouldn't have because I was too impatient to accelerate my career.

Recommended Resources

Application: *Pivotal Greenplum – how to get intimate with vast amounts of data* (link)

Article: *Google Time* (link)

Definition: Skunkworks (link)

Book: *The Audacious Finance Partner: Reveals The Key Factors and Skills for Business Partnering Success, by Andrew Codd* (link)

Book: *The Goal: A Process of Ongoing Improvement, by Eliyahu M. Goldratt* (link)

Book: *The Richest Man in Babylon, by George S Clason* (link)

Book: *Freakonomics: A Rogue Economist Explores the Hidden Side of Everything, by Steven D. Levitt, Stephen J. Dubner* (link)

Book: *Trump: The Art of the Deal, by Donald J. Trump, Tony Schwartz* (link)

Book: *Talking Straight by Lee Iacocca, by Lee Iacocca, Sonny Kleinfield (Author)* (link)

Book: *The Wall Street Journal Guide to Information Graphics: The Dos and Don'ts of Presenting Data, Facts, and Figures (2013)*, by Dona M Wong (link)

"Just disconnect from your job for a one- or two-hour window and that would be investing in yourself."

Stan Besko
LI: sbesko
WS: binspiredfinance.com

Tags:
#networking #catalyst #adding value #specialising #generalising #development #80/20 rule

STAN BESKO after an accomplished career in IT Sales, Operations and Finance co-founded the finance consulting house B Inspired Finance Group. Stan brings 20+ years of experience and best practices to organisations that need help in the three focused areas of: Leadership and Development for Finance; Finance Transformation Engagements; Virtual CFO services for Start-ups and SMB.

Stan also holds an MBA in Financial Management from York University and lives in Toronto, Canada with his family.

On the pitfalls of the reactive nature of finance supporting the business
When you look at a typical week for a finance person they're typically caught up in a workday minus ten or workday plus ten close cycle. They tend to be in a reactive state where the business has demands on them, providing gross margin information, detailing expense reports, in most cases the finance person is the keeper of the keys when it comes to the health of the business. When it comes to the broader organisation, sales & marketing, operations, they need that information and so finance tends to be in this reactive state. And what happens is that they go week to week supporting the business, and not really looking out for their own interests. So when they're ready to move into a new role they look up and realise, *"I'd like to do this new role, but I haven't really built those relationships, I haven't extended myself, I haven't done skip level meetings, I haven't looked at different organisations where I might want to go to at a later date and built up those relationships."*

On the importance of blocking off development time in the calendar for finance leaders and professionals

Across 140 people in the European finance team I blocked off their calendar, I sent out an invite in Outlook, you can put it down as busy or out of office, and they'd have to accept it. I did that because I'd get feedback from that group of people, it was like a poll, to get at what was top-of-mind and interesting for those who were doing the reading, who were going through their skills development. I'd then take that content and put it into a one or two hour block depending on the week, and that finance person who accepted the invite, would then be tasked with making sure they covered the content. So whether it was a video on demand, whether it was a one hour training course, whatever the case was, it forced them to do the training.

However it was really incumbent upon them to make sure that they didn't let another meeting override that blocked time, so that was the communication part of it, you have to protect that window, there's always going to be meetings, there are going to be demands from the business that are going to want you to take that meeting away and move it to another time. If it is critical, move it to another time, but don't delete it. And in doing so I made it easy for them by feeding them the content that was submitted by others who felt that this was really good stuff. It was some soft skills development, taking some of the negotiating skills training that the sales organisation was going through, it was top of mind economic information, maybe it was a Harvard Business Review paper. The idea was giving them the content and that all they had to do was disconnect from their job in that one or two hour window and that would be an investment in themselves and an encouragement to take ownership of their own careers.

On the importance of specialising and generalising in finance

If you look at Finance you do tend to have a lot of specialities. You have a tax person, you have an accounts person, you have a sales finance person, and so there's an opportunity to specialise to be able to offer value. However at the same time you want to also generalise so that you're opened up for opportunities, so that you're not pigeon-holed to help you to have a broader view of the business so that you can actually connect the dots between where the company is going, with what you have to do at your granular field level.

How to become more marketable by broadening your network

They (the most successful in finance) broadened their networks so that people knew who they were, they did skip levels, they did cross-functional engagements, they set up one-on-ones with organisations that were outside of their day-to-day activities. They made sure that they had a network they could rely on when the time came to ask for favours or when they needed to get visibility into something. They also made sure that they had a network outside of the company so if you looked at their LinkedIn profile ninety percent of who they were connected with weren't from inside their four walls and they actually had a network that was in the broader industry. So those people tended to be much more marketable because they were more engaged.

How to become a catalyst for change by spearheading opportunities

How Finance can differentiate themselves is to spearhead opportunities to affect change, become a catalyst. When you look at some of the books that have been written on this, *catalytic behaviour*, it is really about doing something different. Don't follow the status quo, but challenge the norm, because that's often what happens when you get into these roles. It's just easier if I continue to do it the way that everyone has been doing it because that's what's been written in the policy, and that's the way it's always been done. That's what companies are looking for, especially the public companies who are really under pressure with expense management, tight budgetary cycles, they all want to do more with less. Yet the shareholders want more visibility, the company wants more responsive and more timely information. Essentially you're trying to get more information out of your finance team to deliver to sales, in a timely manner with fewer people. And so you're always under this pressure to become this catalyst for change

So where am I going to find this value? It's the *eighty-twenty rule* in action, *"Where am I going to get eighty percent of the value from 20% of my efforts?"* The people who are the ones I've seen to be the most successful are the ones who have this catalyst type approach where they question, *"Why does it have to be done that way? Why can't we do it this way?"* So spearheading those opportunities even if you're not in that leadership position where you've been tasked with it. Just recognising there's an opportunity to do something different and having the foresight and courage to take ownership of it. Not ownership in an arrogant *everyone follow me* or *my way* type approach, but instead as,

"Hey! Let's all get together and talk about this." I'd say that is a way you can show value, not only to the finance function but to the company overall because you're now making the company much more effective.

On the fear of getting out

Get yourself involved with the sales organisation, sit across from a customer with your account team, because you can better understand your product, your market and customer and what the sales person is facing. You can better add value from that perspective because when they speak their language you can better relate to some of the challenges they face and you become much more like a business partner and more of an advisor. You then straddle the balance between making sure there's compliance and making sure you are looking out for the company's best interest from a profitability & risk exposure standpoint, as well as from a revenue recognition perspective. You understand more what the account team is facing and you add value from that perspective because then you can speak their language, you can relate to some of the challenges they face. There is always an underlying theme of don't go native, there's always that risk but that's where you have to strike that balance to build the relationships within the broader organisation.

On the best bit of advice Stan has ever received

I had a manager years ago who's advice was, *"We don't know what we don't know."* I love that piece of advice because it's very simple but it almost drives you to go get information to make sure that you don't say things that are going to come back to bite you because you weren't really completely informed. The worst thing is that you could be giving your opinion on something that you don't fully know and you're not completely informed about. People are going to remember that and the more senior you go in an organisation and the more mistakes you make when you say things like that, the more they remember. So I like that piece of advice is we don't know what we don't know because it really encourages you to get to know what you don't know.

Recommended Resources

Video: B Inspired (link)

Website: B Inspired (link)

"In terms of business, finance has a language and it's very specific. One of the big improvements we can make is become bilingual."

Steve Rosvold
LI: steverosvold
WS: cfo.university

Tags:
#trust #relationships #languages #mentoring #networking

STEVE ROSVOLD who following an extensive finance and accounting career spanning four decades within both multinationals and SMEs then founded CFO.University which is a community of member-scholars, companies and trusted advisors committed to the development of Chief Financial Officers. Steve holds an MBA in Finance from Chicago's Booth School of Business and is also the owner of KRM Business Solutions which provides a range of CFO advisory services and competencies. Steve is currently based out of Vancouver, Washington in the USA.

On the importance of building relationships

You have to develop a strong relationship so people feel really honest and able to share what their concerns are. There is nothing more troubling than solving an issue that isn't really the main issue for somebody. So a big part of developing a relationship is where people are comfortable telling you about what I need to work on today and that means they need to tell you their faults. So they need to say where am I either personally weak or where is our system weak. And sometimes that's hard to do for executives. So develop a relationship where people are open and honest with you so you can help them. The biggest challenge is making sure people tell you what the real issues are and I can help them solve their issues once I know what they really are.

On the key skill to be able to hone in on the business's real challenges

One of the key things is to be a really good listener. That's with all of our financial professionals in general, having good listening skills because this comes back when you're dealing with your operations people, your sales people, your CEO, your Board. To really understand their issues takes great active listening skills. You learn what their pain points are and you can identify where you can help them. Listening skills are super important and that builds relationships and once you have that trust in a relationship it becomes much easier to have really straightforward dialogue and you learn so much quicker. You're not trying to deal with any noise. Having that open relationship where people feel they can talk to each other and share their issues is really a key in the learning that has to take place in professionals today.

On one of the key improvements we can make to be multi-lingual in Finance

I happen to only speak English, I've dabbled in a few other languages but in terms of business, finance has a language and it's very specific. One of the big improvements we can make is become bilingual. What I mean by that is to understand the commercial aspects. So in your business & industry your sales people and your operations people have a different language that isn't about debits and credits. It's not necessarily even about revenues and costs. Learning that language and then the next step is communicating your information in their language, not financial language. That's a hard thing. We've been trained in accounts preparation, we understand income statements, balance sheets, revenues & expenses. As a quick example in my first job I was in the grain business, where we prepared a balance sheet and a P&L every month. But the trading staff, the people who were the commercial managers, they understood different things, terms like long and short. They understood position reporting, they understood elevations. All these words, they're not accounting words but that's how they understood the business. So developing a way to communicate results in their terms, rather than on a balance sheet and income statement, is so critical in growing your ability to communicate, learn about the business and teach people about the business. We know the results that's where we're going to get it, being able to communicate that in a way people can understand is really important. So you've really got to be bilingual to be in a financial role today.

On the role of finance professionals and accountants as teachers

I've grown into that more. I wish I had taken that on earlier as we have this universal language that helps understand any economy whether it's a commercial organisation, a not-for-profit, a country's, or whether it's a person's own financial one. We learn this knowledge and being able to deliver that to other people helps them understand better and get better. So we have a really important role as teachers. Think about it, we have been the custodian of company information for 500 years, since double entry accounting took place. That's been our role and it actually continues to be our role, but there's more challenges in that role today than there were when we just had a simple set of financial statements and people just took our word for it. There's more scope for us to teach now but it means we have to grow out of just the financial statements and be a bit more linguistic.

On the importance of gaining some exposure to different experiences

Getting more exposure not even in your company but outside it. In my experience, I think it might be universal but, finance people work their tails off. We have the month end close, and we put in these fantastic hours, are super committed and super focused, and so sometimes we get caught up, *"Oh I want the numbers to be perfect,"* and we forget that there's this whole other world going on around us. One of my early faults in the first 20 years of my career, I was super focused on the companies I worked with, big multinationals. My whole network was with those companies and the companies that served my company. If I had a titbit of information to pass onto the younger professionals is make sure you stay broad. Get out there with other organisations, gain other experiences that can broaden your curiosity and learning into other areas more than just accounting.

On the best bit of advice Steve ever received

This whole idea of making sure we're talking in the language of those who we're talking to. So that means don't talk finance to a salesperson. Don't talk finance to an operations person. We have the responsibility to learn their language enough to be able to talk in their language.

And on another note and this is a little bit more on the personal side, my father is a brilliant man but he didn't want to answer one question when I was starting out, when I got out of University. I had two offers for two companies and one company was going to pay me a little more. Well he had me talk to the president of his company who knew these companies very well and he told me take the job that's lower paying. I said, *"Why would I do that? I'm worth more than that, the other job must be better if it pays more."* It was the best advice I've ever got. It got me into a company called Cargill, which is a large company that traded very well. The other company went bankrupt within 5 years. So the moral of the story is find wise people and listen to them.

Recommended Resources

Book: *Absolute Honesty: Building a Corporate Culture That Values Straight Talk and Rewards Integrity (2003)*, by Larry Johnson and Bob Phillips (link)

Website: CFO University (link)

"Our job is to make the people we interact with feel a bit better about themselves."

Wayne Ackerman
LI: wayneackerman

Tags:
#EQ #interpersonal skills #less is more #growth #dealing with criticism

WAYNE ACKERMAN is Principal at Seaview CFO Solutions following a career as a successful Chief Financial Officer (CFO) engaged in driving organisational change improving performance & shareholder value. Wayne delivers profitable growth & stabilisation using simple financial strategies; assists in crisis management situations and completes specific projects beyond the capacity of incumbent staff.

Wayne holds a CPA designation and an MBA from Rutgers Business School. He lives in New Jersey, USA.

On how to work with a diverse crowd

The focus on everything in finance right now is so technical, the artificial intelligence, robotics, data visualisation and all these great things and that's all wonderful. I just hope we never lose the emphasis on leadership and motivation and more importantly just the ability to talk to people and to lead. If you have the skill set to be able to work with this diverse group, to manage and motivate, to lead and get a common aligned vision, and coach, you become an incredibly valued asset. That's all assuming our technical skills are on par with our strategic skills but I kind of think it's the EQ, the emotional quotient, that allows you to work with a diverse crowd.

On how to go from good to very good and positively responding to criticism

Where I went from good to very good was when I got some criticism about my ability to interact. I was a little shocked at first, and of course it hurt a bit too. Then I began asking people around me how I am perceived. I received some really interesting feedback, I was told that you're a little disconnected, you don't always seem interested in people, sometimes you're too focused on the end goal. I thought these are all good things until some really wise woman in HR said, *"No they're not, they're really not! Your job is to lead these people. Your job is to be concerned about them and to make sure they feel safe and have the tools to do a good job, and make sure they succeed."* I've been able take all that information and work on myself a little bit since this happened when I was a lot younger and it's important to think about these soft skills. You have to ask people around you, *"How am I doing and how am I perceived?"*

On how getting yelled at helps people feel better if handled right

One controller who used to work for me in a fit of frustration, and probably a little bit of exhaustion after I had asked him to stay late and get something ready for the morning, said to me, *"I have to get home and I don't think you care."* That was like, Wow! A bit like pouring cold water on my head, I said, *"What do you mean?"* He kind of vented and that kicked the whole thing off. It's free to get yelled at. And usually you're going to make the person on the other end feel much better once they're done yelling. If you handle it right they'll say, *"I didn't really mean to yell and get upset, that was unprofessional and I'm sorry, but man do I feel better."* Our job is to make the people we interact with feel a bit better about themselves.

On how to keep your sanity when growing a business from $65m to $350m

The way you do that is by having a terrific team and a vision that we're going to grow and where we need to stay ahead of the growth curve, not be just at the cusp or worse yet behind. For instance, when you bring on a new client, and in our case they were large new clients with million dollar contracts, you have one opportunity to delight them. If you think not having the right people trained on hand is good for the bottom-line it's horrible for a critical implementation. So you always have to have an inventory of people ready to deploy. The leader of the company, the CEO, was a big proponent of that and I really learned some valuable lessons. It was really investing in your short-term and your long-term future by being ready for the growth. Not everyone can do that because you're not always ensured that growth will come but in this case we were confident and that was really the strategy.

On the power of handwritten notes

Every time a particular executive would go on a visit, on his plane ride back he'd hand write a note to someone that he spoke to. He'd write something very complementary and then say here's what I expect when I return for my next visit. They were very well received. In the world of LinkedIn, marketing emails, and instant messaging, taking the time to write a handwritten note every now and then could make a big impact.

On the best bit of advice Wayne has ever received

It was earlier in my career at my first job as CFO. I was high-energy, I was loquacious, I wanted to contribute and one of the board members who happened to have been trained as an attorney pulled me aside and he said, *"Wayne you know when you're sitting with a group, less is more."* I was a little bit puzzled and I said, *"Alex, can you just elaborate a little bit more?"* And he said, *"Okay, I'm going to be blunt, talk less and listen more!"* I've never sat in a meeting since where I don't hear his voice because sometimes you're so eager to, as was my case, to dominate, or lead, or influence. It's so easy just to be the centre of attention but that's not our role. Peter Drucker said it best, our role is really to lead with questions, to listen and then to have a few impactful things to say.

Recommended Resources

Book: *Execution: The Discipline of Getting Things Done (2001),* by Charles Burck, Larry Bossidy, Ram Charan (link)

ASIA & AUSTRALASIA

"Finance has seen its role really evolve now. Where once upon a time most decisions were taken with finance being involved half the time, now finance is being involved all the time."

Anuj VIJ
LI: anujvij

Tags:
#business partnering #career #international #key drivers #oil&gas #transport #common ground #technology #culture #mindset

ANUJ VIJ is a finance advisor at Chevron and has gained rich and diverse experiences in international markets and industries spanning 3 continents over nearly 3 decades. Anuj has a track record of extensive senior management decision support roles and leadership experience in fast paced international environments.

Anuj is currently based out of Calgary, Canada and holds an MBA from Queens University, Ontario, a BComm as well as being a Chartered Accountant of India.

On the benefits of working in an unstructured cross-functional environment
So they said we have a job for you in Houston which we think you'll be a great fit for. I said, *"Okay, what is it?"* It turned out to be a finance coordinator role for the mid-Africa business unit which is one of the largest in Chevron, but in their exploration and development team which was based out of Houston. It was a very fulfilling job because it involved all the elements of financial planning, legal, participation in Board meetings, management meetings, partner meetings. A great opportunity to really leverage cross-functional experience and I also went to work with the business unit in Nigeria. I did new country entries into Liberia, Sierra Leone, Morocco. I also handled the Liberia clerks and wrote most of the accounting procedures myself. It was a very enriching job, as well

as fairly unstructured, needing an ability to roll up your sleeves and get stuff done. Towards around 2012 our Canadian business unit announced the acquisition of our Kidimax project and there was going to be a massive team established in Houston and my boss basically told me that they've asked for you to lead that effort there. I've been fairly fortunate that the jobs have found me.

On how a finance business partner role gets created

We'd grown our operation from around five thousand barrels a day to thirty thousand barrels a day. Since the operations were growing they wanted somebody with a lot of cross-functional experience to be a finance business partner for operations. So they created the role and I was offered the job, took it up, and it's been a fantastic journey just because the operations are so fast paced and I was able to do so much on digitisation, big data, introducing all sorts of things. Again no established role, but an open-ended job description to be the trusted resource that everyone goes to. That was the drift I was given and I think we ended up doing that.

On the biggest evolution in Finance and why it is a good thing

The change has been the way the role has evolved with how finance, which used to be seen as a back-office kind of thing, now people have started to realise that an integral finance participation in all aspects of the business is key to success. Again, it differs from company to company. For example in AP Moeller Maersk finance was always a very integral part of everything because this was the traditional Danish style to maintain control over the finances and everything else will fall into place. Then in a large multinational organisation like Chevron which is highly technically driven, driven by the geology under the ground and the engineering that goes on above it, is one where finance has seen its role really evolve. Where once upon a time most decisions were taken with finance being involved half the time, now finance is being involved all the time. For example, there is nothing that happens in operations that I'm not aware of, because at the end of the day everything has financial impact.

On accountants who can sell

In the book, *"What they don't teach you at Harvard Business School,"* there's a quote, *"I'm always afraid of an accountant who can sell."* Because most people when they're talking about a business are worried about one driver or one lever, whether it is increasing market share, increasing product, and so on. If you have a finance professional who sits at the table who can actually take in many more parameters at the same time, he can calculate and bring in the business aspect, *"Fine we're growing market share but if our overall profitability declines then it's not really worth it, or if we are going to do that strategic move what timeline are we placing on it."* Understanding the business is key.

On how to develop common ground with business partners

When I came into Chevron, after my initial compliance job I was talking to lawyers all the time. I spent time studying the Acts, studying the language around what I was responsible for. When I went to talk to them I would have that basis, that common ground or bent because our key customers were lawyers. When I moved into the Nigerian-African role, where I was working with a whole bunch of geologists and engineers, I spent the time and effort to take courses in Geology 101, Engineering 101. So that when I'm sitting at a table and we're discussing, for example, drilling on a certain thing and people are throwing out whether there is the correct capture seismic shoot and how they're going to be able to use that to get the point. If you don't understand that and you don't understand what value those people are trying to drive, you cannot be seen as a valued business partner. You have to earn their trust, you have to be able to communicate at the same level. You need to understand what the business driver is for whichever group that you are servicing. At the end of the day finance is still a service we are providing to the overall organisation, but if you don't understand what the business drivers are for that organisation you cannot be as good at providing that service.

On an unprecedented opportunity for Finance to rethink what we're doing

Big data and software as a service is what really excites me now because we were always limited by the things like financial systems being kind of static, they were not dynamic. Imagine how things used to work, like for example two years ago when somebody wanted to look at an initiative to launch a new product. They would send an email or call a meeting and then say we need to get information for this particular market and then somebody would go ahead get the data out from the financial system put it into Excel, load it into PowerPoint and then have a presentation. The whole process would take roughly a week or so. I think there's a huge opportunity right now about rethinking the way you actually do business. Things like PowerBI, Office 365, PowerPivot and Microsoft Teams have actually put a lot of computing power into the hands of finance people.

On leveraging various easy to use technologies

When I came into the operation I was like, *"Oh my God, everyone has asked me questions about the same data every single time and I have to pull it every single time and this is ridiculous."* So I ended up implementing a whole data platform configured partly on SQL Server and running off Microsoft Azure and PowerBI. So first we started standardising the data set, what people normally look at and then pull all that data into easy to use dashboards that everybody can access. So now when my frontline manager needs to look at performance he doesn't need to send me an email or give me a call. He will just open up my dashboard on his mobile or on his computer and he can see all the performance of that particular well going back in time until that well first started. The ability to aggregate and present data more fluently, quickly and seamlessly is an opportunity that is really exciting. The point is earlier on, to execute something like that, you needed IT people. You would need specialised skills in programming, you would need all sorts of stuff that mean either you upgrade your skills or you bring in someone else, which is not that easy in any organisation because then you're looking at putting resources, time, effort, money and business cases together. But the capability that the advent of these technologies has put into the hands of a finance person is unprecedented. With very little IT involvement I can actually do far more today than I could even conceive a year or two ago before we moved onto these platforms.

On driving mindset and cultural change

Big data and the ability to predict and look at trends and for example in this particular operations role with the right data being made available to the right people, we've been able to truly improve profitability and drive down our operational costs in so many possible ways. What it has resulted in has been a shift in the mindset from where earlier on it was just one driver after the other that was kind of driving decisions, it could have been production, it could have been reserves, or better design, more efficiency or reliability. But now there is an element of being able to compare profitability along each of them. Everyone is now getting into a return mindset as well, so, *"Fine we are going to be doing this, but what does it give us, does it give us a good return on investment?"* Even small decisions are being driven with that mindset and that cultural change in the whole organisation is what is really exciting me now. It's finance playing a starring role in almost everything. It has even transformed the way IT works now, IT is even part of the main operations team. So you've got Finance, you've got IT, and all the operations people now really working together to drive towards a common goal.

On the best bit of advice Anuj has ever received

From a finance perspective go and work in the field and watch what happens. For example, in my first job we were really short of staff, like 30% or 40% understaffed, everyone was called upon to do everything. But in learning every aspect of the business it really helped know everything that was going on and you could make decisions accordingly. Similarly when we went to Maersk one of my bosses gave me really good advice to forget about everything else and go with an operations manager and see an operation, like what was happening on the docks. It was a really valuable lesson, because when we went there, I walked the ship up and down, watched the whole unloading/loading operation. I knew exactly where everything was when I looked at my financials because then everything else fell into place.

Recommended Resources

Book: *What They Don't Teach You At Harvard Business School (2016)*, by Mark H McCormack (link)

"There has to be a strong element of travel involved because no matter how strong the technology is, we talk on a daily basis. This personal interaction is how you make these relationships and great teams that work together cohesively."

Ashish Arora
LI: ashish-arora

Tags:
#FP&A #global #low-cost #flexibility #culture #strategic #travel

ASHISH ARORA is Vice President at Cvent. Having built a globally respected FP&A team from scratch Ashish has demonstrated that he is a dynamic, results-driven executive with extensive experience in fast-paced and high growth environments. As well as proven expertise in driving efficiency and productivity through evaluation and automation of processes. A strong leader with experience in setting up processes, building and directing highly skilled financial management teams to support achievement of overall corporate goals and objectives.

Ashish holds CGMA and ACMA designations, as well has having an MBA in Marketing & Finance. Ashish is also based out of Delhi, India

On the three main qualities FP&A professionals need to have nowadays
When we look at financial planning & analysis professionals the first thing is they need to have strong critical reasoning abilities. They need to have the ability to break down a large problem into smaller problems and then apply logical reasoning to solve those problems bit by bit. Most people when they look at a large problem they get bogged down by the fact that it's such a big problem and how do I resolve it? But essentially what it is, is you break it down into smaller steps and then try to solve it step-by-step. You might also end up thinking that you're going to go from direction A to B and you might end up going from A to C but that's the nature of business today. Secondly, I definitely look at people who

have a mindset to adopt technologies and systems because as we grow as an organisation you will work with systems. So you've got to be comfortable with using Excel, visualisation systems, with managing large amounts of data. The third key point is that they don't have to be accountants because accounting is something that you can learn. However what they need to be able to do is to sit down with the business and understand how business is done, because if you know that you can really apply your skill set and provide insights to the business. These are the three key points that I look at when I'm hiring for financial planning analysis professionals.

On how to build a team that is strategic in nature and from a low-cost and far away location.

We have approximately 30 people in the team, of which 20 people are in India and the remaining are in the US. So a large part of the team is in India and then we do have people on ground in the US. In today's world you are really just a Zoom call away and there's a lot of collaboration, which really helps So how do you build a team in India or even in Eastern Europe because essentially the first point of going to these countries is cost, to get lower end work done out of these countries which is not strategic in nature. However to build something that is strategic in nature and is very important to the business, how do you do that when you're when you're seven seas away from that? At the end of the day I think it's a two-way street. The first is the core team or the decision makers at headquarters of the business, the C-level suite, have to really believe in it. I'm not saying that it is as easy as hiring someone and then things get done. There is a lot of hard work, a lot of patience that is required to be able to build something like this in a faraway location.

I'll give you an example, our CEO is a great proponent of India, it's actually his baby. So he interviewed the first 250 people that were hired in our office himself. Being the CEO, he made that kind of commitment. For 16 straight years he comes to India every year, he would spend five to six weeks previously, but now it's three weeks and we used to have these recruitment drives because we have this saying in our company that the DNA of the company comes from its people. So you've really got to hire the right kind of talent and once you get that ball rolling and once you've hired the founding team they are the ones that will help you build the team.

On the other side of the picture, let's say I've been hired, one thing that is very important is that it's not as easy as say working for an Indian company. If you're working for an Indian company, you're working nine to six, you're going back home on time. But if you're working for a US company you have to put in a lot of sacrifices. You're saying, *"Okay, I'm looking for a global company I have to be flexible, there has to be travel involved."* We have this program where I travel to our head-quarters at least once or twice a year. My boss, our CFO comes here every year so there has to be a strong element of travel involved because no matter how strong the technology is, we talk on a daily basis, this personal interaction is how you make these relationships and great teams that work together cohesively. It's kind of a slow process with a lot of hard work that is required to be able to scale operations like that.

On managing workforce diversity while maintaining business profitability

The business requirements for people remain the same no matter if I'm hiring in the US or are hiring here in India. There's one added caveat to the requirement which is communication. Now when I'm hiring people here in India I also have to make sure that these are the people who are going to be picking up the phone and talking to very important people in the company. Analysts in my team talk to the VP of sales when they're doing sales forecasting. Now if I'm hiring an analyst or senior analyst, that individual sitting here in India has to be articulate enough so that they're able to talk to their internal clients, and be able to artic-ulate their questions well and to get their input. Likewise in the US, you've got to hire someone who is open to diversity. Like one of the senior analysts that works in my team, she is in the US now and is the only person in that team there. She has to work with the team in India and so after she was hired she came to India for six weeks and spent those six weeks with the team, building that strong relationship. Now she's not going to come back every year but people know it's not just a phone number that you're dialling, it's actually a real person that you're talking to so, I think the ability to communicate is very important.

On the importance of culture to good performance

Our CEO is great visionary and for him culture is very important. He said, *"I want to make sure that if I am in the India office or if I'm at the HQ in the US, when I'm sitting inside the office there should be no difference in culture."* So we started this program for our top performers no matter which Department they were in, and we would send those in the US office to the India office and vice-versa. It had two motivating affects on people. One, because the Top 10 felt something great was happening to them because they're getting international exposure both on the Indian and the US sides. The second was it started spreading the culture and this was one unified culture that was built. Over the years we still continue with the program. There's constant travel that continues to happen. Obviously travel is very expensive for our business, but then we always have felt that this is very important for the business to do and for the long term success of the business.

On the best bit of advice Ashish has ever received

It was when I was really young in the company, our CFO said, *"In what you do, do it well and good things will follow."* I live by that, if I am enjoying what I'm doing and I'm putting my 100% into it and I'm making sure I'm doing it well everything else will follow.

Recommended Resources

Book: *Radical Candor: Be a Kick-Ass Boss Without Losing Your Humanity*, by Kim Scott (link)

Book: *Creativity, Inc.: Overcoming the Unseen Forces That Stand in the Way of True Inspiration,* by Amy Wallace and Edwin Catmull (link)

"A lot of the conversations that I have with finance professionals is that they don't necessarily know what other people are thinking and feeling and need from finance around the business."

Brad Eisenhuth
LI: bradeisenhuth
WS: theoutperformer.co

Tags:
#business partnering #value creation #outliers #career #impact

BRAD EISENHUTH is founder & CEO of The Outperformer, a multi-award-winning performance advisory, training and consulting group dedicated to the accounting and finance profession. His business and team have developed innovative programs to reshape and raise the level of performance of finance teams, resulting in huge gains and benefits to the organisations that have partnered with them. For their work with companies like PepsiCo, Mirvac, Subaru, The University of Sydney, GenesisCare, Westpac and others, they won Education & Training Program of the Year in 2018 at the Young Leaders in Finance Awards, and are currently a Finalist for Professional Development Program of Year in the Australian Accounting Awards.

Brad is also a published author of CFgrOw: Staying in the driver's seat on the path to CFO. Brad is based out of Sydney, Australia.

On why your technical accounting skills don't differentiate you

Fundamentally everything we do throughout our education as an accounting and finance professional, doing our accounting qualification, the general foundational skills we've developed, they're now basically moot points, or hygiene factors as we call them. So these hygiene factors no longer differentiate you, and are no longer seen as important or as valuable to the business, they're just expected. As a result, we've started to see individuals being rewarded for dealing with their organisations to solve problems, being intrinsically involved in complex decisions, and supporting business decisions to be as successful as possible. Being a leader, as opposed to an accountant, that's where we've started to see the conversation move to.

On how non-finance leaders responded to "what do you want from finance?"

When we started to analyse and deal with non-finance leaders and look at what they're looking for. And say, *"Well what do you want from the finance function? What are you trying to capture in terms of importance?"* Now the first thing that we typically see, at a base level, is they definitely want to see accuracy. They want to see an accounting function that gives them the right information, but then again going back to my point before, that is an expectation and now a hygiene factor for most of these businesses that we deal with. And when it goes wrong there's a lot of credibility lost with respect to the finance function. But beyond that it's that ability to understand and empathise and really appreciate what the business is doing.

On why some finance teams struggle with business partnering

It's a really complex question and there's a few moving parts within that. I don't think there's any one issue. First of all there's the infrastructure within an organisation. There's a lot of people saying they don't have the time to address or put their energy into these business partnership activities. Now when you break that down for some people that is actually an excuse or fear. I mean, for them they're very comfortable doing this BAU stuff and reporting. And for them to be exposed and go into some difficult conversations in areas where they're not as comfortable is not easy. Therefore I'm going to call that *I'm really busy* and *I don't have the time.* For other people, it's not that they don't have the time, it's that their leadership group is positioning them as *doers* and *deliverers.* And rewarding their delivery and not necessarily their engagement with the business or other parts of their finance function to look at strategies to partner with them better. So there's a breakdown within the internal finance infrastructure that holds them back from success with business partnership.

On one question that can help you spend time on things that are valuable

Just ask the question, *"what can be done differently?"* So that you start spending your energy on things that are valuable. Those conversations are about what's happening in your world? What keeps you up at night?

What are the pressures in your part of the business? A lot of the conversations that I have with finance professionals is that they don't necessarily know what other people are thinking and feeling and need from finance around the business. Then just stay on that autopilot. So one of the first things you can do is to start to assess what's happening. Empathise and do some research around the needs of other stakeholders and think about that. And anyway, it's a good practice to be doing this all of the time anyway. But starting at that point, listening and capturing some insights around value and what that really means to them.

On the management accounting team who stopped producing reports

One of my contacts at a large organisation in Sydney ran a bit of an experiment when going through a change of their commercial finance function in a large property group. One of the things that he said was that the management accountants in that business were really busy there running off reports. They were producing a lot of information for their various stakeholders So as a first experiment what he decided to do was, and this may not be for everyone to test initially, he said, *"Let's stop reporting and see what happens?"* Now low and behold all these reports that were meant to be sent out by email were never received and not a lot of feedback came back from the business. No one had actually challenged to say *"Hey, where is my monthly report?"* Of course there's a lot of valuable work and information in those reports, but the key is in how you actually deliver that information in a way that makes an impact to that person. How do you engage with that person in a way that makes sense to them.

On the one ability that helps people move forward in their careers

One of the things that you start to really learn when you watch careers evolve and why certain people have pushed forward in their careers is that it comes back to the ability to be delivering stuff that matters to another person and intrinsically by nature those other people feel the need or have the capacity to support you for doing those great things for them.

On the three types of people you find in organisations

Adam Grant, a professor at Wharton came up with 3 types of people in organisations; givers, matchers & takers. And when you look at it, givers and matchers are probably the majority of our population. 20% of people are **givers**, they like to support others. They don't necessarily get a direct return and they just want to help. They're really valuable to have in your team. **Matchers** by nature are probably 60% of the population. These are people that when you do something for they feel compelled to do something back. It's that whole idea of IOU or supporting each other to help create value with this value trading concept. The final group are the **takers**, now it doesn't necessarily mean that takers won't do anything for you but typically they will orient all their decision making to what's in it for them and sometimes these people can be very successful within their organisations. They can manipulate and growth their career and take advantage of other people, but often when it comes to the crunch they may not help you. So when we look at this whole idea of partnership or creating value for others, when we realise that it's not actually about us and it's about other people, we can say that 80% of the people that we actually deal with would be really willing to help us succeed and develop and grow in ways that are important to us if we are clear about that. So there is a relationship between career success or achievement, the things that are important to you and this whole idea of partnership and supporting others around us.

What CFOs & businesses are beginning to realise.

Finance leaders are really beginning to realise that individuals need to drive their own careers and that ultimately they're in the driver's seat. And then giving them the tools, the skills and actually investing in them over a period of time. Not just saying well here's this dog and pony show style of workshop, listen to that for an hour, get excited and you should be fine and you go and apply those skills you've learned. They're realising that if we want to see change we actually have to invest in it and we actually have to spend the energy with our people to make a difference. There was a finance leader I worked with in Sydney, we did some work around that change concept and driving careers and being the owner of your career. The team started producing projects, coming up with ideas and working on ways to create value in their business. Now he's actually a little bit overwhelmed, he's like, *"My team is now starting to really drive interesting conversations and thinking about the big picture and doing some really cool stuff in our business. In fact it's making my job a lot easier because I'm working with my team in a different way now."* And I said, *"That a very good problem to have. Right?"* They're the things that excite me and the reasons why I moved out of recruitment to move from that transactional environment to a place where you can really make a difference in your work.

The best bit of advice Brad has ever received.

Earlier in my life I received the advice which was, *"If you do what everyone else does, you'll end up like everyone else."* There's nothing wrong with being part of the pack, or being average in general, but at the end of the day, if we're going to stand out and make a difference, you just can't do what we've always done. I've applied that in my own career and to some degrees there's a lot of risk that comes with that. So I started to look at outliers. I started to look at those my in my own field and what is it that they are doing that's working, that they are really good at? What is it that they do to have a great reputation? Then I asked how do I start to apply those things rather than doing what the masses in my field were doing? One of the things I learned very early was to appreciate that these people are just like you and me. They have their own careers, they have pressures, they have their own family, they've got all these things going on in their lives. Doing that and being different to everyone else and actually paying attention to some of the details was really good advice that I'm glad I took up.

Recommended Resources

Video: *How to be the Luckiest Person in the World* | Lindsay Spencer-Matthews | TEDxUQ (link)

Book: *CFgrOw: Staying in the Driver's Seat on the Path to CFO (2015),* by Brad Eisenhuth (link)

Book: *Give and Take: A Revolutionary Approach to Success (2013),* by Adam Grant (link)

Website: The Outperformer (link)

"The most important challenge that our IT business partners are facing is to be able to tell their story and help people outside their functions to understand IT."

Geetanjali Tandon
LI: gtandon
WS: dataandfpa.blogspot.com

Tags:
#business partnering #FP&A #IT #storytelling #data #analytics

GEETANJALI TANDON has 17+ years of experience in corporate finance specifically in Financial Planning & Analysis and currently is Digital Transformation Finance Director at Bayer Crop Science an agrochemical & agricultural biotechnology corporation, which involves the strategic planning & analysis, decision support & financial management of a $1bn IT budget. Geetanjali writes regularly at her blog space "Big Data and FP&A" which is about how big data is changing the world of financial planning and analytics. She also publishes a weekly analysis of finance news and how to analyse it within the lens of FP&A.

Originally from India, Geetanjali is now based out of Orlando, Florida in the U.S. and holds two Masters degrees, the first in Agricultural Economics as well as an MBA from Georgetown's McDonough School of Business.

On how to get up to speed as a business partner

When you're moving to a new function or let's take an example when I moved into IT I took the time to listen. Listen when you're in meetings and listen when you're with people who are experts. Find experts, ask the questions of who the experts in the organisation are and go and talk to them about how they function. Don't be afraid to ask questions, asking questions is important. It doesn't matter where you are in the journey of being a functional business partner, but ask the questions. Asking questions today in IT for example might be, what is cloud?

There's a lot of people talking about cloud computing but do you really understand what cloud computing is? Sit down with someone to understand that, go read about it. The same thing when we talk about infrastructure, what does infrastructure in IT actually mean? What do networks actually mean in IT? And take the time to not only ask and talk to people within your company but go out and read about it also. Combine the two and then come back and ask the questions of what you're reading with the experts.

On the biggest challenge IT business partners are facing

IT is a very interesting area because today every company has an IT function which is moving from a back office to a front office area. The most important challenge that our IT business partners are facing is to be able to tell their story and help people outside their functions to understand IT and where the expenses are. Because the way you're moving IT from a back office to a front office means how you budget IT is changing. There was a time when you were investing a lot of money in building that infrastructure in IT. There was a lot of capital expense that you would go get an approval for and then spend that money, and it comes through as depreciation. Now the industry is moving to a more lifecycle management approach within IT to a more subscription type services. In effect, a switch from a capital expense to opex, so it changes from depreciation where it gets hidden to an actual line item expense within IT which goes up and down depending on how you use it. That is a shift in the story line within IT and really gives the responsibility to the business that there is an expense to how you use your resources. Telling that story, talking about that technical debt (legacy IT infrastructure to be migrated), describing the shift to the lifecycle management of IT is a challenge and not a lot of people understand that especially in a company which is not an IT company. It's a biotechnology company it's an agricultural company, where for years we were spending money in R&D. Now IT is investing a lot more in digitisation, and so it's becoming more important.

On the key ingredients to make an impact with storytelling

Let's take the example of a cooking stock. A stock can be used for soups, it can be used for sauces, it can be used for the basis of many things, you can actually put stocks in curries, it just gives a different flavour. What do you want to use the stock for? You should have that understanding and also what kind of stock do you want? Do you want a vegetarian stock? A chicken stock? That helps you understand the ingredients. In the same way let's apply to the story that you're trying to tell, for example, around the IT expenses. What is it that I want out of my story? I want to help understand how you're spending the IT expenses, what the trends are and help budget holders take some responsibility of the decisions that they're taking as a business on the impact it would have in IT. So it's the same thing when I'm trying to tell the story what are the data that I have? What kind of data do I have? How many years of data do I have? Let's put it all together and take a step back and say okay, what are my expenses trying to tell me? What are my limitations? A lot of us are struggling with the systems and data that we have, we've probably gone through a transformation at some stage so we might not have that many years of data that we can compare easily.

Towards the end of the cooking process there's a lot of boiling that happens. Say after two or three hours, there's a lot of foam that builds up at the top of the pot so you need to skim that foam. It's a bit like when you are working with numbers and you're trying to get to the metrics that you want so that you can tell the story. There's a lot of information that is on top and you skim the key bits of information. There is a lot of information that the numbers will tell you, not every single bit of information is that important, or not every single analysis is going to get you to the metrics or to the good discussion that you want. So you remove those and then you're left with the crux, that is your stock. After you filter out all numbers, what's the few main things that it's telling me?

On three things we can do to be better translators of business needs

Firstly you have to understand analytics. You don't have to be a PhD in statistics to do that but you must understand analytics and also partner with people who understand compliance and financial regulations. In FP&A we really love analytics but being part of the finance function we need to understand GAAP or IFRS rules. We don't need to be experts but we need to partner with people who understand those well enough so that we can apply that knowledge to the analytics. This is where I think we bring really crucial understanding to the business to help them if they actually want to do something. What are the rules regarding that? What is the impact and accounting on that? That's the second thing, and the third thing I would say is work with data scientists who understand the latest methodologies of how you're looking at analytics and how you can apply the latest regression rules or neural networks. You don't need to be an expert in doing that, what you need to be able to do is to work with data scientists to apply that to the business within the rules and compliance we have. That is where I think we will bring the most value to the business and this is where someone starting out in finance should really look at.

On the best bit of advice Geetanjali ever received

Take a moment and step back. We are so in love with what we do, especially our love of numbers, that we just want to go ahead and dive into the analytics and go and present these things. But take a moment and step back. Step back and take a look at the bigger picture and really try to understand what is it that you're trying to do before you delve into things? Instead of going to request this person to get me ten years' worth of data take a moment to step back and really figure out what are you trying to do? It helps to really narrow down and focus on what you're trying to do and help you to understand whether you really need to do this at the level that you're doing it or very quickly just prove it out before I request the ten years' worth of data.

Recommended Resources

Movie: *Apollo 13 (Docudrama 1995)* directed by Ron Howard and starring Tom Hanks, Kevin Bacon, Bill Paxton, Gary Sinise, and Ed Harris (link)

Blogspot: *Big Data & FP&A*, Geetanjali Tandon (link)

"I think all of us know intuitively that doing this as a profession, what good looks like. And we all know where we want to get to. But it's bringing everyone else along on that journey with you and getting them to understand that as well."

Jamie McBrien
LI: Jamie-mcbrien
WS: optim2.com

Tags:
#transformation #offshoring #implementation #career

JAMIE MCBRIEN started his Finance career 20 years ago with PwC and then Deloitte. Having also spent a number of years as a management consultant Jamie became a Director of optim2 & optiBPO who both improve Finance operations via offshoring and outsourcing for middle market companies all around the globe via their offices in Australia, UK, US and Hong Kong.

Jamie is currently based out of Sydney, Australia and holds an MBA from UNSW.

On improving our success in finance transformation implementations
I think a critical starting point is making sure that we get a detailed understanding of the current state and engaging the right stakeholders all the way through. I was just speaking to a client today where we are helping them with their offshoring strategy, and a critical pre-requisite is getting their processes right. He said to me, *"Do we need to do this? We kind of already know where we want to get to, why don't we just start moving there?"* I had to have the conversation with him that I know where we want to get to, but we need to bring others along as part of the change. I often forget, and it's easy as a professional who consults on this on a day-to-day basis, that all these things that are in my head on how things should work aren't necessarily in everyone else's. So it's

gaining the understanding and that takes time, and ensuring concerns are heard, even if your natural tendency is to want to push forward.

On why engagement is key to successful transformations

Without appropriate engagement you will not have an understanding of what change is required, not only from a process perspective, but from a people, structure and systems perspective. For one transformation project I was involved with, a client had us engage with 58 different people. After listening to 58 different people, numbers 5 to 58 sounded pretty much the same, you've heard the same record before, you know what is coming up next. However, if you look back on that project, from the client's perspective it is a successfully proven initiative because everyone was consulted on the way through. This meant that when the change was announced no one was surprised, and everyone felt as though they had contributed.

On the opportunities in finance from the democratisation of knowledge

The real big focus for us at the moment is helping organisations plan, build and manage offshore teams in the Philippines. One of the things that I'm realising the more that I do this is that knowledge truly is global. We can see that knowledge transfer is borderless and it's becoming easier and easier to do that. We're seeing the activities change that are getting outsourced and offshored. We're seeing them move upmarket. Ten to fifteen years ago when I started doing this you'd only be offshoring accounts payable. We've just hired a team leader who's going to be the global treasurer sitting out of the offshore location. We've got financial planning and analysis people, and M&A people also sitting as part of offshore teams. Realising that this knowledge is global and easily transferable is an opportunity.

Whilst it isn't directly related to accounting & finance, I went to a client the other day, they're an industrial business. I pressed the buzzer on the main entrance gate. The lady on the other end introduced herself as such and such and she said, *"Who are you?"* and I said, *"I'm Jamie, I know who you are, where are you sitting?"* Now bear in mind this client is in Perth, the woman on the entrance gate buzzer was sitting in the Philippines and she then opened the gate for me from there. That's just a small example of the idea that geography as a constraint is getting reduced really rapidly. That excites me because I think it's a democratisation of knowledge and that sharing is fantastic and it is only a positive for the whole world.

On the financial controller who deliberately made himself redundant

I was speaking with a financial controller of a business and he said that he was giving himself the objective to make himself redundant in the next two year period through building his outsource team. He was given an incentive to do that and he was saying it sounds strange when your job is to do yourself out of a job, but he said it was a rewarding project. Over the two year period to build the outsource team, he transitioned all of that activity, then he kept building up the team, and he actually even hired his own replacement, to whom he then handed over at the right point .They all agreed and he moved on and sailed off into the sunset and found another role. He finally said, *"You're a pretty wanted person when you demonstrate that you can do that in your career."*

On the best opportunities for career success in finance offshoring

Our clients are typically that middle market, we define it is as them having between 50 to around 500 people. That middle market is interesting for me because the bigger end of town will have a CFO that sometimes has been even removed from the accounting function and the transactional processing. However a 500 person company is probably turning over revenue around the billion mark and often have that single senior CFO, an FC, and there may be a commercial manager there also with a team of 20 or 30 in the accounting function. So those sort of firms are the ones that are not going to have the expertise internally to run these sort of projects. The middle market enterprises are at a size where they're never going to have someone on their books that are going to be doing this, but there will be someone who can come in and help them to do that. We see that's where the big opportunities are for us.

On how finance professionals can remain relevant in the face of offshoring

It's a willingness to understand that things are going to change regardless. We always get told that automation is going to kill outsourcing. I disagree completely, but for me I just think it changes the nature of the outsourcing because people are still going to be needed in terms of what they do. There's always things coming along be it automation, be it outsourcing that is reducing those lower level transactional roles, further automating them and there's a need then for finance people to continuously reskill themselves to really change what it is that they are looking to achieve. So be open to it! We had a client who first was against outsourcing, but then realised there is not a big future in being against the initiative. You've got to get on the bus, build up your knowledge, understand what works and doesn't work because if your organisation is going to embark on this strategy anyway, it is better to put your hand up and say, *"Well I know a fair bit about this."* Then you're going to be a valuable person in that business to help them be successful.

On the best bit of advice Jamie ever received

One of the things I was told early on, that's always stuck with me, is that if you have a business mission statement or a personal mission statement that no one would ever argue against, it's a poor mission statement. For example, we aim to be the best at X. You need to make sure you put forward a mission statement that people might dislike, or they might challenge, or they might ask questions about because then you've got the right one. If you've got the answers to the challenges and the questions and it's not just a motherhood statement then you've really thought it through.

Recommended Resources

Book: Maverick!: *The Success Story Behind the World's Most Unusual Workplace (2001)*, by Ricardo Semler (link)

Website: OptiBPO (link)

Website: Optim2 (link)

"Now the sales for that region went up 50%, do I take credit for that? Not really but they are the ones who went out and sold. All I did was free up their time to do the things that they are good at, and at the same time give them tools to make the right decision."

Khaled Chowdhury
LI: khaledchowdhury
WS: beastbi.com

Tags:
#data management #IT #OVOTT #change #innovation #value

KHALED CHOWDHURY is an accomplished and visionary Global Finance Leader with a proven track record of achieving new heights through collaboration and an infusion of technology that enhances organisational capacity and strengthens capabilities with significant experience in the Energy & Chemicals Manufacturing industries.

Khaled also sits on the advisory council of the Association for Financial Professionals as well as being a circle leader for the FP&A Trends Group. His core interests are in Strategic Planning, Forecasting & Budgeting, Financial Analysis, Business Analysis, Process Optimisation, Financial Modelling, Financial Reporting.

Khaled holds a CMA designation, is a Certified Corporate FP&A Professional as well as a Six Sigma Green Belt. Khaled, lives with his family in Dallas/Forth Worth, Texas, USA.

On the key responsibility of leaders in periods of change
What I have learned, especially in today's world of change is that the largest part of the responsibility that falls on the leader is to guide the learning process. Just to elaborate on that, with the amount of technological change that we're going through, we're not going to have the same way of doing things every 5 years forget 20 or 30 years. Everything that you are learning is probably going to become out of

service by 5 or 10 years time and in that case the only way we will survive and thrive is by learning. So one of the biggest responsibilities on leaders nowadays should be to help navigate this learning journey. And true leaders would be the ones that lead their people through that learning process to get to the next stage.

On a practical approach that we can use in finance to help navigate and accelerate the learning process to acquire experience faster

One of the best mentors I've worked for, his name is Marcelo Rodriguez, who was the previous CFO for KMG chemicals. His way of management for every single person on his team was the fact that he gave us resources and feedback. He would say, *"You know your stuff more than I do, however what I can tell you as a customer, these are the areas here that we can appreciate more and here are the resources to go learn."* So he would help us pick things from two perspectives. one perspective would be he would pick something for us to learn and he will let us pick something to learn which he would support as well. That continuous learning process helped us get to a stage where you would not really have seen people get to as fast without having a number of years more of experience.

On the three components of habits and how to change our cues and habits to deliver better outcomes

I have been personally struggling with my weight and I have been trying all sorts of stuff and nothing sticks. I came across this book by Charles Duhigg called the Power of Habit, I said why don't I figure out how and what it means to change a habit. In summary he talks about that there are three components of habit. One being a *cue* that triggers the process, the *routine*, which is your habit and there is a *reward* behind it. Figuring out what is the cue, which tends to be either a specific event, time, people, emotion, or preceding event, that leads you to do your routine which tends to be the habit. Then you get a reward whether if it is that cookie that you pick up, or that socialisation that you need, or the sugar rush that you're looking for. As finance people there are things that we do the same way, we have habits on a monthly basis which is our cue,we go through this routine and our reward is the monthly package. However the challenge becomes in today's world is that the business is looking for a different reward, and to deliver that means we have to change the cue and change the habit so that we can give the business the right rewards they are looking for.

On why it's not technology that disrupts rather it's the application of technology

This is one of my takeaways from Clay Christensen's class called *disruptive innovation*. The idea he talks about is that the technology by itself is not disruptive but how it is used. A good example of that would be the project that I just finished at KMG, where we brought in the twelve years of invoice data and things like that. What we did actually was not revolutionary at all, the difference was how we did it. Traditionally this task would have been given to IT, it would go through a twelve month process, a statement of work, and then maybe in two years you'll get something. Versus us being close to the data and I think it puts FP&A in the spotlight because you know every single problem with the data, how it comes out, and because we own it. If you ask IT why this is this? They will say this is what the system says versus the responsibility that falls on us, where we can usually explain why the number is this and what it should be. However coming back to the point of disruptive strategy, we took technology that was pretty available and the way we harmonised it from the perspective that we brought in data from invoicing but we also brought in data that was booked to the ledger. So the data was always true, it was one version of the truth regardless of how you want to do it. Whether you wanted to see the invoice data that was there, or if you wanted to see the other portion of the data that was there. Now instead of having IT-led enterprise reporting, we created self-service business intelligence. That helped the business perspective because they now had a form of data that was useful for everyone in the sense that we built a dashboard for the CEO but the same dashboard was relevant to the frontline salesperson.

On the most valuable resource you can give back to the business and in one instance drove 50% more sales

When I'm trying to promote an idea I don't always promise that we're going to get a huge value out of this. The one thing that I will promise is that I will give you the most valuable thing back to you, which is your time. People know how to do their business better, so once I free up your time to do the more valuable things, you will. One of the sales team that I dealt with used to spend 2 weeks at a time doing sales reporting, now they don't spend any time. Now the sales for that region went up 50%, do I take credit for that? Not really but they are the ones who went out and sold. All I did was free up their time to do the things that they are good at, and at the same time give them tools to make the right decision.

On why it's more than simply teaching others how to fish

So starting back to the idea about leading, a lot of it is your team learning. Something that I picked up from Trevor Noah's book, *Born a Crime*, is that a lot of times we have a saying, *"Teach others how to fish."* However a lot of times we teach people how to fish but we do not give them a fishing rod. So my philosophy is to give people a fishing rod and teach people how to fish. Stock the pond and give them support when they need it to help them develop their skills and they will be on their own. It's about empowering people to make the right decision and actually give them the support along the ways to build that expertise.

On the best bit of advice Khaled has ever received

It goes back to when I was doing my first budget, I had spent a couple of all-nighters and my sales vice president said, *"it's not about the numbers."* I said, *"What are you talking about? I've just spent countless hours putting this together."* He looked at me and said, *"it's all about the story, the numbers have to flow with the story."* At the end of the day being a good steward of the data is really about being able to get to a story, and a position where our stories jive. If sales are saying that we are seeing weakness in the market from this perspective, then does the story from the procurement team make sense? Are we working towards the same story? That's where you have to take this information and get to a good story and figure out if it fits the story that you want to tell your customers.

Recommended Resources

Book: *Superforecasting: The Art and Science of Prediction*, by Philip Tetlock and Dan Gardner (link)

Book: *Pre-Suasion: A Revolutionary Way to Influence and Persuade*, by Robert B. Cialdini (link)

Website: BeastBI (link)

"The analogy I like to use is the lantern versus the flashlight. If you've got a lantern and you come into a dark room, you can see a lot of things very clearly. However if you come into that same dark room with a flashlight you're only going to see one thing."

Pete Smith
LI: thinkingbehaviour
WS: theoutperformer.co

Tags:
#coaching #GROW #relationships #fixed-mindset #communication

PETE SMITH is a Partner at The Outperformer, an award-winning training & development firm that works with organisations enabling their employees to access best-in-class thinking to deliver better results, all through the power of career development. Pete is also CEO of Humanity in Business, as well as holding a number of training and facilitation consulting roles throughout his career.

Pete is based out of Sydney, Australia.

On a useful framework to break out from our fixed mindset

It really is about the kind of questions you ask yourself in the environment. If you think about something that has a natural cause and effect, it's easy to say A + B = C and away we go. But when you get more complexity you've got to actually analyse things in a different way. So you have to ask questions. I like to follow what's called the GROW coaching model. It comes from John Whitmore:

G stands for *Goal*. First and foremost what is it that you are trying to achieve? What's the best outcome? What's the best use of your time? How can I help you the best today?

R, the *Reality*, is the colour. It's the what's going on around here? The better you can understand under the hood, what's going on in the engine then the more the goal can shift in a more appropriate and effective way. The reality questions are: what's the impact of it? What have you tried in the past? Have you seen this happening in other places, in other contexts?

O for *Options* is next. When you get the answers to those questions is when we come back to the expertise mindset. As we're in a disruptive business landscape the emerging options are the ones that are novel. We explore here what can be done differently? What do we need to look at?

W for *Will Do*. At the end of the day it's just a good conversation unless you've got some action out of it. Unless we know the next time we catch up with them that we've got a starting point about what was meant to be done, otherwise we won't break out of our fixed mindset.

On the importance of listening to avoid solutions mode and the lantern versus flashlight metaphor

In coaching my mouth used to move up a little bit too much and a couple people had pulled me up on it: *"What's going on? Why are you doing that?"* So I really trained myself to repeat what the person has said in my own mind because I know if I don't I'm going to go off on my own tangent. I'm going to go off on what I think needs to happen, I'm going to go into solutions mode. The analogy I like to use is the lantern versus the flashlight. If you've got a lantern and you come into a dark room, you can see a lot of things very clearly. However if you come into that same dark room with a flashlight you're only going to see one thing. If we jump into solutions mode too quick, we're getting our flashlight out too quickly, and we're missing what else is in the lanterns view. I use this as a metaphor that early on in the dialogue with someone, don't get locked in too soon. Hang around with the lantern and see what's going on around it. *Helicopter*

On the importance of paraphrasing to test our understanding and to help our stakeholders lock in accountability for solutions

I recommend that you don't repeat everything that a person says with your mouth moving, a fun way is to paraphrase. I know this is basic, even I have to catch myself forgetting this sometimes. If we can test our understanding with the person, let's say we're delivering some analysis by walking them through a dashboard, and advising them that it suggests there is a different way of thinking about what you're doing. Then take on board what they are saying with the lantern. It means we have to actually stop ourselves drawing the conclusions to better understand the conclusions of the person whom we are engaging with is drawing. This is why we paraphrase, because if we don't test what we understand of what they know, then we're going to go off on a tangent.

On the reasons why reading non-fiction is constructive for accountants and analytical types

Neuroscience actually shows that when you read a story book the right brain is engaged. If you read a boring book, you'll find yourself thinking about your phone bill, or next week's rent or something like that. Then you go to the movies and the movie was better than the book. But if you've ever read a book where you go to the movie and it just wasn't as good as the book, that's because you've created the imagery in your own mind, and that means you've engaged the right brain. Now the finance and accounting professional might enjoy a really good novel because it is actually engaging the part of the brain that they don't often work with as much. So neuroscience has shown that it helps to connect both hemispheres of the brain more effectively by reading a good story.

On the importance of shadowing those who understand the customer persona

Spend a day shadowing folks out in the business, get into their world. Designers, design thinkers and those people that really understand the customer persona spend a lot more time understanding every step of their day. I had a client who spent a day with one of his stakeholders, and it wasn't just the insights he got from his stakeholder, it was the message it sent to his stakeholder about how embracing he was of all these things going on in his world and this was really invaluable.

On the best bit of advice Pete has ever received

I remember as a kid I was in Melbourne with my brother to watch the Aussie Rules Football. I was from a small countryside town and we met with one of his mates, who had this most amazing car. I think it was a Jaguar. I said it was real beautiful and he and I got talking. I then asked him, *"What's your job?"* and he mentioned he worked in sales. I followed up by asking, *"Selling stuff?"* He told me, *"There's a couple things you need to know, 1. It's not what you know, it's who you know. And 2. It's about having the gift of the gab."* Now some of us might put sales in the box with a certain odour, however as I've moved through life I go back to that moment.

I think that what he meant by having the gift of the gab is just about listening and communicating. And his point about it's not what you know but who you know is about relationships. When you listen and ask good questions your focus is on them not on yourself. I guess that's required for a good salesperson. In my context as a facilitator and a coach, it's always about the other person and the success I've had in my career comes from that. It's that people know and trust that I'm having their best interests at heart.

Recommended Resources

Book: *Influence: The Psychology of Persuasion (2007)* by Robert B Cialdini PhD (link)

Book: *Coaching for Performance: The Principles and Practice of Coaching and Leadership FULLY REVISED 25TH ANNIVERSARY EDITION (People Skills for Professionals)* by John Whitmore (link)

Book: *The Lion, the Witch and the Wardrobe (The Chronicles of Narnia, Book 2),* by CS Lewis (link)

Website: The Outperformer (link)

"Promise what you deliver & deliver what you promise."

Rishabh Sawansukha
LI: sawansukha
WS: gststreet.com

Tags:
#outsourcing #value #shared ecosystem #freelancing #technology

RISHABH SAWANSUKHA started his finance and accounting career as a chartered accountant over 20 years ago gaining experience in Taxation, Technology , Change Management & ERP with companies like Schlumberger , Coca Cola , Oracle, Snapdeal & IOCL. Rishabh is also founder and chairman of GSTStreet and BizStreet.biz which leverages a shared ecosystem of a 400+ strong partner network to facilitate Clients in Business, Tax, Technology, Tax Talent Hiring, Debt Management and Transformation services.

Rishabh is currently based out of Gurgaon, Haryana in India, is a Chartered Accountant (CA), Certified Strategist from IIM-Ahmedabad, Certified Mediator & Arbitrator as well as holding a Masters in Business Finance (MBF).

On how to avoid burning the midnight oil
When I started my career I was exposed to a data room. I was told forty locations would send data into you to process it and it would take three people ten days to produce three to six reports for forty locations. After 2 months of working in this environment burning the midnight oil I figured I needed to automate the repetitive processes. This was back in 2001, and my boss said to me we don't have any budget for any technology because we were implementing SAP. So at best he could approve some technology trainee/intern and then I was supposed to work after office hours with them. I was strictly told that you cannot work on any projects within office hours. At that time I was young, I was not married, so I decided to work on those process automations and after one month we created a very simple visual basic tool, a basic macro, and in half an hour we were able to process one location. So we

could run all the processes and by the time we came in the next day all our reports were there. It was like a dream come true because we told our boss we are going to have this party quite often now. We will come to office for 10 days but we will have fun because the reports will be available in one day. That was the power of cutting down the processes which required human intervention which can be done through machines or via coding languages. However that was a very long time ago in 2001, and I think that times have changed with artificial intelligence and so there are many things we can actually make smart use of it for any function like Tax, Financial Analysis, MIS , Accounting and so on …

On why technology is really helping finance do what we should be doing

If we see the new technologies that are coming to market, for example, mobile technology. Before last year, there was business forecast & planning we used to do for a telco business. People always said that India is a vast country and it is very difficult to reach out the last mile. However now India has 900 million active mobile users, so the whole country is connected. It is very easy to reach out to anybody at any given point. This is a big change we have actually seen in our lifetime and has created lots of business opportunities for accountants. As an example we have started a small mobile shared service compliance centre and we started by targeting clients outside India, particularly in the Hotel and Hospitality Industry where processes are more or less same. Only the city and currency changes but customer expectations do not change drastically. However we are actually now getting more clients from India because more and more companies are comfortable with giving their non-productive activities to us. We do it in a very methodical process only supported by using technology. We are giving them the results in the form of dashboards, of key metrics, which they never got through the manual support of accountants both in-house or external. The business owner, the CEO and the CFO they're not interested in how we've captured the data and how we've transformed it. They're interested with the insights in the data so we can identify the opportunities and answer whether we have identified the threats in time by using senior and seasoned experts on board with BizStreet. Because if the company has a governance failure it allows us to make sense of it and sort it out before it is too late!

On breaking down making sense of shared services into three simple steps

I will just say that in 2007 when we set up the global shared service Centre for Oracle it was set up in Bangalore, India. We had over 400 people handling accounting for every country in every part of the world except North Korea. They found the Indian accountants were smart enough to get into the shoes of their country accounting teams. The three things I'd like to share is that first, you have to have the mindset at the top. For the accounting and the controllership functions there are a lot of things that are non-core that can be outsourced. The choice always remains with you, however you must get your house in order first because whatever I cannot do I cannot outsource.

So firstly, I should know my business and if I don't know my business there are people who can slice, dice and tell you what the core processes and the non-core processes are. We largely do this part for our clients who intend to adopt automation. The second thing is you have to create process champions within your organisation who are going to control the processes because you can outsource the process, but you cannot outsource the controls. The controls should always remain with you because it's your business, it's not the business of the shared service provider. The third part is change management, because the technology is changing fast, your business scenario is changing fast, and your transactions tomorrow can be getting more complex as you might be buying in China and selling in Singapore. So you might have to be more aware of the global taxation impacts because the taxation of the global digital economy is a new and developing area. So we need to know about the relevant developments that we need to be cognizant of. So there you have to develop either an in-house capability to decode the taxation systems of all the countries you deal with. However if you are a small start-up or business you should focus on implementing some tools or applications which are easy to use and not very expensive so that you can better understand your business.

On how shared ecosystems and economies are working in practice

The shared economy is not a very new concept, it was around nearly 1,000 years ago. Even before telecommunications and the Internet the shared economy was still there. We all started with bartering, and the barter system was there before currencies came. Barter was nothing but shared economy. So now in our model of shared ecosystems we require experts who can deliver the projects. It is not freelancing, it is not aggregation, it is very different because consulting is not a commodity. Whatever shared economy we have seen so far, things like copper, or gold, or hotels are commodities, you can always price them. However, I cannot price the time of myself because it will vary depending on the subject, the situation and the client. Sometimes it will be worth $2,000 other clients might value it at $10,000. If we create a marketplace situation where everybody's work is price tagged, then that will not work. So we decided we will only work with the premium expertise, which is by far not easily available or accessible in a consolidated form. And in our ecosystem, we onboarded 400 seasoned experts worldwide. On our website you will not find them intentionally because we do not want people to be labelled, we don't want people to be tagged when you're looking for some work in the market because they are not. We work with the people who can promise what they deliver and deliver what they promise, because the biggest flaw in the freelancing business is people can promise the moon but they can't deliver the earth. So we work with them, we develop their capacity and enhance their network so that when the user comes they will at least show up. This means we can deliver complex projects very easily because we believe in the power of the shared economy globally.

On the best bit of advice Rishabh ever received
One of my bosses told me that we work for three things, knowledge, money and fun. If anything is missing in your life then you are in the wrong profession, so change your profession. So if you don't get the knowledge every day, or don't get paid well for your work, of if you don't enjoy your work then there is no point continuing that work.

Recommended Resources
Book: *Work Wise (2010)*, by Rahul Kapoor (link)

Book: *Zero to One: Notes on Start Ups, or How to Build the Future (2015)*, by Blake Masters and Peter Thiel (link)

Video: TaxStreets Global (link)

Website: BizStreet.biz (link)

"In the consultancy environment 70% is good enough. Perfecting a task is not expected or asked for, you're not making anyone happy apart from yourself."

Shruti Kapoor
LI: shruti-kapoor

Tags:
#confidence #diversity #presence #common ground #values

SHRUTI KAPOOR is a global finance professional with extensive commercial finance, business partnering and consulting experiences. She currently works with Sodexo, leading the global transformation project for the order to invoice and cash processes.

Shruti is a Singaporean and currently lives in Paris, France

On how to connect with non-financial stakeholders and get their attention
What I found is, learn to simplify things so you can get your message across in a simple and surprisingly non-financial way. You've got to tailor your questions and concepts to a non-financial target audience. So what I try and do is, I try and throw some humour in. I try and throw as much practical information into it. I really tailor it to their business even if it means coming down to their individual site, and saying, *"Okay, let's talk about Mister XYZ for example."* Bring it down to a level that is relatable for them, I think that's where you get their attention.

On how to develop your confidence by learning what not to do
I think when it comes to the Big 4 experience that I've gone through I've been in that environment for about eight or nine years and it's a really accelerated learning curve, at least for me. I learned probably 80% of what not to do, and what I don't like, and 20% of what I saw that I wanted to emulate. I learned that very quickly. I know I am not a subject matter expert, I cannot win an argument if someone goes down the path of say accounting policy. That kind of stuff doesn't interest me however you would need this kind of confidence in consultancy environments.

On how the junior finance professional in the room can demonstrate their presence

One very simple way is to offer to take minutes. You'll be amazed how easy it is where people instinctively will trust you if it's your words that they're reading at the end of the meeting, because that's what they will remember.

On Shruti's experiences as a minority and the importance of food

To be fair Europe is used to diversity, so it's not a region where I'm coming in and trying to bring a different perspective. They are used to it so that really helps. What I've found is because I'm a minority in my own country (Singapore) I'm used to being the odd one out. So I'm comfortable in that space. What I always do, and I do this at home as well, this is not specific to Europe again, finding the commonality is key and a lot of times the easiest way is just to connect, on business principles and business concepts. That's one way of keeping it technical and slightly more reserved which works within Asian cultures and personalities.

If you're brave enough to try and venture into more personal conversations a great common ground is food. You'll be amazed the number of people that can spend hours and hours talking about food and it doesn't matter which region they come from. I know that that's such an easy thing in Asia to talk about, and for the Europeans & Americans too. I guess in terms of the differences that I bring, number one, especially in a physical meeting, I am a visual representation of diversity. Whether I like it or not, again I stand out, it forces people to realise there are different languages and cultures in the room. So I think that trying to be comfortable in that space and not to take it personally is something that I would recommend because people are not uncomfortable with you in the room, but you just have to accept the fact that you look different.

On learning to accept and not fight business values & decisions

What's worked for me is to learn to accept and not fight the business values and decisions that are made. There's that grey space of being miserable and not agreeing with why your company is either being ruthless with cost cutting, or your company is being too slow and inefficient by allowing people that are inept in their jobs to continue doing what they're doing. Being in that grey space is very negative. It's extremely demoralising, so learning to accept it or saying, *"Sorry this generally doesn't work with me, and I just need to go."* The sooner you can make that decision for yourself I think the easier it will be in terms of coming to work everyday because you really have to line up the business values with your own personal values. If you feel at some point that the business is going against fundamental principles that you agree with, it's time to go, be brave enough to go.

On the best bit of advice Shruti has ever received

As an Asian I think one of the things we strive for is perfection, it's in our DNA, we can't help it. That gets exasperated with going through a consultancy experience. I really had to be told, close to my breaking point I would say, that in the consultancy environment 70% is good enough. Perfecting a task is not expected or asked for, you're not making anyone happy apart from yourself.

Recommended Resources

Book: *A River Sutra (2007),* by Gita Mehta (link)

"When a person actually has that curiosity, in general, they tend to be a lot more receptive and open about change and I can foresee there are going to be more changes coming along."

Wei Chien Yoong
LI: wei-chien-yoong

Tags:
#business partnering #internal audit #risk management #diversity #value chain #margin analysis

WEI CHIEN YOONG is Audit Lead Asia Pacific at the diversified conglomerate Cargill, the largest private company in the world, and as such she's a regular business traveller across Southeast Asia. Wei Chien's other prior roles included finance transformation. implementing Cargill's Global Business Services Strategy in Malaysia; Finance Director Southeast Asia Process Automation and controls at Invensys with other leadership roles at Diageo, Honeywell & KPMG.

Originally from Malaysia Wei Chien has an Executive MBA from Singapore Management University, is a member of CPA Australia and is based out of Singapore.

On how the expectations of the modern finance professional have changed

The profession is no longer secure per se, it is evolving. Nowadays it requires a very strong people focus and stakeholder-centric mindset along with the ability to translate, understand and interpret the numbers into insight therefore supporting the growth and development of the business.

On how the internal audit team can become more valued business partners

The technical capability needs to be there, that's the foundation, that's where you can have a constructive and knowledgeable conversation with the stakeholders but that in and of itself is definitely not enough in the current environment, which is about partnering with the business, translating the numbers into insight and sharing it with the business. I would think internal audit's capability to call out some of these strategic risks the business is facing at the macro or broad level, particularly around sustainability. One thing that I will recommend for anybody in a finance, accounting or audit role in particular will be having a global and broad perspective about the risk areas that the business is facing. A lot of the audit profession within which I have worked, both external and internal, tends to have a very checkbox mindset, it's very structured, it's very square, you check off the box and get your job done. But I don't think that is going to sustain us because that is not what the business is looking for.

On what businesses are looking for from their auditors
They are looking for an auditor that is more well-rounded, who understands the business, connects with the business, understands what is the real risk to the business and what is the practical mitigation plan or control plans that need to be put in place, because we're not talking about the perfect scenario. When you run a business there's always risks, so the auditor needs to have that perspective to come in and figure out what is practical for the business to do in terms of mitigating these risks or what are some of the risks that the business will accept and continue to operate in that manner.

On how diversity in audit perspectives can unlock innovation
You do need that diversity to unlock innovation. With different views, opinions, and I truly believe collectively as a group, we are going to improve on the group thinking and the approach as well. This is what I see in audit. For example I'm going on an assignment shortly into Australia. I'm going to work with people from Turkey, Latin America and of course, Australia. We didn't want the audit team to pick people from just one country and that really excites me.

On the white space in between two value chains
The main differences between Diageo and Cargill are that Cargill is a commodity agriculture supply chain company, so money is made on moving out shipments of goods as compared to what Diageo does as a premium alcohol company where you sell on brand, on differentiation, and your premium offerings. That was when I would say I got involved in terms of looking at the value chain and margin analysis, with an

emphasis on where profit margin is taken by different players along the value chain and its impact on the final price that we're paying as a consumer. With that, I reflected upon the business model at Cargill then in my mind thinking that it's probably going to be a matter of time until a number of businesses will need to make a strategic shift or choice in terms of where they want to play, how they would want to position themselves versus the gap in their current capabilities and how to close them. And indeed, that was the case when I re-joined Cargill, when I was in Malaysia. I saw that happening across a number of businesses and when we started to look at what the customer needs are versus what we can offer and what our competitors are offering of course there's a white space or blue ocean there. That untapped market that everybody is hoping to get, to capture the maximum margin and also opportunity.

On why the human element is so important for accountants

I'm not sure if you know this book, it's called the Little Prince. In that little book I always remember that there's a phrase, *"it's only with the heart that one can see rightly and what is essential is invisible to the eye."* Again, coming from an accountant that sounds a little odd, but you must have that human element, have the ability to empathise and connect with people to be a good business partner. And this particular book has taught me a lot of about being authentic and true to myself.

On the key quality for the finance professionals of today and tomorrow

Having that global and open mindset and having that curiosity about change. When a person actually has that curiosity, in general, they tend to be a lot more receptive and open about change and I can foresee there are going to be more changes coming along, be they technology, globalisation or just even politics impacting some of the trade policies that will impact the work of finance professionals. So keep an open mind, be curious about things, that will ensure your relevance into the future.

On the best bit of advice Wei Chien would give to her younger self

The advice I would have given myself back then is the same as now, is to be true to yourself. I think that's very important to know what your passion is and go for it and never give up. I guess that has given me an attribute that I'm always very proud of is authenticity. To be a good business partner, a finance person or business leader one needs to be authentic. Authentic as in be honest about your strengths and weaknesses and not to be afraid to be vulnerable, with your peers, or even with your boss or your colleagues. You can only do that when you are true to yourself.

Recommended Resources

Article: *Auditing Sustainability and The Greater Good, by* Wei Chien Yoong (link)

Book: *The Little Prince*, by Antoine de Saint-Exupéry (link)

EUROPE

"There are definitely two types of approach to business, one physical and one digital. Accountants cannot stay away from the digital business model so they need to understand it and be able to support it."

Agnès Hugot
LI: agnèshugot
WS: fasttracktrade.co

Tags:
#collaboration #younger generation #networking #curiosity #digital

AGNÈS HUGOT is the co-founder of Fast Track Trade and Cites Gestion. Agnès also has an extensive background in international financing and corporate development. Agnès is a believer in technology as a strong commerce enabler and her key focus is on the needs of Small & Medium Enterprises and she helps facilitate their inclusion into international trade networks because they are essential for driving the economic growth in any market.

Agnès holds MBAs from both HEC and INSEAD, France, and is based out of Singapore.

On collaboration tools making efforts more visible
The way we're working is very different from any other traditional corporates. Firstly because nowadays you stand and put post-it notes on the wall for anything that needs to be done and you need to characterise in short stories on those small pieces of paper otherwise they stay on the wall and you don't pick them up until the stories have been completed. When you stand there it takes a lot of thought, so basically you don't want lengthy meetings to last. You just want to get right to the point. If anything, with using collaborative tools and software, you can see what people are delivering. This can also very tough because those who are not delivering their tasks need to be supported by others. However you can see what they have done during the day, whereas in a more tradition-

al organisation you don't see anything because people either don't come up with anything good or they just play political games.

On why team momentum comes from the youngest team member

The team's momentum comes from the youngest. You need to make sure that they can be heard. That every single decision in terms of the team's organisation and the future of the firm is taken with young people in mind, Why? Because for those of us above the age of forty, we have been taught and we've been used to working in organisations where paper and centralisation is huge. This is completely the opposite of what is happening right now with the emergence of digital networks and platforms. Sometimes we might not get it and it is okay not to get it, so long as you can listen to the youngest and you make sure that their views are influencing the business, and are taken into account for your organisation. If you believe that your organisation has too much inertia you need to do it outside of the system, but you would want to make sure that you have young people coming out of Universities, bringing their tools, and bringing their ways of behaving and collaborating, because these are the ways that are going to help you win in the digital age.

On the importance of luck and random factors

You need to be patient, you need to observe the game, the competitors, and to stay in it, but it's about character. Now it's not worth spending three years trying to push something that would never happen, but you do need to make sure that you create random networking opportunities. By that I mean you need to go to random networking events. The people who were key in Fast Track Trade, and in developing the path to value met randomly. So you need to be open to go and talk to people, to be just curious about what they do before you start introducing yourself. This is the way that you create your network and then you create brand messengers who are going to relay your message and value even though they are not your employees. It is not only about patience; it is also about luck and the random factor.

On how to stay relevant by focusing on digital tools

So two things. The first is looking at digital transformation and digital tools with a lot of openness and curiosity. This is going to play a big part in our professional lives. The second aspect is the distributed ledger technology because this can help record a lot of data and help your work to be more meaningful without adding more effort. It's about using the technology to become more of an advisor to smaller and medium-sized companies who cannot afford that for now but would appreciate the support. There are definitely two types of approach to business, one physical and one digital. Accountants cannot stay away from the digital business model so they need to understand it and be able to support it.

On the best bit of advice Agnes has ever received

When working you need to try whatever comes your way and don't give up when you don't like it at first sight because it might bring some value to you later on. So just be curious about everything. I participated in the financial crisis in Greece and helped restructure the banking sector. I've never refused any kind of engagement which was considered as risky, as it will bring a lot of things that there was no guidance for, no checklist for, and this is a good lesson for someone who started their career as an auditor. Your career is about having fun and developing yourself. There is a point where it needs to make sense and be consistent with the pleasure you have at work. Also always have an eye on what is digital, because this is going to have a large impact in our lives.

Recommended Resources

Book: *On China* by Henry Kissinger (link)

Website: Fast Track Trade (link)

"Our business partners want to make good decisions, because that creates more value and that makes them successful."

Anders Liu-Lindberg
LI: andersliulindberg
WS:businesspartneringinstitute.org

Tags:
#business partnering #relationships #value creation #stakeholders #insights #trust #credibility

ANDERS LIU-LINDBERG is a Senior Finance Business Partner at Maersk supporting its largest product and has 10+ years of experience working with Maersk Finance both in Denmark and abroad. Anders main goal at Maersk is to show how others can be successful with business partnering and drive value creation as a trusted partner. Anders is also the co-founder of the Business Partnering Institute, the owner of the largest group forum dedicated to Finance Business Partnering on LinkedIn with almost 8,000 members, as well as the co-author of the book "Create Value as a Finance Business Partner" and a long-time Finance Blogger with 40.000+ followers.

Anders has a Masters in Finance & Accounting from Copenhagen Business School. When he's not working & contributing to the finance community Anders can be found spending time with his young family in Copenhagen, Denmark.

On the 4 specific skills areas to develop for a successful career in finance
Our competence has four specific areas: business partnering skills, technical skills, analysis skills and leadership skills. And when we hire people into our financial roles we say that they need to already have the technical skills, we do not spend a lot of time developing technical competencies. Of course, it could be that you're in a specialised function like Tax or Treasury where you might need to go to some technical course from time-to-time, but in general no that's not what we train for, we train for the partnering skills and the analysis skills. The analysis

skills are mostly around how to solve problems in a different way than people typically do. These are our two core areas which means that they are the most critical to finance professionals of the future. If you can partner with stakeholders and want to create a successful collaborative relationship, then in order to do that you will need to solve their most critical problems. So those two go hand-in-hand together, you help them solve problems whereby you build relationships, and also the other way around, and if you do that, you will always add value to your stakeholders, which will probably mean you'll always have a job.

On what business partners really want

Obviously our business partners want to make good decisions, because that creates more value and that makes them successful. So that's what they're looking for us to provide. In fact, it's about helping them make better decisions.

On 4 simple ways to provide great insights

To get to the insight phase we have to stop running tons of analysis and handing out reports that never get read and trying to figure out what the right data source should be. If we can't get outside our office or away from our desk to sit down with our stakeholders, we'll never be able to deliver that impact for them. So all they want is for us to help them make better decisions but we can only do that if we get out there, talk to them, understand from them what is the real problem, and help them solve that by finding insights in all the information that's available to us. We also need to improve the speed to insight tremendously because right now it's either non-existent or way too slow.

On why the future for our profession should be seen as half-full

If you're an accountant who's heavy on the transactional side, a billings clerk, or A/P supervisor, or whatever it maybe, I think your job is likely not going to be there in the future so what is it that you could do instead to get ahead of the curve? Generally, there are 2 roads to take. One is to specialise. The accounting profession itself is growing because it is focusing more on specialisation as the environment we operate in is getting more and more complex, with countries trading more and more with each other, with transfer pricing and all these other complex issues that require Treasury and Tax people to be in that space, so it's not going to go away. Of course another approach is to go up into the value chain, getting more into analytics and business partnering, because that's a way to add value right here and now. No one knows what's going to happen in ten years or so but those jobs will still be there in the future. So you have to decide for yourself what it is that you want to do with your career. Those choices are better made now rather than when you're forced to make them because technology is coming to take your job away. It's for the individual to decide of course, but I see the future as half-full, because I made my choice a very long time ago.

On how every stakeholder interaction can help you add more value

In every meeting you're sitting in with your stakeholders they will be talking about issues you might be able to do something about. Even if they're not speaking directly to you, even if they are having a conversation with someone else, you can pick up on that. If you can solve this, it will be solving the problem for a key business stakeholder. You can turn out something that helps the business relationship and also helps you to add value.

On the most important quality for a finance professional to have today

The most important quality is the ability to develop relationships. If you can develop relationships with your stakeholders, then you can come out a winner. Being able to develop relationships takes in all the things that a finance professional has to be able to do, because if you can't do analysis, if you can't solve problems, if you can't do all sorts of things that are related to finance, you will not be able to develop that relationship.

On how doing the right homework is important to developing relationships

You can do a lot of homework before you get up from your desk. I don't mean refining your analysis a bit more, what I mean is look at what kind of tools can I use to partner with my stakeholders. So first of all, what is your own personality profile? What preferences do you have for interacting with people? And what is the profile of your stakeholders? Because typically they could be the same, they could be different but you cannot always just do your own approach to the work and developing the relationship. So try and figure out what kind of profile they value. Are you someone that likes to speak to the result, or explain the process, or talk about what happened over the weekend or on your last vacation? They could be the same, or they could be different to you. But if you don't consider those preferences, more often than not, the relationship will not develop in the right direction.

On the best bit of advice Anders ever received

We also need to look at the trust equation, because trust is key to any successful relationship. So are you credible with what you do? Do they trust your product? Are you reliable, do you deliver what you say you will deliver? Do you have outside interests so you can have a good conversation with them around things that are not just business related? And then do you have something, some personal experience you shared together, maybe a team building or whatever it might be? Are you oriented towards your stakeholders or yourself? So do you listen more than you speak? If you listen more that you speak this will also help you in building trust. After knowing that trust equation then all you need to do is communicate, so you create some touch points with your stakeholders. It could be some elevator conversations or it could be at the coffee machine. In every interaction you have with the stakeholder use it to advance the relationship. Listen to what they have to say, make sure you've understood what they've said, and then offer suggestions to advance their agenda. Those things will help you build a successful relationship and that is one key thing finance professionals have to do to stay relevant and add value.

Recommended Resources

Book: *The Power of Full Engagement: Managing Energy, Not Time, Is the Key to High Performance and Personal Renewal, Abridged edition (2003)*, by Jim Loehr and Tony Schwartz (link)

Book: *Create value as a Finance Business Partner: Transforming the finance function into a profit centre Paperback (2018)* by Bo Foged, Anders Liu-Lindberg, Henriette Fynsk (link)

Website: The Business Partnering Institute (link)

"In Finance we've some tremendous strengths & assets that sometimes we're guilty of taking for granted."

Andrew Codd
LI: andrewcodd
WS: sitnshow.com

Tags:
#business partnering #assets #society #impact #influence

ANDREW CODD is the producer & founder of the #SITN podcast which is listened to in over 150 countries and aims to create more influential finance professionals worldwide who solve meaningful problems for their organisations and in return have fun, rewarding and successful careers in finance. Andrew has improved the financial success of many well-known brands during his 20-year career and nowadays scales this enterprise-level experience to medium-sized enterprises in Europe, the Middle East & North America. He has also authored a category bestselling book on finance business partnering and regularly gives keynotes and workshops to finance teams worldwide.

Andrew lives and works from the southwest of Ireland. He has a CGMA designation, an MBA in Finance with distinction from Manchester Business School, is a certified mind coach and NLP practitioner.

On how the impact of finance & accounting extends beyond the desk

When I took on my first proper management role I had a team of 15 people and I was very lucky because my first hire was an MBA graduate. He was previously a manager from IT himself who really helped me see how much I sucked as a line manager. I really felt that up until then in my career I was able to do everything myself, even when I was at university, I was able to get the team projects done, largely by myself. I had very high standards and willed things to completion, I was always 'A' grade, I even left school with the highest leaving results, I achieved a first class honours every year at University. So I had been very strong academically and always had a great belief my own ability. But if you're only focused on yourself and doing the work yourself, you're never really growing with others and actually there is more to life than just trying to do everything yourself. I realised that if I was ever going to be successful or have my work given credit for or even do anything meaningful it was always going to have to be with other people. So the two years I spent in that line management position allowed me to make a bucket load of mistakes on how to manage people. I also learned a few things that seemed to work along the way and as part of that process I grew because the people around me grew, which allowed me to grow some more, and then they grew some more. It just seemed to be a bit of a snowball, rolling down the side of a mountain, gaining a momentum all of its own. That's when I discovered that it was important to come out from behind the desk, work with people, understand their haves and wants, and it was just applying a lot of stuff that I learned from sales but sometimes in finance we can just get a bit lost. It's easy to get caught behind our desks staring at our computer screens.

In Finance we've so much more to offer. Obviously, we can count on the great technical knowledge we have learned and can offer our organisations. However our impact is bigger than just that because prosperous enterprises lead to prosperous societies. Particularly given those organisations and their staff pay and generate income taxes, their customers pay taxes on the value added, and when you add up all the numbers it's a benchmark of the financial success of an economy, which is judged on, guess what, their numbers. But also its success is judged by the level of its employment opportunities and income per capita, which again are outcomes from having successful indigenous enterprises. So there's a bit more to finance and accounting than simply sitting at our desks all day.

On the great assets we have in Finance

In Finance we've some tremendous strengths and assets that sometimes we're guilty of taking for granted. One of them is our access to data, another is our access and proximity to the key decision makers, as well as that perceived independence from political interests. We also have that broad visibility across our organisations of the value chain, as well as having the technical training to be able to deconstruct the value drivers, quantify the outcomes of potential courses of actions to make a difference to the bottom line. We can turn such insights into financial outcomes to figure out where organisations could be getting bigger bangs for their buck and the best returns are on their investments. There is a lot there in terms of what we can do.

On turning Finance into a game

The thing is with mental models is to continuously test them and refine them to make them better. At the end of the day the models are only worth as much as we've gone and applied them and tested them out, to know what works well and what could be better and that's part of the fun. Actually when I work on anything, I turn it into a game to try and figure out how much I actually don't know and a key phrase that's stuck with me is from Frederick Hayek, *"I am ignorant of my own ignorance."* Or more colloquially, *"I don't know what I don't know."* So I'm always questioning what it is that I don't know and what has to have happened to acquire this knowledge either for me personally or my team to help stakeholders make better decisions.

On the best bit of advice Andrew ever received

It's got to be from the book, *How To Win Friends And Influence People*, by Dale Carnegie. I know it was probably written nearly 100 years ago now but there is timeless advice in there. My favourite though would be, *"First seek to understand, then seek to be understood."* A lot of what we do in finance is actually wanting our insights to be understood and the most effective way to do that is to actually take a genuine interest in other people and invest the time to seek to understand what it is that they want and what it is they think they have. Because the difference between those *haves* and *wants* gives us gaps that if we close the gap between *the haves* and *the wants*, we can actually add some value to people. I've always found that has been at the cornerstone of my success in connecting with people and adding value for people over my career. Early in my career I sucked at management, this was also one of the resources that helped me be a better manager, person, partner to my wife and father to my kids. It came along at the right time when I needed it in my life and I still use it very regularly to look back on it and find things in myself that I hadn't seen before when I re-read it.

Recommended Resources

Book: *How to win friends and influence people*, by Dale Carnegie (link)

Book: *The Audacious Finance Partner: Reveals The Key Factors and Skills for Business Partnering Success*, by Andrew Codd (link)

Website: #SITN Portal (link)

"To stay relevant is all about the value that you create in the business. It's no longer good enough to turn up at 9:00, move the numbers around, go home at 5:00, and say my contribution is producing this report."

Andrew Harding
LI: andrew-harding-fcma-cgma
WS: cimaglobal.com

Tags:
#management accounting #value creation #change #relevant #not-for-profit #trust #stakeholder value

ANDREW HARDING is the Chief Executive of Management Accounting at the Association of International Certified Professional Accountants which represents 667,000 members and students in public and management accounting and advocates for the public interest and business sustainability on current and emerging issues. Andrew is a Deloitte alumnus, having started his career in the mid-1980s as a trainee auditor. He progressed into training and development from there, and then began professional body work in 1991. He joined CIMA in 2009, originally as Executive Director for Global Markets, and became Managing Director in 2011—a position he held until 2016, when appointed as Chief Executive. Andrew has served as Non-Executive Chairman of GTS Chemicals PLC, a Chinese company listed in London, from 2014 to 2016.

Andrew holds FCMA, CGMA and ACA designations as well as an MBA from Henley Business School. Andrew is based out of London, England

On how we keep ahead of the rapid pace of change
There are things where you can get ahead but once you're ahead you're only ahead for a short period, you have to keep that rapid change going. If I think about things that I learned as a trainee from 1983 to 1986 and what did I learn then that's relevant now? Well all of the statutes have

changed, all the tax legislation has changed, a lot of the techniques have changed, What hasn't changed though is that primarily you're working with people and you have to get things done, you have to influence people, you have to get the right decisions made, that's all still there. So that becomes the really key sustainable part of it which lasts forever, but the other pieces, you've got to move, you've got to change, we need to look at the world, we need to anticipate the world.

On some simple ways for us to stay relevant

To stay relevant is all about the value that you create in the business. It's no longer good enough to turn up at 9:00, move the numbers around, go home at 5:00, and say my contribution is producing this report. Now what you have to be doing is for anything you produce, what's the result of that? What does that create? Who's mind does it change? Who's thinking has it changed? How does it impact on the business? I was with a finance business partner this last week at a leading IT company and he said, *"I don't have finance in my job title anymore. I am assessed on the impact that I create with the data I have at my fingertips. I no longer do the analysis. We've automated that. It's all about how embedded I am in the business, how I understand the business and now I don't have to seek permission to be in a meeting. Now people look to me for the solutions. It's very different from where finance was 5 years ago where you were regarded as the back office. Now you are the owner of the understanding of the business. People want to know if they pull a lever here, what's the impact over there. I'm that guide to them and I create solutions. I also help them develop their own solutions."* So a very different role and you can see how this feeling of influence and impact really becomes important and that stuff can't be automated.

On a real challenge but also an opportunity for finance professionals

There are a number of finance roles which if I'm going to be honest are about moving data from one system to another on a spreadsheet. That is stuff which is ripe for automation. To the business advisory sections of the consulting firms, that is their bread and butter, they eliminate those, roles disappear, and cost is just eliminated. The people doing those roles, they need to be adapting their skills, they need to be moving into that business partnering role. When we've talked to corporates, those that have made these big changes, most of them to date have not been eliminating huge numbers of jobs. What they've been doing is creating new roles, so the roles which would have been back office suddenly become business partnering roles because the front line of the business is also experiencing this huge, rapid change in speed. That means they need information, they need data at their fingertips. They don't have time to wait, they don't have time for analysis to be done and they need that business partner who is embedded to have that deep understanding and that's the shift that has to be made. The challenge to the mid-career professional who has been moving data around is really, you've been moving that data around, that's given you an understanding of the business, so get out into the business and start using that understanding. Sometimes we actually get people who have done those jobs saying, *"I felt like a robot."* Well the great news is a robot will do that now and you can do the stuff you want to do and you can add that value the business is looking for. That's the way we see it going but there is also a hard message in there which is, we have to adapt, we have to move, we have to change, and we have to recognise the world is changing and no one is going to turn the clock back for us.

On The advantage of becoming known as a Value Creator

Let's say we go back to what is relevant and what are people looking for from you in your job? They're looking at the value you create and if you can build a process and automate that process, that creates value for the business. You then become known as a value creator. Your personal reputation and your personal skills base is around creating value rather than crunching numbers for a report. That adds value to you and the business. That starts to take you from that position where you're doing analysis to that position where you're influencing and having impact, that's where the value is. I wouldn't look at it as making your own job obsolete, I would look at it as reinventing that job and creating time so that you add value in other areas.

On the perceived trust deficit in society and our role to play in addressing it

What have management accounts been doing for the last 100 years? We've been measuring more than the money. We've been measuring productivity, efficiency, and we are now starting to measure outside influences. So now we need to start measuring trust. We need to start referring to that in the metrics in the boardroom. And some might say you can't measure trust. Well perhaps there are surrogates that exist to measure trust. You might start with, what do your customers think of you? What do the communities your business operates in think of you? And once you start looking at that then you start to get a focus on it.

Again it's a key part of the management accountant's world because that's a key part of how business value is created nowadays. If we think about stakeholders, think about stakeholder value, it's no longer just that old concept of shareholder value that needs to be maximised. There are other stakeholders who need to have their value maximised, customers, employees, the communities they operate in, the governments of those countries which they operate in. You see the current discussion around those companies who report their profits in territories other than those in which they do their main business. What's that all about? That's there to build trust and confidence and how do we deal with it and get a line of sight into it? It's all about getting the reporting right.

On the best bit of advice Andrew has ever received

"Set ambitious targets and chase them down relentlessly," and that was certainly something which helps to energise a business, particularly if you're working in a business which is notionally not-for-profit. You need things to build momentum, drive energy and drive enthusiasm. That kind of thing really does energise. If I'm talking to someone about what they would like for their career advice, what I would say is, look for opportunities, explore things that are interesting and focus on genuine impact. An impact is not about attention seeking.

Recommended Resources

White Paper: Future of Finance Resources (link)

White Paper: Business Models Concepts (link)

White Paper: Building trust in a digital world (link)

White Paper: Global Management Accounting Principles (link)

Website: AICPA-CIMA (link)

"If you're in finance, you're not just about posting journals, doing the bank recs, the year-end accounts or even the monthly accounts. All that is there in order to drive the performance of the business."

Andy Burrows
LI: andrewburrows
WS: superchargedfinance.com

Tags:
#business partnering #performance management #purpose #value creation

ANDY BURROWS is Founder and CEO of SuperchargedFinance.com which not only helps accounting & finance professionals drive business performance, but also provides useful & practical advice for those same people working in and with finance on how to improve and grow. Andy qualified as a chartered accountant in the UK more than 20 years ago. He's held many accounting & finance leadership positions and continues to advise on and drive many Finance change and transformation projects at various well-known businesses. Andy is also an author publishing 3 non-finance related books and is based out of Basingstoke, England.

On the culture shock of making finance director at the age of 29

I was made finance director at the age of 29 which was a big career move for me, a horrendously steep learning curve, bigger than I expected. I knew the business very well but the commerciality was a culture shock. So I worked long hours and learned loads. I moved on and in my usual way thought what else can I learn? What different things can I now do? And so I went back to a big PLC (publicly listed company) where I worked in the corporate centre doing quite technical accounting type things.

On the best finance team he ever worked in and why

It was central finance within a PLC which was new for me and again even though the role was quite dry and technical I learnt loads partly through the people who were there, they had some fantastic finance people, and that was Centrica plc, which I consider the best finance team I've ever worked in. Really because of the Group Finance Director at the time. He knew how finance works and business works and it's taken me probably the 15 years since I left there to really pull all that together in my mind and workout actually, he really did know what he was doing, it all fitted together. That's where I tend to use the phrase, *"finance drives business performance,"* and that was their strapline in Centrica.

On why would a business want to hire a CFO in the first place

What I was trying to do at the time was some part-time finance director work for smaller organisations. And one of the things I learned from my marketing gurus is to systematise things down into a nutshell. I had to really think about what finance is all about? Why would any organisation employ a finance director? Why would you want one? And I thought about what is it that finance brings to the table? It's that finance, more than any other function, gets involved in every area of the business. You could say HR or IT they support every area of business but finance has a unique position in needing to know the numbers for each and every function, each and every area of the business, and to know what's driving costs, what's driving revenue, margin and growth. When you look at the bigger companies who gets the flack for the performance of the business, well it's the CFO. That's because the CFO has that influence and position of interest in every function, it's the whole business they're interested in.

Then when I was trying to put together what does business performance involve and how do you manage business performance, I realised that all the elements involved in managing the performance of the business are elements where finance is involved. You've got the strategy and planning, the reporting the analytics side, the transaction processing, the resource allocation, the cash management even risk management, control, they're all things that finance is involved in. That's quite interesting from the point of view that all those things are there in order to manage and drive performance. That's why I'm quite keen to get across the message that if you're in finance, you're not just about posting journals, doing bank recs, the year-end accounts or even the monthly accounts. All that is there in order to drive the performance of the business. Once you start to understand that it changes the way that you think about what you do. I found that it can give you the motivation and boost that you're there for a good reason.

The purpose-driven CFO

I've a series of articles on LinkedIn called the purpose-driven CFO and the premise of the series is really, let's look at different things we do in finance and ask why we do them? As soon as you do that, you realise that if you think about it hard enough, the reason that you do them isn't quite what you thought. It's a bit like budgeting, people just assume budgeting is just what we do every year. But when you delve into what budgeting is all about and what it is there for, it is more about controlling the spending of the business. When you look into that and say well it's about controlling what people spend. It doesn't really do a very good job of it and then you start asking, well how can we do it better.

On a reporting quick win

Reporting I'd say is probably one of those areas with a lot of quick wins. Think of the old adage about measurement, *"Measure what matters,"* and, *"What gets measured gets done."* That one in particular is quite an interesting one if you unpack it because what it really means is what you report drives the behaviour of the business. So if you take that a step further, then what we ought to be reporting is the stuff that drives the performance of the business, so that what people are seeing is what they can influence. And if they can influence those things then the business will do better. So taking a sort of data balanced scorecard approach, looking at what actually drives performance and reporting on that is much more powerful than just turning out the management accounts every month.

On why we need to shift our mindsets to be more outward looking

We need to focus more on driving business value and become a little bit more outward looking if we want to see ourselves as driving business performance. We're all about supporting the business, driving the business, protecting the business and its performance. If we start being more outward looking, and answering, *"What can we help the business do to make more revenue, make more profit or cash, etc?"* Then we will become more valuable to the business. I think that mindset shift is what we need more so than those cost cutting, finance transformation type programs. I've developed a bit of a bug bear with transformation initiatives that just try to make finance cheaper, and actually it gives the wrong impression. Finance can be more valued by what it does, rather than cutting down the number of people who are in it, within reason. We do need to be efficient, but I do think it's that mindset shift.

On the best bit of advice Andy has ever received

Always learn, but I think also ask for help and never give up. From the bad things that have happened to me I would say that most of the things you worry about are not actually worth worrying about as much as you make them out to be. Just try to do the best job you can and not worry so much.

Recommended Resources

Book: *Good To Great (2001)*, by Jim Collins (link)

Book: *Start With Why: How Great Leaders Inspire Everyone To Take Action (2011)*, by Simon Sinek (link)

Book: *The Little Book of Beyond Budgeting: A New Operating System for Organisations: What it is and Why it Works (2017)*, by Steve Morlidge (link)

Articles: The purpose driven CFO series of articles (part 1 of 10) (link)

Website: Supercharged Finance (link)

"You've got a lot of very bright people but they undersell themselves, sitting there quietly doing stuff but no one would know. It's one thing using the spreadsheet to get results out, but then actually doing some thinking based on it, it's under-appreciated."

Brian Donnelly
LI: brianpeterdonnelly
WS: synapseinformation.com

Tags:
#spreadsheets #IT #people #impact #OVOTT

BRIAN DONNELLY is CEO & Founder of Synapse which uses innovative Cloud technology to provide bespoke spreadsheet solutions that provides simultaneous multi-user functionality around consolidation of spreadsheets enabling one version of the truth on every desktop. Previously Brian started and led a number of Venture Capital backed organisations in Silicon Valley, USA & the UK following a stint out of college working at the British Tax Authorities on their databases.

Brian holds an Msc in Computer Science and lives in Birmingham, England with his family.

On the importance of getting to the point and having great people

I was having to give a presentation in Singapore and the organisers of the investment conference, like they all do, said just get to the point, keep it crisp and less than 10 minutes. So the first presenter, an MD PhD, he had a forty-five slide feature which was packed with lots and lots of detail and then he read out each line. After nine and a half minutes, he had only gone three slides in, it was never going to work. So Dr. John Diekmann (inventor of gene chips and founder of Affymetrix) who's this luminary in the field. he turned up with 3 slides. And on the question on how do you build a fantastic company and for that matter a finance team, his first side just went up on the screen and it just said, PEOPLE! He talked about People and it was a wonder of eloquence, we were just glued to it. And then he put the next slide up, and it said, PEOPLE, and then he spoke very eloquently about a different aspect of it. Amazingly his final slide came up and it just said, PEOPLE.

To this day, I walked away with this simple message, that you can't build a great finance team or a great company without getting great people and one thing he said that really struck home was, you can build a silk purse from a sow's ear, however wouldn't it be easier to start with silk. Life's much easier if you hire good people, who are really smart, particularly for a start-up like ours. If you get the wrong people, well, let's just not go there.

On why Finance are allergic to sales people

None of us are naïve, and in finance, as well as all accountants I speak to, they are antigenically sensitised against salespeople, a bit like when you have to protect yourself from hay fever, because it's just so crass. Particularly if you're deploying a fintech solution. We're working with the Bank of England at the moment, you just go and have a chat with finance, it's fantastic what they tell you they're doing. There's some big problems and we may be able to fix some bits of that. Why do you need someone just to come in and well, tell fibs that are so obviously over the top, some of these are a bit like having a second hand car salesman sell to you.

On why the entire world of Finance is built upon spreadsheets and the tension between Finance & IT

Everyone knows that the entire world of Finance is built on spreadsheets. Another thing, without trying to be provocative is that the finance team are, bright! They just are. These days we are probably not allowed to say that but it is true. They're considerably brighter than a lot of the rest of the departments in business and yet the IT department who are often not well liked by Finance come along and say, *"Thou shall not use spreadsheets. They are very bad, wrong, and you don't know what you're talking about."* Of course the dichotomy of this is you need to use spreadsheets in finance for so many different purposes and yet they have got obvious downsides. You get multiple people trying to use them and lots of other problems, as you see with sensationalist headlines in the FT and other journals how tens of millions got lost due to an error on a spreadsheet. So we built something which, when we showed the finance people, they loved it. You have a spreadsheet and as you type into it captures all the stuff you type in and it ripples through to Fred who is in New York or Mary who's in Sydney and everyone gets a single view of the truth. And when we solved that problem, the world beats a path to your door.

On why Finance is guilty of underselling its impact
You've got a lot of very bright people but they undersell themselves, sitting there quietly doing stuff but no one would know. It's one thing using the spreadsheet to get results out, but then actually doing some thinking based on it, it's under-appreciated.

On the best bit of advice Brian has ever received
When they drag me out to Silicon Valley, the VCs (Venture Capitalists), said, *"So, you're a great guy you know, we get this whole thing but, less words, less words."* So get to the point, especially when you're raising funding or if you've got a presentation with your boss. When you're chatting with people what they want from you is the summary first. Don't give me a life story first. So briefly chatting with a great investor one summer's day in New York he said to me, *"I had this guy coming in the other day, he spent 20 minutes telling me all about the wiring in this complicated thing, and then some other stuff, and the VC turned around and said so let me get this right. You make and sell software?"* and the entrepreneur says, *"Yeah! I've been telling you that."* So I think get to the point to help people as rapidly as possible figure out what you're talking about.

Recommended Resources
Website: Synapse (link)

Video: What Synapse Do (link)

"I think the more you share with people, the more you will get those different views and the richer you are basically."

Charly Landy
LI: charly-landy

Tags:
#reverse mentoring #career advancement #value creation #experiments

DR. CHARLY LANDY is currently a Financial Controller at GSK. Charly has 14 years of working experience in various finance and leadership roles across many different business units and services areas.

Charly holds a CGMA designation, MA in Natural Sciences and a PhD in Cell and Molecular Biology. Charly is based out of London, England.

On how long to spend in a role
I think it depends on the culture of the company. It depends on what you need to deliver in that role. You need to show you can perform and clearly deliver results. For me I'd probably spend around 2 years in a role or along those lines.

On growing in a less scary way in finance
I used to be a scientist, and science is about doing experiments. I always feel like I've applied that to my career because you've got to try something in order to know what it's like? Whether you can do it? Whether you enjoy it? If you're just sitting there doing the same role for your whole career then I think you're limiting your impact. In today's world you just can't do that, so you've really got to take the leap. You'll find sometimes that the role isn't what you were hoping it was going to be or isn't what you thought it was. Then in those situations you just have to hope that you fail fast, move on, or just decide you're going to put up with it for a few years and then take another step. And that's what comes from doing experiments. I find most of the time they go well and

I've learned a lot. You've got to be brave, and you'll find each time, it pays off and it gets easier.

On the importance of seeking out more viewpoints

I should have sought more viewpoints from different people earlier on in my career. I'm very good at doing that now and I find it tremendously valuable, because it challenges my thinking and I love it when people challenge my thinking. I really encourage that in my team and from people whom I talk to. But early on in my career I didn't do enough of that and just thought I'd have to make all my own decisions. This probably meant earlier on that I probably didn't progress as fast as I could have. However, some people have been wary about sharing information, I'm the opposite of that. I think the more you share with people, the more you will get those different viewpoints and the richer you are basically.

On the value of mentoring and reverse mentoring

There are also things like reverse mentoring where there is a more junior person in the organisation who might mentor a more senior person for example. But I think the key point is that we learn something from those interactions and as the mentor right now I've learnt a lot from my mentees, as they have from me. So I think it's a really valuable relationship to have.

On the importance of having a value creation mindset

I've been in some roles where I've never really had to question my value in a way as a finance partner. It's just been a given that I would be in involved in everything, that I would sit with the marketeers, with the sales guys and we'd do stuff together. Then there were other roles where I felt that I was really having to justify why I, or even my team, were in existence. I think that can be really helpful because it really makes you think, *"Well I can be paid to do a job, but what am I actually contributing? What am I really driving for the business?"* In some cases it can actually be challenging to question, *"What am I achieving, what are my accountabilities, what am I really providing?"* It doesn't have to be very often, but I think when you can start the question what you're doing you'll end up driving more value.

On tapping into what's readily available

We have so much available to us nowadays as finance professionals, we're so lucky and it's so easily accessible, and above all the majority of it is free. I've been on LinkedIn for years and only recently discovered it properly. It can be a bit overwhelming sometimes but there's so much you can tap into. There's so many free events you can go to, there are so many people to meet, there's just so much out there. The more you open yourself up to all of that, the more you'll get from it. So I just encourage everyone to tap into all of that.

On the best bit of advice Charly has ever received

I remember quite early on someone telling me to get breadth, to get as much breadth as you can to lots of different experiences which I think is quite good advice. Someone else said to me to get a mentor, and I remember ignoring that advice for a long, long time. I remember thinking I already know what I'm doing, but it was really that, I don't know who I would ask and why would they want to talk to me, or even why would they want to give their time to me? There is a lot of value to mentoring. Finally, just go outside of your comfort zone. Don't always think of doing something just because it seems like the obvious next step. Get some different viewpoints first and then decide on the different challenges and opportunities.

Recommended Resources

Book: *Michelle Obama: A Biography (2009)* by Liza Mundy (link)

Book: *The Whole Story: A Walk Around The World (1997)* by Ffyona Campbell (link)

"If I have a fiduciary responsibility as a CFO to check that the company is operating as a going concern. And if I set up systems that only show me the exceptions, via my analytics. This saves me lots of time, but am I really in control of the company? Is it not on us to check the Greens as well as the Reds."

Chris Argent
LI: christopherargent
WS: generationcfo.com

Tags:
#digital finance #transformation #data visualisation #data scientists #analytics #exceptions

CHRIS ARGENT is a "Future of Finance" thought leader and Founder of Generation CFO which is one of the more active, 'must-go-to' peer groups for accountants and finance professionals on LinkedIn with 70,000 members all over the world. It examines new trends in finance transformation, digital transformation, CFO role revolution and the growth of the modern strategic business partner. Chris has an impeccable résumé delivering highly valuable Finance transformation projects for blue chips like Vodafone; BAT; Amazon; John Lewis to name a few. Nowadays Chris is a highly rated independent Finance transformation consultant & speaker. Although he started his Finance career as an entry-level accountant in finance operations he soon began leading finance teams and ascending to the Divisional CFO level. Chris is based in the Surrey Hills near London, England.

On how to present the case for sponsorship of digital finance transformation
I've been in the digital finance transformation area for about 8 to 9 years now and people still don't really understand it. In fact, I did a survey through Generation CFO and only 32% of people were really aware of the technologies that could enable finance in this area. I'm talking about reporting, data visualisation, data analytics and nothing radical like

machine learning, R-scripts and all that sort of stuff. So 32% of people got it, which means there's a lot of people who don't. So you've got to present the case. I've seen a lot of projects over the years that have started with an ERP transformation and they've tried to add the AI and analytics elements on top of it. But by pairing the two together you're running a two-speed race on the one big project. Your BI & analytics team will be more agile and able to go much faster than your ERP implementation, which is a central IT project most of the time and will slow them down when the business needs more analytics now. So I would say really focus on your high value decisions, the high value insights that you're trying to create. If you sat down with your CEO or commercial director and said, *"what's the biggest pain point for you this year?"* It might not even be on your finance team's radar but go focus on that. By presenting the value in pounds and pence, and not just a nice whizzy dashboard, that's what's going to get you further sponsorship for the budget and for you to build out your more agile team.

On the benefits of adopting an innovation pioneer mindset

There's been talk for a very long time about finance business partnering and trying to get in front of a business. That's kind of sat within commercial finance's world but I think it's starting to spread out across the whole of finance. Even FP&A and statutory accounting need to get much better at using data and innovate more. Innovation for me is primarily a mindset change. You'll hear lots of people talk about more agile ways of working and being data-driven. And yes, there are several ways of working, methodologies that the likes of the Google's and the Facebook's would call out as a way of working. However what it means in finance is we have to adopt a mindset of getting up from our desks, talking to people about the decisions that they're making and then having an open mind to the solutions and partnering with them on what you're going to develop together.

I'm finding, 9 times out of 10, it comes back to surfacing data, turning that into information and insight, but it's difficult. I speak to people regularly about this and sometimes it's tough and frustrating, because we're putting something on them that they cannot do without additional help, without finding a partner. That's where the enabling comes in and that's where I've seen this gap between accepting that it's ours to own but not being aware of the time, skills and resources that we need to bring in to enable this. Not being aware of the technology, the ways of working, and not really being able to drive it, which must be so frustrating. So we've got to start thinking in terms of education, innovation, about our technologies, or even partnering up with people that understand the processes and the technologies.

On a scary example of how data scientists view traditional finance work

I'll give you a classic example of this. I've come from core finance. I'm finance at heart, I'm into the numbers detail and you can get lost in that sometimes. The team that I'm working with now are predominantly computer scientists. When I first joined the company I sat down and had an introduction with them and these guys are open-mouthed listening to me talk about what my job was and they said, *"Chris, you spend nearly two weeks of a month generating numbers, structures, reports, and analysis from a standard set of data. Then you try to interpret it, put some commentary on it. You just about cross the line and then there's about a week of getting your head around what just happened before you go and do it all over again, really?"* The computer scientist's brain cannot understand why this is a job. Their approach to this is, right, give me the data, let's understand the model, let's understand the lineage, let's crack the data quality problems, let's standardise the reports for the interface that sits on top of it, let's make it repeatable and there we are. Now there's potentially a disposable proof of concept to begin with, however there's an industrialised way of doing this which drives huge wins. I'm oversimplifying it a bit, but they're looking at us as doing a soon to be redundant job if they could only get their hands on it.

On the slow Finance adoption of digital technologies

I've also had this almost knee-jerk reaction from some people saying it's too difficult, I can't get my head around it, it not for them. However I would say, hang on, look at your track record. You've implemented new IFRS, we've got things like GDPR done, you've signed off IT spend. You're able to spin up teams to deal with that sort of thing, but the reason why you do that is because they're *'must-do's,'* where you must rise to the occasion. Whereas adopting digital technologies is still seen as optional, but it's really not an option, no more than accepting social media and smart phone usage.

On an example of some data visualisation tools

The technologies have moved on so far now that you can download a whole host of no cost demos. We use Qlik as a data visualisation tool

but there are many others like MicroStrategy, Tableau, PowerBI, etc…
. So the technologies are much more user friendly now and there's almost
no need for coding. If you use something like Qlik, there's QlikSense
which is less coding heavy. I'm not a technical expert at all, I rely on
partners and IT to really help me on that side. My value is understanding
what the business needs, what it does, how it operates. What I would say
to all business partners, commercial finance leaders, and the like, is that
you have loads to offer and don't overlook your strengths, leverage
them. Most of the time you're talking to non-finance people, so it's on
you to interpret the data in a way that they're going to get it quickly, and
make conscious decisions on. That's the strength of data visualisation
tools, you're highlighting something specific, a headline or an
exception, very quickly.

On the dangers of only looking at exceptions
We're getting to a point now where if we can automate some of our
decision making with robots, you only need to communicate the
exceptions to the humans. That poses quite an interesting theoretical
question, it's a bit like the driverless car and accident liability. If I have
a fiduciary responsibility as a CFO to check that the company is
operating as a going concern. And if I set up systems that only show me
the exceptions, via my analytics. This saves me lots of time, but am I
really in control of the company? Is it not on us to check the Greens as
well as the Reds. How humans and robots work together is a new field,
and there's a long way to go on this argument.

On how we should view some of these new data visualisation tools
Most people start by learning the tools but there's also answering the
right questions that the business needs answering, which is the key.
You've got to understand the business, define the key questions, you've
got to understand the drivers and decision timelines and make sure
they're the right KPIs. You've got to understand the data, the data linage
and the data quality that supports those decisions. Otherwise you're just
showing them a pretty picture with no depth. Data Visualisation is an
enabler only. Think of it in terms of another really good tool for supporting non-finance people in the business.

On the best bit of advice from Chris to help Finance remain relevant
Be positive and do the following! Set yourself some targets to test yourself. One target may be, *"How many standard reports out there can I*

automate versus the total number of reports that I have?" Or, *"How many how KPIs do I have and how many can I automate their production?"* Or even, *"How many post-close queries can be reduced by providing better insights or better self-service tools?"* And it's not just about productivity. Yes it's real tangible time savings that we're moving into, but think about the big problems in the business that may be answered with more people, process, data and tools. This isn't just a "nice to have" anymore, it is a "must-do" to remain relevant.

Recommended Resources
Website: Generation CFO (link)

"It is an incredible passport if you qualify as an accountant."

Ed Harding
LI: edharding

Tags:
#confidence #value proposition #practice #interim #banking

ED HARDING is an internationally mobile Interim who has operated across Europe and Asia. Ed has two decades of leading companies through complex situations including crises, transformations, turn-arounds and M&A. His Interim CXO assignments have addressed cost reduction, scaling for exponential growth, restructuring the change agenda, strategic and financial planning, launching new brands, risk management, talent strategies, acquisitions, divestment and transformation (finance, business, regulatory and service culture).

Ed is also a Mentor to The Mayor of London's International Business Programme and Vice-Chairman of The Investment Business Committee (Professional Standards) at Institute of Chartered Accountants England & Wales. Ed holds an FCA designation and lives in Brighton, England with his family.

On how Ed's training helped improved his ability to wear so many CXO hats
I think my confidence to do different (CXO) jobs comes from my interest in business and my training. I had an incredible training with Mazars, where I touched on everything from building a set of accounts out of a shoebox of receipts, through to auditing very large companies as well as raising financing. Seeing the overall picture of a business has been quite easy because of having to build a financial picture of my clients back when I started out of these shoe boxes. I've never lost the interest in doing that and I've never lost the ability to dig into stuff and take something that looks quite complicated and turn it into something quite simple. It is an incredible passport if you qualify as an accountant.

On the biggest challenges of stepping out into non-Finance related roles

I think it's a really useful exercise to move outside of finance to take the finance message outside of the function. I think it's a critical part of what accountants need to do in the future. All of the basic accounting work will in the end be automated. This means the valuable qualities of rigor and discipline that finance people have will be still required everywhere. Actually I've really found it quite difficult finding the right badge for ourselves. It's particularly difficult for recruiters too to sell a generalist, into what is effectively still a specialist market. So quite often, let's say, if you're looking to be the CFO in a private bank, you need to have been a CFO in a private bank previously, or be on the route to being one having been in a bank for the last 10 years. I don't necessarily subscribe to that opinion. I think someone moving across industries and across functions can bring a completely different insight and so new thinking into a business too.

On how Ed has constructed his career story into 4 pillars to make it an easier job to sell his value to potential recruiters

You are always the best seller of yourself, so nobody else can sell you as well as you can. I've done a number of things I've found interesting or grown from. What I've done is created a story, in which I describe the four pillars to my career. I have financial services: I've been all across financial services from insurance, to wealth, to commercial banking and trading. I've got finance as a subject matter and I've been CFO at a number of outfits. I've got transformation and change: which would include M&A and any kind of crisis, basically non-BAU (Business As Usual), as my 3rd pillar. So if it's tricky, then I'm interested, and I'm someone you should speak to. The last one is technology, or let's call it technology and disruption: I've spent a long time working with early stage technology companies, that's the place where I'm getting my thought leadership from that I can take to the big companies, and I can take my big companies' experience to the smaller ones. They're a really great source of keeping me fresh and relevant, and interested in the new operating models coming out. So the way that I say it is that I've got these 4 pillars, financial services, Finance, change and technology. And if you're looking for someone to fill a job and you need two of those skills then I could be useful, three of them we should definitely be having a chat and with four of them then I'm absolutely the first person you should be speaking to.

On why there's a gap between consultants and practitioners
I joined a large consultancy firm to be a partner in their Swiss finance transformation practice, it's a great business, but it's a consulting business, not like a business run by operators. So the guys there are experts at the finance transformation practice of that firm, setting up their processes, they are not experts at running functions, they have never done it. However the gap between consulting and operating is a big leap.

On the idea of intelligent simplicity
I'll dive into the detail with the experts at the business, the people that run the business and I help them remove some of the clutter that's built up around the outside of their core processes and core business. In doing that you've then got to the essence of a business that you can then grow and transform. It's very difficult to transform something that's messy. It's very easy to transform something that is clean because you can see what it is you've got to change, so your *from today position* is much easier. If you look at companies like Airbnb, Uber and the newer, younger, and smarter exponential organisations. Those guys, they have no legacy thinking. It is very simple for them to grow quickly and that's why it's so hard for the incumbent businesses to change. So I'm looking at all areas of friction in big companies to close the gap between them and these exponential organisations. I describe this as growing them with *intelligent simplicity*, that is what I do.

On how to get involved helping the next generation of start-ups
The first one I did was a music gaming business with some family members of U2 and I was introduced to them by a lawyer. It was iTunes, meets Trivial Pursuit, meets Facebook. At the time we were trying to build a social network and then Facebook came along. So we were probably working with the wrong thing. I think volunteering is useful. Nobody buys something that's untested. I made myself available to a number of different projects that I was interested in, I met some really great people that I continued to work with regularly. I got picked up by a group called Hack Forward, which was created by the founder of Xing, I think Lars Hendricks made tens of millions in his early thirties. So he had done really well and he realised the guys who made the money out of the business were the suits whereas in his words it was the geeks, the coders and developers that generated the true value basis. Then I met Lars, with a couple other people, such as, David who was one of the first

Google people into Europe, and Tom from IDEO. We set up this thing, Hack Forward, and from there that became a another badge. When you get the badge you get the pull of other people coming in.

On the best bit of advice Ed has ever received

Be enthusiastic and energetic. If you're not and you don't feel enthusiastic and energetic about what you're doing, then it's quite likely you're in the wrong place. If you're leading people you have to inspire them to do great things. Words like empowerment are really, really important, but you're not going to empower anybody if you're not enthusiastic in the first place. So I think having energy and turning up like you're excited, like I am when I go to work. It's not work, it's fun, and when it's fun you do cool things. My dad sums it up well when he said to me and my brother when we were starting off in accountancy, he said *"don't live to work and don't work to live, but live at work, and be you at work, and you'll always get the best out of everything you do."*

Recommended Resources

Book: *Exponential Organisations: Why new organisations are ten times better, faster, and cheaper than yours (and what to do about it)*, by Salim Ismail, Michael S. Malone, Yuri van Geest, (link)

Website: Investopedia (link)

Podcast: Strength in the Numbers Show (link)

Report: DNA of CFO of the Future (link)

"If I was to perhaps start the year as if I was going to give myself an "A" for my performance for the entire year, what qualities would I need to be demonstrating throughout the entire year to be delivering an "A" performance?"

Glin Bayley
LI: glin-bayley
WS:simplyglin.com

Tags:
#business partnering #career advancement #lateral #empathy #fun

GLIN BAYLEY is a holistic performance coach that works with individuals, entrepreneurs and organisations to drive better performance. Glin is also an accomplished Head of Finance & Business Strategy, with a career spanning over 17 years working in global blue-chip companies such as Coca Cola, General Electric and Associated British Foods.

Glin is currently based out of Sydney, Australia and qualified as a CGMA.

On questions to consider to get the most out of your career experiences
One thing I probably haven't done as successfully as I've seen other people do is to be really planful about where they are heading in the future. When I joined Coca-Cola my early 20s I was just so super excited about the brand and that kept me there for the next four years. I had two roles there, got my first promotion into middle management and felt like I was on top of the world. Then when I moved to ABF it was a very different model. You're starting at a middle management level but also recognising that for me my journey was around answering, does this role give me something new to learn? Did it excite me and did I get some enjoyment out of being in that environment? And did I feel that I can make a difference and was I being rewarded in that role as well as I would want to?

On career development advantages of working at larger brands

It really got to a point where if I got bored I looked and that's probably not what most people want to hear from a senior finance person. So is that really as planful as it got? It really was like that. If I had a line manager or leader that I was super inspired by it just meant I stayed longer in the role because I had a fountain (of knowledge) that I was learning from. If I got to the point where I thought, okay, I've delivered what I needed to do in this role, I feel like I'm stagnating what do I do next? Then I started looking. I think the benefit of working for an organisation like Associated British Foods was that they encouraged moves around the divisions and what made it better for me was I could take my learning from one organisation to the next without feeling that I was stealing content. Typically when you leave a company, you might think, what can I take with me? And it's sort of frowned upon that you're taking stuff away with you. However, when you're moving into another division within one company it was almost like I had permission to take what I needed to take from one organisation straight into the other organisation, and I could take all of my contacts and connections too. So even though I worked for lots of different brands and businesses I still felt like I was in one organisation, my network relationships were building, my experience was significantly greater because I allowed myself to be immersed in the different business challenges each of them faced.

On the career benefits of lateral moves within the same business

Kingsmill being a bread business was mass volume, low margin, high level of production and therefore the focus was very much about how did you manage costs, how to manage manufacturing efficiency and what can you do to drive value in an environment where it's a commoditised business? Then you look at the opposite in Twining's (tea) whilst it's still to a degree manufacturing it's heavily focused on the brand and the experience. It's a high value proposition, so you're looking at the premium end and it is a business that wasn't low margin because it was differentiated and it had a lot of innovation in that space. So whilst tea at the lower end might be seen as a commodity, I didn't feel Twining's was. It was really interesting going between two different companies within the portfolio that had very different external pressures that drove ultimately how the business internally was being run. I feel whilst I've moved a lot, it hasn't hindered me in any way, if anything I feel like I'm much richer for the experience.

On what really matters with your next career move

Time has always been the measure that most of us have used to go, *"If I do two to three years that's deemed to be appropriate,"* but realistically what is appropriate? This is your one shot at living your life. You get to choose where you're headed and as long as you're adding value and you've got really clear deliverables and you're surpassing them, then I don't see that there's any issue in moving sooner than a timeframe that someone else may or may not have decided is appropriate for you.

On a practical way on how to be a linchpin in Finance on a daily basis

I love Seth Godin's work, but for me that (linchpin) book was really about understanding what does it take to be indispensable and how do you be remarkable on a daily basis? Because I think we can get ourselves into a rut of going, *"Okay, I've got my objectives for the year. I may not have regular check-ins with my leader. I may or may not have a mid-year performance review, but I know I will have my year-end one where I will have to talk about what I've delivered in the year. And can I think back to the last month or last year of what I've delivered to warrant an outstanding grade?"* For me being a linchpin doesn't wait until that twelve month mark before you start assessing your performance. It's about going, *"Okay, if I was to perhaps start the year as if I was going to give myself an "A" for my performance for the entire year, what qualities would I need to be demonstrating throughout the entire year to be delivering an "A" performance?"*

If you can have that mindset to know what an *'A'* performance looks like or whatever the grading is at the top of the chain now and you're looking at it going, *"What will that need me to do and how would that need me to show up in order to deliver this."* That's what for me being a linchpin is about. It's surprising and delighting people. It's going out of your way to make an impact because recognising that in today's world especially with the digital evolution, the map that we once had that we were encouraged to follow, is being diminished. What a linchpin is really stating is you now need to create your own map, you need to determine where you fit and how you add value. And also demonstrate to the organisation that you are indispensable so when it comes to making choices about humans or robots, it's a no brainer when it comes to you because you've demonstrated that your ability to connect the dots, you're insights, your ability to leverage relationships is far superior than any artificial intelligence is going to be doing. That for me is what being a linchpin is about and I would say that's probably one of the things that's helped me in my career is about widening the scope of your impact, so don't limit it just to finance. You're a finance expert, you're qualified, you've got the examination results and the letters behind your name to prove your credibility in the field, but allow yourself to widen your scope and think, okay, well I've got credibility here but how can I build credibility elsewhere?

On the importance of empathy and spending time with others

I do that by being more empathetic and in my case spending time with sales guys the majority of my commercial finance days. Often, many thoughts travelled through my mind, some of them complimentary, some of them not so complimentary, so I used to ask myself, *"Why do they do what they do?"* It's only when you allow yourself to go, if I saw what they saw, if I knew what they knew, if I believed what they believed would I be making the decision they're making? And nine times out of ten the answer is yes. So if you can allow yourself to really understand and get behind their thinking, behind the decision or choice made, it allows you to really start going, *"Well what can I do to influence their worldview? What new information and knowledge can I present and share such that I can change the insight that they have around the decisions they make? How can I show up as a partner rather than as someone who's just a challenger and say, actually, we've got the same goal here but we're coming at it from different perspectives and how might we do that in a way that's more effective?"*

I just think, certainly from my own experience in finance, that it's so easy for us to be a bit more black and white in our thinking because a lot of the way we've been taught is that there's a formula, we can figure things out, and we've got an insight. Also sometimes I think we forget how much we know, and you assume other people have got the same lens, the same knowledge and insight that you have. If you can allow yourself to go, well these individuals that I'm trying to partner with haven't had this same training or discipline in the background that I have, they don't see the world the way I see it because of my own experience. So how can I give them a bit of insight into what I know, what I see and what I believe and therefore why that leads to a different decision than they are making and jointly work together to go identify where our world views differ. Empathy is a huge one in finance. If you can find more empathetic finance folk, I think the impact that we would have across the organisation would be immense.

On the best bit of advice Glin ever received

It's don't take yourself so goddam seriously, that's the best piece of advice I've ever been given. It serves you well when you realise actually you can have a little bit of fun. You don't have to be so serious and you show up with more playfulness in what you do, you lift the energy of the environment and of the people you're with, you're fun to be around. People are drawn to your energy because you're sending out a signal of, *"Hey! Come and talk to me because I'm approachable, I'm friendly, I'm interested and I'm not so wedded to my computer that I'm looking like I don't want to be disturbed."* That was definitely the best piece of advice I got because I did take myself incredibly seriously at the early part of my career. I found my career success was exponential once I allowed myself to relax and have some fun. We spend a lot of time with the people we work with and there's plenty of times in our lives when things are tough, that require us to be serious, but we don't have to be serious all the time in order to be successful. So, I'd encourage you, don't take yourself so seriously and be a bit more playful in how you show up.

Recommended Resources

Book: *The Art of Possibility: Transforming Professional and Personal Life (2002)*, by Rosamund Stone Zander and Benjamin Zander (link)

Book: *Linchpin: Are You Indispensable? How to drive your career and create a remarkable future (2010)*, by Seth Godin (link)

Website: Article (link)

Website: Simply Glin (link)

"Ultimately what we're talking about is not only about bringing value into the business but also bringing intelligence, i.e. identifying things that the business was not actually previously aware of as well as the regime of testing the controls, the technologies, the processes, the people."

Howard Cosby
LI: howard-cosby
WS: aveiroe-europe.com

Tags:
#forensic #business process audits #learning

HOWARD COSBY is the Managing Partner at Aveiroe Europe LLP, who excel in the development of Outsourced Forensic Accounting, Audit and Business Process Review Services.

Howard also qualified as a Chartered Accountant and Mensa Member, served on the Cabinet Office SME Panel and the BRC Retail Audit Group, and is based near London, England.

On forensic business process audits and how they are done

Most of the groundwork is done by deploying an audit program and data routines which identify where there are things that are perhaps worthy of investigation. It is then the expertise of our personnel that comes into play to make sure that those things are then investigated thoroughly and to a conclusion. It is an interesting mix of science, data, and of course expertise, so in some respects it's not that dissimilar from the silent witness (crime) type of programs without anybody ever being sent to prison.

On how to succeed with business process audits

One of the key attributes is stakeholder engagement. The organisations we largely work with in the past have tended to be of some considerable size. As a consequence you are working with a multiplicity of stakeholders. One could be dealing with procurement functions, one could be dealing with logistics, one could be dealing with finance, internal audit, people responsible for the tax areas of a particular client business. We therefore require a skill set which enables us to engage appropriately with all of those people, and to be frank, also across a number of levels from the C-Suite right down to the people who are responsible in the accounts receivable functions, etc, etc, etc.… .

On how business process audits can add value

In the first instance it's about finding out what is not going the way that it should be, and the only way to do that is to undertake a review, an audit. Then you work on how you can help the client improve their processes and it is often the case that we don't know what is going to be found within the client organisation. Of course, through our experience we have an idea of all the processes that need to be reviewed, and indeed the things that we are likely to find, but we can undertake up to several hundred different process tests. In any organisation that mix is very varied. Ultimately what we're talking about is not only about bringing value to the business but also bringing intelligence, identifying things that the business was not actually previously aware of, as well as the regime of testing the controls, the technologies, the processes, and the people. You're providing that assurance and if you do the job properly, you're also bringing those learnings to the client organisation via a flight path towards improvement.

On why business process audits tend to get overlooked

The type of work we undertake is never on the top of the "To-Do-List" even though it's important work that needs to be carried out in organisations. In fact, having pioneered this work with very large organisations we can now make this available to smaller enterprises. So organisations that have not previously undertaken this type of work now actually have a service, which is essentially an information service, that pays for itself and provides a very good ROI. It's an organisational review process which can be undertaken any time but it often only comes to the top of the To-Do-List when organisations are going through significant changes with systems transformations and the like.

On why accountants make the best CEOs

A while back I was mentored by somebody who's extremely successful and has been involved in raising finance for a large number of organisations particularly in the UK. As a consequence he really has worked with the top levels management within the UK. One of the things that always stuck with me was when he said that in his view the best CEOs were accountants, followed pretty closely by engineers. Those analytical skills we something he felt were hugely important to business and all I will say is that for the people who go into the finance and accounting profession nowadays, don't see it as a single route into CFO type positions, but also for the top spot as well. I do tend to agree with him based on what I've seen over the years. There's no limit to what the people who go through our profession in the right way can achieve.

On the best bit of advice Howard has ever received

It's advice that plenty of other people have heard before but really it's two bits of advice from my father, from whom I first heard them, which wer, enjoy your job, do your best and learn from it. If you've got a passion and you're able to get yourself into something that you really enjoy, inside and out, like I have. Then everything becomes a lot easier. It is always about continuously learning and that's the great joy that comes from working with this huge variety of people and organisations, which without a shadow of a doubt is something I wouldn't had, except for going down the route I did, into accountancy.

Recommended Resources

Book: *Black Box Thinking: Marginal Gains and the Secrets of High Performance: The Surprising Truth About Success (2016)* by Matthew Syed (link)

Book: *Guns, Germs and Steel (1997)* by Jared Diamond (link)

"For me it's very simple. Let's take a look at what is the key value proposition of finance. It is simply to enhance decision making, that's all, nothing else."

Irina Steenbeek
LI: irina-steenbeek
WS: datacrossroads.nl

Tags:
#data management #information value chain #KPIs #decision-making #data lineage

DR. IRINA STEENBEEK is a data management professional with an extensive financial background. Irina works with medium-sized businesses on a strategic level, assisting them to optimise their decision-making processes and company performance by implementing a data management framework around the information value chain, supported by an effective set of business capabilities. Irina is author of 'The Data Management Toolkit', 'The Data Management Cookbook', and 'The "Orange" Model of Data Management', various white-papers and series of blogs on the topics of data management and FP&A.

Irina holds an MBA in Finance, PhD (Engineering) and CGMA designations. She is based out of Amsterdam, The Netherlands.

On realising the importance of (financial) data management
It was very interesting. I had just joined a small bank as their management information systems officer to optimise the management accounting reporting. At some point we realised there were different reporting platforms for finance and risk, so our reports were never reconcilable. Eventually the management came to the decision to implement a data warehouse as a solution and one of the consultants mentioned the term, *data management*, I had no idea what it was or what it meant? That moment was the start of my career in data management. The deeper I go into understanding the business processes of a company the more I'm convinced that data are the real source and life blood of any operation

in a company. Based on my experience, I can say that 80% of the data circulating in any company is financial data.

On how data lineage impacts driver-based planning

People speak a lot about driver-based planning, which of course you use for deriving your KPIs. However, if you take a look at the situation or picture from the data point of view, KPIs are your data, and business drivers are also data. So the question becomes how do these business drivers make an impact on your KPIs? Because to know which drivers do make an impact on your KPIs you need to know the path of how data have been transformed. In data management we call it the *information value chain*. I see a strong relationship between data management and finance at this point. I translate the finance concepts of KPIs and business drivers into the concepts of the information value chain and critical data elements in data management, which gives answers on the following business questions: Which information do decision-makers need? Who does what? What do information and data mean? Where do data come from, where do they go to, and what happen to data on the way? And last but not least, how good is the quality level of the data?

On why some data elements are more critical than others and how to identify them

If you take a look and the number of data elements which are circulating in the company or even the data elements which are in your reports, there are a huge amount. So we must use the concept of Critical Data Elements (CDEs). Finance people call them KPIs, however both CDEs and KPIs have the same meaning. They make the biggest impact on your company's performance because they focus attention on those drivers that make the greatest impact on the business. Such an approach allows finance to significantly improve the value of financial reporting .

On the role of finance in improving our data management

This first step is to become a data management initiative sponsor. From my point of view finance is the key user of data in the company and it uses data the most. Very often finance even feel that they themselves are the owners of the data that they are dealing with, but it's not true. Finance is not the owner, finance is the user of data. For me it's very simple. Let's take a look at what is the key value proposition of Finance. It is simply to enhance decision making, that's all, nothing else. It's the same value proposition as data management. The role of Finance is to specify their information requirements and deliver these requirements to data owners. Data management coordinates these activities. When finance gets the required information, it will provide insights from this information to advise a company's management on possible business decisions.

To ensure correct decision making you need to have the correct information at the right time, right place and delivered to the right person. The role of data management is to build the chain that transforms raw data into meaningful information. This chain we data management professionals call the information value chain

On the Information Value Chain concept and the importance of optimising it
To be able to deliver the right information requirements to the data management team finance needs to know the decisions it is supposed to make or support. Then data management professionals will look for what data do you need to get the required information. Data management will also specify and design the way to process the data into the required information.

On the steps required to build a better Information Value Chain
The first step is to find business drivers that require a data management initiative. The second step is to find business sponsors for the initiative. The CFO can become the most influential sponsor. The third step is to involve data management professionals. Some large companies here in Europe already have data management teams, however small- or medium-sized companies might not have such a team in place . What's interesting is when I speak to financial professionals they say, *"Yeah, data management is one of our biggest issues,"* but my question back is, *"What are you going to do about it?"*

Smaller companies can find people that already work and who have some knowledge in data management. Each company already has data management to some degree. Some companies have already formalised the function and others are yet to do so. There are also a lot of professionals in data management who came from finance, audit, or IT.

The next step for finance is not waiting until somebody starts doing something. Finance can start with optimising its reporting. To do so finance should ask, *"What information does management need for decision making?"* And compare this to what you deliver to optimize the information delivery.

On two common challenges with KPIs

There are two challenges with KPIs. Number one, it is possible that KPIs with the same name have different formulas behind them, so you get the same name but different figures; and number two, there are different KPIs but they were calculated in the same way.

On why finance professionals are ideally placed to improve data quality

There is great potential for finance people to improve data quality. There are a lot of financial staff who make data error corrections in Excel, but this is absolutely not their work to do. Of course this makes an enormous influence on the quality of their work and what they're doing. So to improve their work and to motivate them to do higher level work, the data quality issues need to be resolved before data and information get delivered to finance. Financial people very often feel themselves responsible for all data within the company and it's not right. The solution is to get a real data management professional so that finance people can do their job, which is analysing data or delivering advice to management. Only a proper data management approach can facilitate finance contributing towards the discussion about how best to improve the value being delivered by finance.

On the best bit of advice Irina has ever received

When I started writing my PhD thesis I got a book about writing it successfully. I never read it further than the first page because on the first page it said the following, *"The most difficult in writing a PhD thesis is to start writing it. Every morning you need to wake up, sit at the table and write it."* Later on I got the second most valuable bit of advice, which was a bit obvious, but to get your PhD, you need to finish it at some point. So if you want things in your life to be done you have to start doing things on a regular basis. However, you also have to deliver results along the way. So concentrate on delivering your results.

Recommended Resources

Book: *The Data Management Cookbook: A pocket guide for implementation of data management 2018,* by Irina Steenbeek (link)

Book: *The Data Management Toolkit. A step-by-step guide for the optimisation of the Information Value Chain* by Irina Steenbeek (link)

Book: *The "Orange" Model of Data Management,* by Irina Steenbeek (link)

Website: Data crossroads (link)

"The other thing in terms of mindset is whenever things go wrong, and they will, what are you going to cling onto that's going to drive you through?"

James Perry
LI: jamesperryaccounting
WS: accountingsuccesscoach.com

Tags:
#exams #mindset #anxiety #coaching #meditation #psychology

JAMES PERRY is owner of www.accountingsuccesscoach.com. Through his tailored coaching techniques, he delivers a unique & fresh perspective to exam & career coaching in a relaxed & interactive environment. This means accountancy students will have the best opportunity to succeed in their exams, enhance their careers and achieve their full potential. James is also a Lecturer, having worked with Queens University, University of Ulster and the private sector. Previously he was a Financial Controller in industry and Senior Audit Manager in a global accounting firm. James holds a CA designation and is based out of Belfast, Northern Ireland.

On an invaluable tip to help you learn more easily
The best way to learn is to teach somebody else. Say someone is struggling with consolidations, control accounts or whatever accounting technique, you can go, alright let's have a look at it, you can do it this way and that's how you learn to get it to click into place.

On why psychology is no longer a fluffy subject for our profession
The word psychology to me five years ago meant a very different thing to what it does now. Five years ago to me the word psychology was what I would call fluffy. It didn't mean very much to me as a qualified accountant who is pre-programmed, articulate and logical. My head works like a spreadsheet, so let's imagine whenever you're pushed maybe by the corporate culture or other stuff that happens in your life to the verge of that spreadsheet disappearing, and going, *"Oh my God!"*

That's when you actually understand your mindset and your psychology is key. So that's why I now help people with their mindset. It's not necessarily about the corporate culture or about people passing the exams, to me it's the other stuff like mindset that is just as important.

On why being a well-rounded advisor is now becoming more important

Accountancy is an incredibly wonderful qualification because it is so much more than just numbers. Today you have to be a rounded business advisor. And that's where the personality, the softer skills, actually building rapport with either your staff or a client to me is so important now. Of course, you have to have an awareness and knowledge of the technical stuff, when a new accounting standard is coming out you need to be aware of that. Although the skill of getting people on your side if you've got a wonderful idea or project, getting those people on board to follow you and support you, for me, that is more key now.

On the first question he asks his exam coaching clients

The first question I ask with anyone is, *"What's the most important thing in your life?"* And they go family, partner, whatever, and then I go, *"Is it not your mind?"* Because without your mind you will not be able to comprehend any of this. And they look at me sideways, exactly the same look I would have given about five years ago. And I've got to prime them because passing exams is a very psychological thing. The vast majority of people who fail exams they actually know the stuff, it's just something else, either it's their technique, time management, that they haven't read the question properly or they have a mental block. That's where the mindset comes in again. The other thing in terms of mindset is whenever things go wrong, and they will, what are you going to cling onto that's going to drive you through? For instance, my mother had MS for 47 years, she was in a coma for the last 14 years of her life and she was my driving force. So, I challenge people and accountancy students that when this goes wrong, which it will, *"What are you going to cling onto that's going to drive you through?"* Whether it's owning your own business, being a partner in a firm, or if you do it for the job satisfaction or the money, what's your driving force? And that gives you a much different perspective on exams and the mindset for it. It's not just this drudgery, or this process you have to go through, there is a light at the end of the tunnel.

On the student who successfully overcome her exam anxiety

There was a student who failed one paper of her ACCA exams five times, and it was the one she had to do to become fully qualified. It was actually one of the easier papers. The first time she failed it she couldn't believe it, the second time it put a fear in her mind, the third time the snowball effect happened. So I mentioned to her about meditation, and she looked at me as if I had two heads and said, *"What?"* So I said before every study session I wanted her to unplug her phone, lie down and count her breaths for half an hour. You need to get your mind ultra relaxed to be in an appropriate state to absorb information, but most importantly, if you panic in an exam you do a mini-meditation. Try some deep breathing for a minute, and that will get you to refocus again she passed the exam. Undoubtedly the reason why she passed, it wasn't anything technical, it was for the simple fact she was better able to manage her anxiety in an exam.

On what an accounting exam coach does

There aren't many exam coaches out there. So yes, I am a tutor, I am a lecturer and I do that in a different guise. However an exam coach is similar to when you've got a coach for the gym, or if you've a coach to play sports, so why not have me to be your coach for helping you through your accountancy exams. It's really the prompting and the advice rather than going through the whole syllabus content, which let's face it, you're probably going to go to a lecture or financial training institution for those.

On two bits of advice to his younger self

Start reading, big time! Because at the age of twenty I was studying so much I didn't actually go read about other things, I didn't expand my mind to go in other directions. And also go get a mentor, get someone who is like-minded as you and will help driving you in the direction you want to go and be that devil's advocate if you've got a problem.

Recommended Resources

Book: *Entrepreneur Revolution: How to develop your entrepreneurial mindset and start a business that works (2013)*, by Daniel Priestly (link)

Book: *7 Strategies for Wealth & Happiness: (2009)*, by Jim Rohn (link)

Website: Accounting Success Coach (link)

"It's no longer enough to be just an accountant. You have to be able to be a much more rounded person."

Jenny Okonkwo
LI: jennyokonkwo
WS: jennyokonkwo.com

Tags:

#career advancement #flexibility #change #diversity #uncertainty #inclusion #women #leadership #bfannetwork #networking

JENNY OKONKWO MBA FCMA CGMA CPA FPA CMA is the founder of the Black Female Accountants Network (BFAN). BFAN's purpose is to create opportunities for female accountants of black, African and Caribbean origins to share knowledge and empowering their experiences of diversity & inclusion through a process of engagement and personal reflection. Jenny is also a women's leadership ambassador for CPA Canada, a CPA Mentor, a member of the FP&A Certification Development Committee, a DECA Judge, as well as giving back to her local community through her numerous other volunteer roles.

Jenny is also a regular keynote speaker, author and is based out of Toronto, Canada.

On building early career foundations in a corporate environment to gain work-life balance later on

Drawing on my personal experience, working in a large corporate environment in the early part of your career has certain advantages. For example study support and financial assistance during the time you are looking to obtain your accounting qualification (designation). The workplace environment provided a variety of roles and professional development opportunities to build a strong foundation in my core areas of expertise, enabling me to forge an independent consulting pathway later on in my career. This allowed for greater flexibility and work life balance while raising a young family, as well as the ability to be strategic in the projects I undertook for building my professional brand.

My consulting work gave me the opportunity to showcase my communication skills, my expertise in managing stakeholders, relationship and project management, brand myself as a change agent and complex problem solver. This led to being nominated for high profile roles in a volunteer capacity. My work in the 'giving back' space enabled me to make a difference in the professional community at large and to utilize my leadership skills as a social entrepreneur.

On how to move forward in accounting & finance

Align yourself with other successful people. Success breeds success. Choose your networks carefully, choose your circles carefully. Align yourself with other people who want to move forward – it encourages you to do the same. Your network is truly your net worth! Think of it this way: if you want to improve your personal fitness you would ideally choose a gym buddy who is at a higher fitness level, which motivates you to aim higher and do better.

On developing BFAN to increase opportunities in accounting & finance

Since the launch of our network in 2016, our accomplishments include

- Successfully positioning the membership as a high calibre professional talent pool that continues to attract employers from various industries
- Two immigrant professionals were recruited by market leading firms as a direct result of being members of the network
- Partnering with market leading employers from professional development and sponsorship perspectives
- Launching the Annual Women in Leadership Summit program, now going into its third year
- Invitations for our members to engage in speaking opportunities, therefore elevating their profiles and building their personal brand as part of their career development
- Introduction of a group mentoring program.

On the need to embrace a more flexible mindset

As accountants, we need to embrace uncertainty. In my opinion, our profession by nature is one where $2 + 2$ equals 4. However we have to develop a mindset where we understand that sometimes $2 + 2$ might equal $3\frac{1}{2}$ or sometimes $2 + 2$ might equal $4\frac{1}{2}$. What do I mean by that? In the past we've always been very comfortable with the fact that we would work with data that was just in-house, where we had full control. Since we are now operating in a dynamic environment, we also have to take account of external data sources. This may give us a sense of discomfort as accountants, because we no longer have automatic reconciliation capabilities when dealing with external data sources. It's in our nature to ensure we can reconcile everything back to a familiar source. Increasingly we will need to get comfortable with making some more qualitative and anecdotal type judgments, regarding additional data sources in the realm of Big Data, the cloud, the Internet of Things, etc... . These are just some examples of areas where there is still work for us to do in terms of developing a more flexible mindset. Developing a capability to capture insights from external data sources and integrating them into our internal information systems and models to give a more global view of what is happening in a particular industry will increasingly become a sought-after skill by organisations now and in the future.

As the world becomes more uncertain, we as accountants need to embrace the cultural change of dealing with ambiguity and uncertainty. The challenge is that we are obliged to maintain our role in corporate governance, maintaining integrity over our data sources that generate the numbers, and ensure they pass the audit. By no means is this an easy challenge and yet it's something that we have to focus on and determine a course of action that addresses this issue.

On other functions taking on previously accounting-owned tasks

There's another side to all of this which is a growing trend towards the business taking on traditional duties and tasks that historically sat in the finance and accounting department. Increasingly I'm seeing a trend in industry, where sales, marketing, human resources, operations and other business professionals are enrolling on finance-oriented MBA programs and assuming direct responsibility of managing their own department budgets and profit and loss (P&L) accounts. In the past, these activities were very centralized to the finance and accounting department. This is no longer the case. In many workplaces, your business colleagues are now managing their own P&L's, putting together their own budgets and forecasts, being equipped with their own financial training, not to the same depth of course, but enough to challenge an accounting professional in a financial management conversation.

As finance and accounting professionals we need to determine what our profession in the future will look like and how the next generation of Finance business partners will successfully add value to an organisation.

On tomorrow's area of opportunity & value for accounting & finance

Tomorrow it's going to look considerably different because of the way the business is changing, the way the business is taking on these types of responsibilities. The area of opportunity for us is to be able to work with that uncertainty, work with the ambiguous data, help to overlay and get that narrative from these external data sources to support business decisions. That's where our value is going to come from. It's our responsibility to explore and identify what our role tomorrow is going to look like and carve out those opportunities to make sure we are able to perform in that future role.

On why it's no longer enough to be a good accountant

The bottom line: it's no longer enough to be just an accountant. You need to be a much more rounded person. What does this mean? Your verbal and written communication skills have to be top-notch. This includes giving presentations and gaining recognition as a public speaker. These skills are now so prevalent in today's global marketplace and in the war for high calibre talent, the extent to which you do these activities well will determine whether or not you *"stand out from the crowd"*.

If you've written, spoken publicly, or volunteered in a professional capacity all of these activities are opportunities for you to start building your career, your platform, your personal brand to become a standout candidate. Yesterday our workforce competition was local, now it's global. If a candidate from another part of the world has the required attributes, they also have an opportunity of being hired.

On the best advice Jenny has to those starting in finance right now

Through university outreach with BFAN and CPA Ontario, my conversations with 20-year olds include the fact that it's never too early to start building your professional brand. I advise them to embrace social media sites such as LinkedIn in a way that helps them to start building their professional brand. Examples of how you do that are through article writing, opinion-editorial pieces, thought leadership, commenting on other people's articles and social media posts.

Recommended Resources

Article: *"Diversity Matters,"* McKinsey & Co., February 2015 (link)

Website: BFAN (link)

Website: Jenny Okonkwo (link)

Twitter: @BFANNetwork (link)

Instagram: @BFANNetwork (link)

LI Group: Black Female Accountants Network (BFAN) (link)

LI Group: Leaders In Finance LinkedIn Group (link)

"It's like in the start-up scene where you say fail fast and move forward. So I think more and more that this start-up mindset is also coming into the finance function."

Johannes Vogel
LI: johannes-vogel

Tags:
#international #digital transformation #failure #digital finance #disrupters #strategy #networking #relationships

JOHANNES VOGEL is Director of Finance Strategy & CFO 4.0 Services at BearingPoint, responsible for helping improve client finance teams' visions and roadmaps, processes, ERPs and reporting system architectures, as well as assisting them to develop their Finance strategies and solutions for the "Digital CFO Office" (CFO 4.0 Solutions). Johannes brings more than 20 years of experience gained within Industry and Consulting of running finance operations, across Europe and the United States.

Johannes also lectures in a masters program on digital communications at the Berlin Universität der Künste; writes blog posts on finance, and is a native of Nuremberg, Germany.

On how employers are putting a premium on international experience
In Germany when we hire people in finance we are placing a premium on international experience. In my view, the people that come in from University, they have had a number of different internships or semesters abroad. So I do see a pickup in international exposure earlier than maybe way back when I went to school, That's a very positive trend and I would reinforce and recommend to anyone still in the process of formation and study to get some international exposure.

On why he's seeing a tolerance for failure appearing in Finance

I had a conversation with the CFO of a major German automotive player who's also heading up a big finance transformation project globally and he also reflected that within his finance transformation program they have started to create smaller teams to try out new technologies. They have really gotten into a mode where they also accept some failures and that not all projects will be successful. So this tolerance of having some mistakes, having some project failures, is starting to sink in. Like with most digital technologies you need to try things out to see if it brings value to your company. This is the mindset that I'm starting to sense much more now at least in German finance teams.

On what's helping Finance teams be more accepting of failure

It's a cultural thing. It is something that the CEO and the management team of that group has really started to push over the last two to three years. There is a big opportunity in digital for all kinds of aspects for the company, in having a better customer experience, in having better product development processes for cars, etc... .This cultural change, like in this automotive example, is really being led by top management. Two or three years back they would have gone around with their suits and ties. Today they go around with polo shirts and maybe a sports coat, but you don't see any more ties. If it is driven by top management it will trickle down also into the finance teams. And from a pragmatic point of view we can try out things on a smaller scale. If it fails it's not going to be a big financial impact. It's like in the start-up scene where you say fail fast and move forward. So I think more and more that this start-up mindset is also coming into the finance function.

On how cost concerns can distract from making the right digital investments

That's the destiny of being an overhead function. The investments into finance being an overhead function have always been very cautious and there's a constant pressure on finance teams. We're seeing that in surveys year-after-year that cost pressure on the finance function is still one of the top concerns of CFOs. At the same time creating value for the business should be the primary purpose of finance. They really can add and create value, so a lot of finance teams and a lot of companies may still need to do some more homework. You have to assess: How good are our accounting and controlling processes? Are they lean or is there still some waste in there? A good way to look at it is can we improve our finance excellence? So being good at what we do, getting the processes right, having systems standardised etc… . This is a task that every finance team should look at and try to continuously improve their processes in an incremental way.

On what CFOs should be considering when it comes to setting a digital strategy

In the times that we live in we have so many shifts in terms of business models, you also have other shifts in terms of demographics with the generations Y&Z coming in. With these changes in the business context both from a HR talent point of view, but also from a competitive point of view, which business models are the ones that we need to support? CFO's are really finding themselves in a position where they have started thinking about how will my finance team need to look like in 3 to 5 years? How will the finance function look in 2023 versus how are we set up today? Once you get into those thoughts then you're very close to starting to think about finance strategy in terms of where do we stand today? What are the requirements that we have from the business? What are the requirements we are facing as a company from our competitive situation? What can we do in our finance team to start addressing that? So how do CFOs get from where they are today to where they have a function that is better set up to address the challenges of both today and tomorrow? It's about doing the basics right, getting the homework done in terms of being process-oriented, not working in departmental silos but looking at the end customer of each process and looking at your systems landscape.

On four digital technologies that are the biggest disrupters to finance

The impact on finance will be on different levels. On the one hand there is RPA (Robotic Process Automation), where you really have rule-based engines that do simple transactional rule-based activities in an automated way, 24-7. So there's a good automation potential in Finance. That's the first tier. Then I would go into the more artificial intelligence type solutions that would create, for instance, service chat bots or more intelligent ways of handling exception work. For example SAP is trialling a mixture of technologies that have OCR and machine learning to identify the payment advice numbers and match them to the outstanding accounts receivable that when it receives a payment or remittance advice from a customer which usually comes in as a PDF. That will be the second step. Then we have this third layer of working with big data and working with predictive analytics tools. In a way they all have a potential to change processes or change the setup or finance as they are. A lot of automation will basically free up human workers who could then be skilled in a different way to provide more analysis and insights. A fourth area would be using standard office technologies like, Sharepoint or tools like Slack or Microsoft Teams. Having these social collaboration tools and ways to share data across an enterprise network or across networks that include external vendors or customers, will also make month end reporting, variance analysis and other processes much easier.

On the best bit of advice Johannes ever received

It was from a colleague actually back at Thunderbird which was my international MBA program. So the piece of advice I received there is really to maintain a good network of former colleagues, of alumni, to really keep in touch with them. I'm still in touch with a lot of my friends from school back then. We're sharing opportunities and we're bringing people back and forth. For me, having a good alumni network in consulting has resulted in some of the most interesting job opportunities or consulting opportunities that were in the end much easier to realise than having to go through an official tender process. Designate time to actively maintain your network. It also adds a human and nice personal touch to your work and I really enjoy calling back on my old customers and asking, *"How are you doing? What things are going on?"* And it's always very interesting.

Recommended Resources

Book: *Reinventing the CFO: How Financial Managers Can Transform Their Roles And Add Greater Value (2006)*, by Jeremy Hope (link)

Group: The FSN Network (link)

Website: Bearing Point (link)

"Don't think of a role as a series of boxes to be ticked on a job profile. Instead think about how a role is going to suit you in terms of your capability and how you want to develop that capability."

Jonathan Evans
LI: JonathanEvans

Tags:
#agility #capability #recruitment #CV #job hopping #career advancement #relationships

JONATHAN EVANS has over 10 years' experience in Executive Talent Acquisition, spanning Agency, RPO and In-house roles. His early career was spent as a specialist Actuarial, Audit and Risk Head-hunter, in the Insurance, Investments and Pensions Industries. He then moved to Pontoon Solutions, the Recruitment Process Outsourcing arm of Adecco, to set up, develop and deliver their Executive Search solution in the UK. Jonathan is currently a Global Talent Scout & Capability Lead at AstraZeneca, a leading global bio-pharmaceutical company, with responsibility for senior hiring for Corporate & Digital functions across the group (including Finance).

On how to avoid getting boxed in
It is quite difficult because you have to do two things that might seem quite counterintuitive. You have to both be mindful and plot your career to a certain extent but it's equally important to be opportunistic. I mean this from an internal and external perspective.

On what is learning agility and the importance of having a capability profile for career progression
Internal succession planning is really contingent upon people being able to be agile. The one skill set that I'd really advocate developing above all others is what I call *learning agility*. That's the ability to think laterally in the first instance about what an opportunity is going to do

for you in the longer term rather than thinking about a linear pathway to success because that's probably non-existent now anyway. The way to do that is to be building a network within the organisation your work in, as well as externally, so you can actually get a full understanding of what a particular opportunity is going to offer you. It's really important to take as broad a view across both the organisation and the market as you can. Then think about what you're going to enjoy doing, but do so in an open-minded sense. Don't think of a role as a series of boxes to be ticked on a job profile. Instead think about how a role is going to suit you in terms of your capability and how you want to develop that capability. The importance is to build a kind of capability profile for yourself that means you're regarded as somebody who can take on a number of different challenges.

It's about the ability to operate strategically as well as operationally. It's about the ability to conceptualise very difficult and complex things and then translate them to other stakeholders both above and below you, in a way that allows everybody to understand what the principle objective underneath all of that complexity is. This isn't just for leadership roles in general. Even if it's, let's say, a financial controller position that you aspire to, it's of equal importance to develop that capability. So when you're thinking about your career, plot out the roles that are going to allow you to build that capability as well as that technical expertise and overall experience. However also remain open-minded and opportunistic to what a role can offer you because roles are very different depending on the type of organisation you're in and also where that organisation is in its own development.

On the topic of job hopping

Apparently we're only one percent the way into the digital age. Think about how much has changed in the last 15 years and then think about what's going to happen over the next 15 years. What is technology and disruption going to do to the finance role in 2 or 3 years, let alone, 5 years. Being opportunistic is not a negative in that context and actually finance professionals can be risk averse to a point, because of the nature of the training for the job that finance professionals do. However there's a risk factor in being risk averse because if you're not going to take advantage and be slightly ahead of the curve at times, then that's a risk as well. Conversely, I was at an event last year, and one of the partners of one of the big head hunting firms was presenting at it. He shared a statistic that over the last 5 years, 80% of the CEO hires within the FTSE100 were internal. So it's kind of indicative of the fact that you don't want to be seen as a fidelity risk, because you've hopped around. That will hurt your immediate chances in an assessment process. There's no getting around it, if you haven't had longevity at organisations then there are always going to be certain companies that will factor that into an assessment on the decision for an individual role. However it also means that you're perhaps not giving yourself the full opportunity to discover what an organisation could offer for you.

Every individual circumstance is different and frankly, good people are always going to have options. But those options within the market are different now to what they were 10 years ago let alone 20 years ago. So nobody expects people to be in an organisation for an infinite amount of time. And actually the counterbalance of it is that you can be perceived as being slightly institutionalised if you have been in an organisation for 20 years. It's about balance and the key thing to understand is how can you attain your development needs within the company that you're working at now? Again, that comes back to building that internal network as well as the external network. If you're in the right sort of organisation you should be able to carve out those development opportunities. Be opportunistic and creative with it. There are going to be chances to take on secondments, there are going to be chances to move into areas that are, green field, or new builds or turnarounds. Those are the kinds of opportunities that might seem like a lateral move or a slightly left field area to be going into at the time, but over the longer term they're going to help to continue to build that capability which is what people look for in those more senior roles.

On CVs (résumés) and how to get recruiters excited
Number one, keep it short and keep it impactful, two pages. Pull out the relevant information for the roles that you've been doing but also paint a bit of a picture as to how you developed through them. At the more senior end, it's a little bit different, because yes, CVs are always important, but it is more about the narrative and the kind of career that somebody has built. What you see in the best CVs are people who really have been able to take advantage of a number of things. By using their technical ability, network, innate commerciality or entrepreneurialism, whatever you call it, to drive themselves into roles where they've been given a lot of responsibility and autonomy, or they've been put into

position where it's either been a new build or they've been parachuted into save something and turn it around. Generally speaking, those are the kind of things that get me excited when I'm looking at a CV. If it's BAU all the way through, there's nothing wrong with it but it's always a bit more exciting when somebody's been able to get that role where it's been crucial to turn a business or department around, or it's been launching a subsidiary, or just that kind of diversity and experience where people have been able to take a step out of corporate life for a period of time and have gone to a start-up for a few years. It's just those points of difference I like. Now, not all companies and not all head-hunters are going to feel the same way, it's my personal preference. My organisation is a big global organisation but we are fast-paced, entrepreneurial and that may be kind of specific to me, but that's the kind of mix I like to see personally.

On the best bit of advice Jon has on recruiters

Cultivate relationships with a select number of recruiters as you go through your career. Have a couple of head-hunters and a couple of big organisation recruiters. I used to work for a relatively niche headhunting organisation in insurance and asset management. If you are in an industry where it's a smaller pool of individuals, then definitely have a relationship with one or two of those sorts of organisations. Then finally and increasingly important, build relationships with people such as myself. This is becoming really essential because probably the most important part of my role is identifying those key talents in the market, six, twelve, twenty-four and thirty-six months in advance of the role becoming available. Recruitment pipelining is the way forward for us. So speak to recruiters but don't make it a transactional conversation. Don't talk about just an individual role in the here and now. Instead the recruiter has to understand what you're mid- to long-term aspirations are because frankly the company that cares about that is probably a big company that you're going to want to get into because it's going to do the most for you.

"The reality is that the world when we just qualified, when we thought that we were set for life, this is gone."

Larysa Melnychuk
LI: larysamelnychuk
WS: fpa-trends.com

Tags:
#FP&A #creativity #proximity #adapt #analytics #CVO #value creation #culture #key drivers #impact

LARYSA MELNYCHUK is founder and managing director of FP&A Trends Group, which helps companies to realise their FP&A potential through training, consulting, professional networking and debating. Larysa is an experienced FP&A practitioner and has held senior FP&A positions at Invensys plc, Ace Group, Key Bank and HSBC Bank before setting up the International FP&A Board in 2013- a global and well-recognised FP&A best practices think-tank. Larysa is also a member of the exam content writing team for the Association of Finance Professionals (AFP) FP&A certification.

Larysa holds CGMA & FP&A designations, as well as an MSc from Kiev Technical University. Larysa is based out of London, England, although she is a regular traveller to accounting centres worldwide.

On why the accounting profession is creative

When people say that the accounting profession is not creative I would disagree with them, especially in terms of modern management accounting. It is a very creative profession if it's allowed to be creative, if you're allowed to go outside of the box and use different analytical skills. I would say that the atmosphere in the Department of FP&A is also very important. If management encourage their teams to do creative analysis, to go outside of the box, beyond simple trend analysis to create the models that influence the decisions of the company, this is how you can really make a difference. Proximity is one of the paramount skills that is needed from people because if you just sit in your Finance Department or FP&A team and just prepare to meet one deadline and then another one, and not go outside of this box. Then it's very difficult to make any impact and influence those making the decisions.

On why it's no longer enough just to be a qualified accountant anymore

The reality is such that when you're an FP&A director and you try to find new people, say you're looking to hire staff for your Department, you've half a million qualified accountants in the UK to choose from. However, I must say that this is a very difficult task. When you interview these people, you understand that it's not enough to be a qualified accountant in order to be a modern FP&A practitioner. Interestingly enough we started to discuss this at the London (FP&A) Board quite early on and what we discovered was that quite a few of my colleagues started to experiment with people outside of the accounting profession. So people with engineering backgrounds, with mathematical backgrounds and so on. The interesting thing that many of them said is that they are exceptionally good. They have very mathematical minds, are really good business architects, they can see the big picture and they can go outside of the box. So the reality is that the world when we just qualified, when we thought that we were set for life, this is gone. So as qualified accountants we have to work very hard in order to adapt to the current trends. We really have to be much more analytical, we really have to understand what is going on otherwise we will become redundant.

On why CFOs are saying FP&A is the hardest position to fill

When we brainstorm the attributes required of being a good FP&A professional it was quite a long list and the reality is that to find the combination of all those skills in one person is very difficult. This is the reason why it is so difficult to find good FP&A professionals. The statistics show that in the UK up to 70% of CFOs say that this is the most difficult position to fill because the requirements are incredible. So one of the solutions is to build teams with some of these complementary skills and attitudes.

On why FP&A is a framework rather than just a department

FP&A is not a function anymore. It is not just a Department. FP&A is a framework used in business. The framework that is used for all strategic decision-making and also for operational decision making. It's not only the CFO that is becoming this CVO, Chief Value Officer, but I have seen situations where FP&A directors became part of the Board and I believe that there will be more and more examples like this. Now it's absolutely normal, especially for group FP&A directors to sit at the Board, not as the executive members of the Board, but as the providers of information because they can position ideas very quickly. I can see it in many companies now, so it has already started to happen. If you think about value analysis and adding value to the company, this is the ultimate goal for FP&A. It is to support a very quick and flexible decision making process in this incredible business environment.

On where FP&A can become less traditional and more valuable

This is what we are discussing around the globe with our international boards, that have experienced CFOs and Finance Directors of large organisations. The reality is that everything starts from the culture and this is currently one of the most topical areas in modern financial planning and analysis. If there is a more traditional culture where there are very traditional budgeting and planning processes embedded into the organisational culture, then it's very difficult to change anything. You could be a wonderful FP&A practitioner within a team of analysts, but the reality is that probably you wouldn't be easily allowed to share and implement your ideas if the company is very traditional. Budgeting is all about judgment. It's very rare that the traditional budgeting process is analytical and independent in creating goals. It is really about negotiation between top management and operational directors around their targets and future goals and bonuses. In reality this is what the budget process is and if you still have this embedded in your company it's very difficult to change it.

However, I've seen some situations when it could be changed from the bottom up, and by FP&A professionals with some very interesting analytical insights they've shared with their organisations. So the first one obviously is that the culture must support it. The second one is people also have to be ready. They need to be more than traditional accountants, not just the consolidators of information. People should be thinking outside the box, they should be more proactive. They also need to be brave because sometimes it's not easy in an organisation to say we have to change this and that since our analytics are showing that this is what we are going to have in the future if we don't take corrective action. Sometimes it's not easy when the company doesn't allow this free thinking and doesn't allow these analytical ideas.

On the best bit of advice from Larysa to stay relevant

Think about the key drivers. Think about how these key drivers are going to change. Think about internal and outside external drivers. Also create the architecture of your models that allows you to very quickly adjust to support almost real-time decision-making processes. If you ask me whether many companies have managed to achieve it? No, it's not happening yet, so the majority of companies are still very traditional, and we have to change our processes to remain relevant.

Recommended Resources

Website: FP&A Trends (link)

Website: Certified Corporate FP&A Professional (link)

"Storytelling is the most powerful way to put ideas into the world and to connect people."

Marco Singh
LI: marco-singh

Tags:
#storytelling #expectations #stakeholder management #technology #digital IQ

MARCO SINGH is a Commercial Finance and Business Partnering leader who has extensive experience working with global companies across the Payments, FinTech, Tech and Financial Services industries. Marco originally trained in engineering before finding his way to finance and then commercial finance further along in his career. Marco also is a treasurer at the Vitiligo Society and Mentor at Warwick Business School.

Marco is currently based out of Maidenhead, England, holds a CGMA designation and an MBA from Warwick Business School.

On moving into Finance from Engineering & Product Development
The biggest challenge actually was when moving over to finance to resist the urge to be very commercial and almost getting ahead of the numbers. First and foremost the thing you had to do was to get the month end right, then get the numbers right, believe the numbers, nail those down and then move on from there.

On why storytelling is important and how to do it effectively
I've got a Golden rule, something I did time again and it's about storytelling. A guy called Robert McKee who was a professor at the University of California talked about storytelling as the most powerful way to put ideas into the world and to connect people. We're hardwired to listen and absorb stories. So something that I would always do is once you've got the numbers, put as much time as you did in getting those numbers into putting together a story. Make it interesting, make sure

you've got some short strap lines that you can hang that story onto and then focus on the delivery of that story. Often I've seen people put lots of effort into the numbers and then the insights just get lost because it's in a dense set a text. Or there's 15 to 20 KPIs all merged into one and it's just not interesting. They demonstrate how hard they've been working but all you need is just two or three key messages.

On an important lesson on managing stakeholders' expectations

I do remember once when I could have better managed stake-holder expectations. It was when I was presenting my results for the first time and the reaction was quite mixed. I realised later it was because for some people I hadn't taken them through the results beforehand and they had reacted against it. Next quarter when I did it I made sure I pretty much man-marked those people and it was exactly the same people with similar messages but their reaction was so different because I had taken the effort to grab them beforehand for ten minutes. To go through the key summaries, key strap lines, make a few changes in terms of some syntax and off you go.

On a top rule on managing stakeholders and line managers

One of the top rules is *"no surprises"* and that's something that I think applies to every single boss that I've ever worked for. When it comes to your stakeholders it's the same for them. They don't have to agree with you, it can be intimidating particularly early on in your career but ultimately you're not going there to change your answer so that they agree. You're getting their input. Even if they don't agree, you've been courteous and as long as you haven't been emotive about your conclusions, because language is so important when you're applying conclusions to your numbers. Once you've taken your stakeholders through your conclusions and they're factual, they're not emotive, they don't really have anywhere to go apart from, *"I have a different view."* Well that's fine, let's have a conversation, that's part of the job of commercial finance, to have conversations about the numbers.

On why technologies and systems are a bit like yesterday's factories

Maybe it's because of my background, but technology and systems are a bit like yesterday's factories. They can't be changed easily, they need lots of investment, and you can't plan a future without understanding their limitations. So I'd always encourage someone to get close to your IT team and your systems people. And to also be careful because in today's environment there's almost a danger that you can love your technology and you should be careful because it won't love you back.

On improving our Digital IQ

One of things I'm really trying to do is to improve my digital IQ. It's a phrase that I've stolen from PwC. They apply it to companies but I'm taking it and applying it to myself. One of my missions is to become more digital IQ savvy and encourage others to have a think about what their digital IQ is and whether that needs improving. Questions like do you understand cloud computing? Do you understand big data, its limitations, and what you can do with it? Do you understand automation? There's lots of hype around artificial intelligence but what is it? Is it an incremental step to take rather than a magic wand? Do you understand data protection? All of those together make up your digital IQ.

On the best bit of advice Marco ever received

I was lucky enough to work with a fairly senior executive and he was absolutely brilliant at presenting. One day I asked him what his secret was, and he just looked at me as said, *"Practice, practice, practice."* I know it's not really advice, but it's stuck with me because he was a guy at the top of his game and he didn't mind admitting that he put in the hard yards to remain at the top of his game. He could have just told me anything really, like natural talent, or whatever, but he was very open that before every speech, before every presentation he practiced loads before it to get it right.

Recommended Resources

Book: *The Innovator's Dilemma: When New Technologies Cause Great Firms to Fail (Management of Innovation and Change) (2016)*, by Clayton Christensen (link)

Video: Robert McKee - *The importance of storytelling in Business* - Seminar 29th November 2013 (link)

Website: The Vitiligo Society (link)

Article: Business partnering with an everlasting impact (link)

Research Paper: PWC Digital IQ (link)

"If you challenge your colleagues and the thinking of your colleagues in the right way in order to influence them, they will then recognise the value of the interaction with finance."

Marco Venturelli
LI: marco-venturelli

Tags:
#sustainability #adaptable #ESG #strategic #influencing #international #surveys

MARCO VENTURELLI has over 35 years of experience in finance and accounting and currently leads Performance and Financial Strategy at Novartis where he is CFO of the Oncology Europe Region, as well as being on the CFO Board of Directors (CFO Consigliere di Amministrazione). Marco has held various roles such as Country General Manager, undertaken international assignments and led global teams. He's also regularly commenting and contributing on LinkedIn particularly with the handles #HappyFinance and #theHappyCFO.

Marco is currently based out of Milan, Italy and also volunteers with Action Aid, looking to alleviate poverty with a constant flow of support to different programs in Arica and India.

On why sustainability is becoming important for finance professionals
Investors like sovereign funds, pension funds and so on are asking companies to be sustainable, not only in the usual financial sense but also in a broader environmental, social and governance sense. It will change the way we work in our companies but also could change the way our governments work. I find this topic of sustainability relatively innovative because so far it's more utilised by investment banks and so on. While the CFO's involvement, at least this is my understanding, is still a little bit on the outside with the exception of some companies. One

thing I suggest to my teams is that we must be adaptable now and in the future. Anticipating the future is always very difficult to predict but we have to adapt to the future. We all know the classical example of Nokia, Kodak, and these big companies that did not adapt to the market. Let's say if you're in the energy area and you do not look to change the way you produce your energy, you put your company at risk because there are external signals that for various reasons are showing that wind or solar generated electricity will take more and more share. What sometimes happens is that the politicians are quicker and faster than the organisations are so maybe we can help our organisations have a different perspective.

On why Finance are well positioned to drive better sustainability

In Finance we are well accustomed to having very well-structured, robust, accurate and coherent financial reporting and concepts. So we can really add value to our organisations by facilitating this move towards sustainability. Because I see more of these sustainability-type measures coming. We are moving from the Corporate Social Responsibility (CSR) agenda, which was a self-promoted and self-acted approach that companies did in the past towards a more structured one. Nowadays there's this new acronym, ESG (Environmental, Social & Governance). Under this new approach you not only share your financial perspective, but you are also expected to share your environmental, social and governance perspectives as well as your plans to become more ethical. At this point society not only expects organisations to be fully ethical but also that they help society to fully develop.

On the components that make up a Strategic Business Partner

A strategic business partner should also be able to influence others, such as, propose simplification projects, because you have the position to look at across the various functions in an organisation's value chain. We are also seeing more CFOs who are driving their companies' operational excellence programs and technological evolution.

On a couple of surveys pointing to the importance of being more strategic

A recent study done by McKinsey said that 41% of the CFO's activities today still belong to the more classical type of financial activities. However there are already 40% of CFOs that are leading transformational projects and nonrecurring strategic activities. There was also another interesting survey done by Ernst & Young that says it's also the CEO who wants the CFO to be more strategic. In Novartis we also did an internal survey of two hundred of our business leaders and we asked them very simply what you would like a business partner to be and where is finance today against that? I think this is a basic question if you want to be a better business partner.

We also asked them how we are doing. Then we asked the finance team, now you rate yourself against certain variables as well as asking the business now to rate your finance partner against them. Every businessperson said that you guys are very strong in advisory roles, you are very competent, very strong in your technical skills but you're lacking strategic understanding and overall business understanding. On the other hand, most of the finance organisation were actually thinking that we are much better in strategy and understanding that their business partners had given them credit for. Of course, all of us like to say okay, I'm great at those things, but it's important that we establish and do these internal surveys because if we want to be better finance business partners, if we want to add value, then we need to know what to do so we can build a practical development plan to get there. It's very like a lean six sigma approach, since you're also asking your internal customers if they like what you're doing and how you can do it better.

On how his first international assignment helped him in his career

When you enter into an international company you get to know people from very diverse backgrounds and you really learn a lot. That's why even though many of us Italians, for various reasons, like our country very much. I still encourage younger people to really take the opportunity of moving out of your country because you really learn much more in a very short period from these international experiences.

On why we shouldn't look at the word influencing so negatively

We need to become better at influencing and sometimes in finance with our integrity, we look at the word influencing with a negative meaning. Especially more junior people to finance who think, that because I am a fact-based person, and that I've given you the analysis, then that should be enough. I've learned that this is not enough. Whatever the analysis is you also have to explain it in a way that is really understood by the other party. I read a book by Adam Grant called Give and Take. It's a book of how in the future you can be successful in a more network-based and matrix-based organisation. What he's saying is you have to give not only to get, basically because if you always wanted to take it from your colleagues in your company you will not be successful, but you also have to give. At the end of the day if you challenge your colleagues and the thinking of your colleagues in the right way in order to influence them, they will then recognise the value of the interaction with finance. People don't like flattery. Let's say they come to you with a project and you say, *"this is a wonderful project, it is the best project I've seen."* This type of flattery does not help the project owner to improve the project one bit. However if you get the project or proposal and you are able to challenge in a positive and constructive way, influencing, then you get more appreciation for being a positive challenger.

On why people prefer sometimes to listen to the CFO rather than the CEO

The financial analysts of investment banks and so on listen more to the CFO than the CEO because the CFO to a certain extent is less about selling a proposition and is more adherent to a particular communication style. However the CFO must also be able to communicate well the vision of the company and how this fits with the sustainability and financial results of the company.

On the best bit of advice Marco has ever received

First always try to work with great people, this is very important. Select if possible or influence to try and go with a good boss, but also with good team with good players. Don't be afraid of having strong peers. Don't be afraid of internal competition, because it much better to play with a strong team and be a medium level player within a stronger team than to be the strongest in a medium team. And enjoy the game. Enjoy what you do, we are all professionals, we are well prepared so we have to really enjoy our daily activities, meetings, whatever we do, because it's also a good way to appreciate what you are doing.

Recommended Resources

Article: *"The Happy CFO: How Finance helps Society,"* by Marco Venturelli, 2017 (link)

Article: Measuring the impact of Impact Investing (link)

Article: The Business Value of impact measurement (link)

Article: Survey on CEOs expecting more from their CFOs (link)

Article: McKinsey report on where CFOs spending their time (link)

Article: *"The Imperial CFO,"* Economist article on the influence of the CFO (link)

Book: *The Audacious Finance Partner: Reveals The Key Factors and Skills for Business Partnering Success*, by Andrew Codd (link)

Book: *Give and Take: A Revolutionary Approach to Success (2013)*, by Adam Grant (link)

"Knowing the business that you are working in is key. Knowing what your stakeholders are interested in is key, because often 80% to 90% of the work that finance departments do, is not of interest to the business."

Marcus Thelwell
LI: marcusthelwell

Tags:
#technology #digital #new entrants #stakeholders #career advancement #motivation

MARCUS THELWELL is a business transformation manager at Deloitte in their Financial Advisory team where he works to improve profitability, employee experience and client experience through more modern ways of working. Marcus has worked between both Europe and Australia over the past nine years developing his Finance and commercial understanding via his work with globally recognised clients and also internally working with a range of industry renowned partners.

Marcus is Chair of the Sydney CPA Young Professionals Committee, a keen musician and has recently become a (novice) triathlete. Marcus also holds CGMA and CPA designations and lives in Sydney, Australia.

On what new entrants to Finance should be looking out for and why we need to be more than our stereotypical image

Traditionally new people entering finance and accounting would be very technically good with numbers and would often be quite introverted. It's well known that there's a stereotype behind accountants that is still fixed in the industry. However nowadays people need to be a lot more than that. Knowing the technical aspects of accounting is almost like a given, whether that's through a degree or whether that's through an additional academic qualification such as CA, ACMA or CPA. Additionally people coming into the industry need to be interested in either the technology that supports finance, and the data aspects of that, or they need to be interested in the actual business they are working in, and they need to have that commercial element to be interested in how the business they're working with operates. To do so they need to be able to represent their soft skills, by being a people person, being curious, and they need to ask questions, get out from behind their desks and get into the business.

On three things new entrants to finance can do immediately to start unlocking value for organisations

I think knowing the business that you are working in is key. Knowing what your stakeholders are interested in is key because often 80% to 90% of the work that finance departments do is not of interest to the business. Whether that's putting out reports they've compiled that way for years or consolidating different data sets of numbers. I think a lot of the time people in finance and accounting are doing those tasks because they are part of their working day schedules and have always been. What they haven't done is actually look at the bigger picture of what they're doing and question, *"What is it that the business is looking for from the information I'm providing them? Is this information hitting the mark in terms of the decisions that are being made?"* I think a lot of the time as finance practitioners we're waiting for the business to come to us asking what they want, but actually it should be the other way around, where we continually test and ask questions of the business in terms of what they want. Because I think we often expect the business to know what they really want, but they don't, not until they've actually seen something that's been really useful. And that's when they will go, *"Actually that's really useful can we have more of that information please."*

On the importance and benefits of new entrants being inquisitive

I think trying to instil a culture of inquisitiveness and curiosity about what it is that we're doing on a daily basis is really important. Especially providing the room for younger people to be able to put forward new ideas or new ways of working on what we're doing. Often we find that people who have been in a business a long time can kind of get stuck in their ways a lot in terms of how they work. Whereas actually younger objective minds come without the constraints of what's possible and what's not. So we should utilising these minds and how they see the world especially with new technology and new ways of working. A lot of the time young people are coding for fun, but the more senior people in the business wouldn't know what coding is or what it's capable of. Actually, the changes are so drastic now that we should actually start listening to younger people who have exposure and an interest in these new ways of working. Particularly because the capability and possibility of the time efficiencies are just enormous, especially for the finance and accounting part of the business.

On how to keep finance professionals motivated to run mundane finance processes

Especially for new people to finance we should set them challenges to solve. So let's say they've got a mundane finance process to run such as putting together a report, we could say to them, *"I'll set you a challenge. If you can improve the efficiency of this process from 5 days to 4 days then you can have that extra day to look into something within finance that you're interested in or something in the business that you'd like to learn and get to know more about."* Almost let them set out the challenge themselves and give them the opportunity to critically think about the process they are putting together. Let them actually come up with suggestions on how to improve it. And once you find those efficiencies, you can then reinvest them back into actually supporting something else which could deliver additional value to the business.

On how conversations that identify a common interest can help boost your career success

Just being able to have a conversation with someone and trying to find that common interest that you might have with somebody in the business is very useful. For example, I remember my final interview to my graduate program, it was actually mainly about football. The reason why it was about football is I actually support a team called Shrewsbury Town, which is in the third league of English football and the interviewer happened to support Barnet, also in the third league. Both teams had a fixture coming up that weekend and we spent the whole of that interview talking about the form of the teams, what football grounds we'd been to, what our predictions were for where our teams will finish in the League. From there on he actually became a bit of an informal mentor for me in my career for the next few years and that was purely based off a common interest and actually nothing to do with finance and accounting. So my advice would be to get out there, meet people and talk to people about things that you're interested in and passionate about. Have a conversation about it and if you can establish that baseline relationship. Then things become much easier for your actual job from the finance and accounting perspective too.

On the importance of understanding how systems work end-to-end and flow through to the end customer

Because I started from the technology side in finance in terms of systems I can kind of understand the concepts of how databases and how data flows through systems. As well as how it needs to be treated before it's ultimately analysed and insights taken from it. Now I would not claim to be a technical expert, however I think that early understanding was really helpful. I would recommend, even if you're technical or not, just to have a habit to read some information in terms of how the systems work, from a purely conceptual perspective and just to get that base level understanding. I think LinkedIn do some kind of open learning sessions on these things so I really recommend people to take that one on.

The best bit of advice Marcus has ever received

Be inquisitive and expose yourself to as many different ways of working in your career as possible. I think people will ultimately have a view of where they think their career should go, but until you experience it you won't really know what you like and don't like. A number of times in my career I've actually quite liked something I didn't think I would like at all, and didn't like something that I thought I would really like.

"Building your career is not a function only of your technical skills, you have to have the interpersonal skills, you have to have the presentation skills, communication skills, and business development skills."

Mark Lee
LI: MarkLee
WS: bookmarklee.co.uk

Tags:
#soft skills #mentoring #giving back #volunteering #career planning

MARK LEE has had a career that spans more than 30 years, during which time he stood out as a top accountant, the partner of two top accounting firms, a frequent financial commentator and one of only a handful of accountancy qualified magicians!

He is now primarily a speaker about the immediate future for accountants. He is also treasurer of the world's most exclusive magic society, The Magic Circle, deputy treasurer of Norwood, a top 150 charity, a member of the ICAEW's members and commercial board and is regularly asked to judge industry awards. Mark holds an FCA designation and lives in London, England

On why technical skills alone are not enough today
I recognised quite early on that building your career is not a function only of your technical skills. You also need to have good interpersonal skills and it really helps to also have presentation skills, communication skills, and business development skills.

For instance, I was invited to become a Fellow of the Chartered Institute of Tax because of the profile that I'd built up as Chairman of the ICAEW's Tax Faculty. When I say invited, I mean that instead of having to sit exams I had to present a body of work in lieu of writing a thesis. I remember going to Guildhall, a big fancy place in London, and being presented with my award. This was really special to me because I hadn't gone to public school, hadn't gone to University, and there wasn't an admissions ceremony when I became a member of the Institute of Chartered Accountants, there is now. That was a really special day and I still have the photo in my office. Being Chairman of the Tax Faculty and then that leading to me being ex-officio member of the Council of the Institute of Chartered Accountants was really cool.

On the importance of giving back and the right traits for success

Once I stood down from my tax activities I was invited to chair the Ethics Advisory Committee of the Institute. In other words, once you start volunteering they find ways to keep you involved if you're contributing in a positive way.

I always felt this was part and parcel of giving back to the profession. As so many of us have realised, you get a lot back from what you give rather than sitting back and hoping stuff is going to come to us regardless. The people who you admire have done that themselves and recommend it.

The challenge I think in professional life, whether in commerce, industry, or in practice, is there's sometimes a tendency to admire and look up to the people who others might see as bullies, or as very single-minded, focused, and determined. And that those attributes and personal qualities are what have got them to where they are.

Whenever I've done that, and I remember when I was younger thinking I wish I was a bit more like this one or that one, I then felt, actually, I don't want to be like that person. I don't like those personal traits and qualities, and if that's what it takes to get on I don't want to do it.

I looked around and I found plenty of other people who were successful who had more nurturing qualities, more positive qualities, and have been successful because of those qualities.

Actually the more I look around, I've realised this as I get older, I've realised there are more people with positive, inspiring, nurturing, attitudes in their approach to colleagues, to staff, to clients rather than being solely single minded and only looking out for themselves. I don't want to be like that and I wouldn't encourage anybody else to be like that because in the long term you might get there, or to wherever it is you're looking to go, but you'll probably be alone and that's no fun.

On how you can become just like those successful people you admire

The best tip I can remember along those lines is to identify 10 people you admire at the top of the career ladder you would like to be on. Start listing out the qualities that they have and that you admire. Look for the overlaps and then look for the gaps between where you are now and those qualities, attitudes and approaches that those people have. Then you can start looking to close those gaps and this gives you something specific to aim for.

On what our work will look like in the future

One of the things I do a lot now is talk about the future, write about the future, and the evolution that's required within individuals operating within the accounting and finance professions.

When we look to the future more and more of the day-to-day tasks that we all originally learned to do will be done through robotic process automation, machine learning, artificial intelligence, call it what you will depending on how far your time scale is.

The skills that accounting & finance people will need in the future will be less technical in some respects, less detail orientated, and may therefore attract different people to those who were attracted into the profession ten, twenty, or thirty years ago.

On the three ways you can look at our future

There's a lot of hype out there about how quickly the robots will be taking over our jobs.

When people are talking about, AI, robots or whatever, you have to question how far into the future are they talking? Most of them are talking 10 to 20 years down the line, at least, and in my experience few accountants are really planning their careers more than a few years ahead and certainly accountants in practice or running accounting firms rarely look out that many years down the line.

How the changes which are coming will impact us are dependent on the timeframe we look at. A friend of mine Rohit Talwar, a global futurist, recommends, and I have adapted his recommendation, that we recognise that there are three time scales to account for when you're looking into the future.

The first one is the immediate future of the next 12 to 18 months. Then you've got 18 months to 3 or 4 years out and then you've got 4 to 10 years. And beyond 10 years? Well nobody in their right mind is making definitive plans for more than 10 years down the line.

On the difference between key business skills and soft skills

Historically accountants have always made time to keep themselves up-to-date technically, either they don't want to be sued, or they don't want to lose their job.

There has been a historical reluctance, not across the board but very commonly, to assume that everything else is a soft skill, not hard, not difficult, not important perhaps, and we'll learn it on the job or we'll learn it by watching our peers, colleagues and bosses.

That's really sad because in my experience the people with the better personal and business skills are the ones who really develop their careers and achieve much more whether again that's in practice or in industry & commerce.

Therefore I think it is crucially important, it's almost a campaign I'm running if you like, to stop talking about 'soft' skills and to recognise that there are a range of key business skills that finance leaders will require whether in practice or in industry & commerce in the future.

Also taking the time to identify the gaps between where we are now, and where we want to be as regards each of those skills. There isn't a finite number of them because the skills you will require depend upon what you're doing now and what you want to be doing in a few years' time.

However, the list certainly includes effective communication, persuasion, influence and presenting type skills. Certainly if you're in practice they also include business development, networking skills, recognising the difference between pitching for work, selling work, winning work and knowing how to price the work.

On how to plan your career in the next few years

Think about how you would like to see your career panning out, at least for the next few years. Look out for people who may have already achieved what you're looking to achieve and ask to have a conversation with them.

There are plenty of people out there who will willingly mentor younger people earlier in their careers now. There are plenty of people out there who will give you at least a short amount of time, some tips and advice, out of the goodness of their hearts, because they want to give back to the profession and perhaps also because somebody once helped them.

On the best bit of advice Mark has ever received
It was to assume good intent and cockup over conspiracy. I found life is much easier for me now that I stop assuming people are trying to harm me, hurt me, or take actions to screw things up. On most occasions that assumption has been wrong.

Other people by and large are out there to help us help each other. There are some nasty people out there, but, in the wonderful words of the children's song from the film Frozen, *"Let it go."*

Recommended Resources
Book: *7 Habits of Highly Effective People (2001),* by Stephen Covey (link)

Book: *You Can't Teach a Kid to Ride a Bike at a Seminar: The Sandler Sales Institute's 7 step system for successful selling (1995),* by David H Sandler (link)

Website: Mark's personal website (link)

"… but we've got the credibility, and credibility leads to conversation, and conversation leads to opportunity."

Martin Gilchrist
LI: gilchristaccountants
WS: gilchristandco.com

Tags:
#practice development #networking #resilience #conversations

MARTIN GILCHRIST is a founder and manager of Gilchrist & Co. Chartered Accountants, a 300 client boutique practice that specialises in looking after professional freelancers and people in independent practice. Martin has mentored many businesses and start-ups through his work with Business in the Community, Digital Circle and the Social Media Association for Business, of which he was a founding member. Martin has been described as probably one of Northern Ireland's best-networked professionals and is known for saying there are so many networking events going on in Belfast that, *you could eat breakfast, lunch and dinner for free every working day.*

Martin holds an LLB from Ulster University and is currently based out of Belfast, Northern Ireland.

On why practice development isn't always about finding more clients

We are very lucky in that we don't have to sell. We have built a practice and although I don't like the word, it is a livelihood practice that sustains the lifestyle we want to have. What we want to do is get satisfaction, reward and recognition for the work that we do. We want to be very good at the work that we do. Practice development for me is not about going out to find clients because the clients come to us. What practice development means to me is going out and building a very strong and stable network of good people who understand what we're about and that we understand them as well. If you have that network it supplies you with everything you need, not just clients, but information and loads of support.

On the distinction between internal and external resilience

It doesn't take you to be in business long to realise that you need to have resilience. You need to have the strength of character and the ability to stand back up after being knocked down. There's internal resilience, your own strength of mind and your own stability, but another important thing in business is the resilience that comes from the people around you. If you have to do something difficult, if you come up against a difficult problem and you have a network of people, if you have other people you can turn to, even to ask, *"have you had this problem before, how did you get through it?"* And to have that response, *"Yes, I've had that happen to me and I've got through it."* That helps develop resilience. Resilience is key in any businessperson's toolbox.

On the five things you can do to build a more resilient network

So how do you build that strong, supportive, productive and useful network around you. I'd suggest there and five things that you can try, and these five things work very well for us at Gilchrist & Co. The first thing is start something. By **start something** I mean, start a group or a club, a get together, a meet-up. Because if you start something you get the credibility of it. And we've started a number of things over the years. For example, the Social Media Association for Business which had more than 2,000 members, it had well over 1,000 people attend the real events. We had a steering committee and we had speakers and sponsors lining up the support it. So what has that got to do with Gilchrist &Co, which only looks after professional freelancers? We've got the credibility, and credibility leads to conversation, and conversation leads to opportunity. In our case the opportunity was £20,000 over the course of the year. That's nice, it's not world changing, but how much time did I spend on that, about maybe two or three hours a month, on proper work.

The second thing is, starting stuff is hard, so it's much easier to *join something*, to join somebody else's club, group, or association. There's a brilliant TED talk on this about not being the leader but being the first follower and being a good first follower. Essentially what it says is that you can't be a leader unless you have followers, but unless you become a good follower or member in any group, you essentially get credibility through that as well. Not as much, but then you're not investing as much.

The third thing is to find a physical space or location where you can *become part of the furniture*. Now we have our own office however if

I'm having meetings I'd go down to Loft Space and pay the fee because I know that when I arrive there will be other people, friends of mine, connections, people I don't know, people that I want to get to know and just being in that space gives them an opportunity to see me and to say hello. The serendipity that comes out of having a space where you become a regular participant or involved in their events is so valuable.

The fourth thing is, and this is one of the most important things that has worked for Gilchrist & Co, it really has been a game changer for us, is do stuff for other people, and it has to be genuine, **give without the expectation of reciprocation**. It allows you to be a contributor, to build a relationship, something meaningful. Even though I'm not giving away a professional service, I'm not giving away a product or doing something that benefits me and not expecting any return there is real value.

The final one is, **have a party**. That's a little bit flippant because I don't actually mean alcohol, dancing and all that stuff. What I mean is find an excuse just to bring together the people whom you really admire, respect, and like. People that enjoy your company just as much as you enjoy theirs. People that excite you, people that when you're having a conversation with them you're all lit up and motivated. Because if you bring people together, whether it's just five, ten, fifteen or fifty of them, we've done this a lot, you don't have to preach to them or give them a presentation, or try and sell them anything, or set out a direction for them, or tell them how wonderful you are and how you're going to lead them. Literally put them in a room and let the magical happen.

On why technology will not put us out of jobs

From a work perspective, am I worried that technology is going to put me out of the job? Absolutely not! I am absolutely not worried. I'm fully confident that technology is going to make me more effective. It's going to make me more efficient. It's going to make me more useful to my clients. Technology can do a lot of marvellous things but what it can't do at the moment and it will not be able to do for a long period of time is two things. It can't put stuff in context. So no matter how good your robot is, even if it can punch through walls, it cannot be you. It cannot be in your skin. It cannot have the 100,000 conversations that you have had in your professional career. It cannot know the people that you know. All that stuff that creates the context, understanding and meaning that is required in order to be a professional. The second thing is empathy, being able to read someone before they even say a word, or read between the lines, or understand nuances in human interactions. I'll share a small story that proves what I mean.

On why mirror neurons matter for accountants and finance professionals

I bumped into an old friend who asked me what do I know about mirror neurons? I said that I thought they were something to do with empathy, and he said *"mirror neurons are the most important thing in business and I can prove it to you."* There's one test that you can do to prove that you can both read and control other people's minds through this idea of mirror neurons. He said the next time when you're speaking with someone, you don't have to be sneaky about it, you can tell them what you're doing. The next time you're having the conversation, when you're standing face-to-face, just smile. Put a smile on your face or even just smile through your eyes, or even just think about smiling. And I bet that the person across from you can't help but start to smile back to you, even if you have told them that is what's happening. It's almost impossible. So empathy, the ability to understand how well the person you're communicating with, and the information that you're trying to get across or the job that you're trying to do, how is it impacting the person that you're actually doing it with? How are they accepting, receiving or understanding it? And are you communicating with them in a way that's creating the result you had hoped for when starting the conversation? Robots can't do that yet.

On the best bit of advice Martin has ever received

I had a senior partner in a law firm say to me once, *"Martin, just keep in mind when you're in business or professional practice, your clients will grow with you."* When you have a professional practice those relationships are going to last for a very long time because as their businesses grow your business will grow. As they develop, get better and can really start to get the satisfaction out of their business as they move along, you will win from that as well. Your network grows with you.

Recommended Resources

Book: *Tribe of Mentors (2017)*, by Timothy Ferriss (link)

Video: How to start a movement Ted Talk (link)

Website: Gilchrist & Co (link)

"It's all about learning who your audience is, learning what information they really need, and doing the best you can to impart that information to them."

Michelle Gasson
LI: michelle-gasson

Tags:
#exams #prioritisation #communication #budget cuts #healthcare #family

MICHELLE GASSON has had a fascinating journey in finance and accounting, from hairdressing, to being a mother, a wife, managing her studies, career and what gave her the idea to become a qualified accountant. Michelle is currently the Financial Controller for Play Design Ltd, a strategic retail design agency specialising in the design and production of branded retail spaces, units and customer experiences.

Michelle holds a CGMA designation and is currently based out of Saint Ives, England.

On dealing with a challenging environment and budget cuts

When I joined it was a very challenging environment. They were very reliant on local authority funding and at that time a new government had just started. It was a case of these budgets are going to be cut, so we had to do more or the same, with less. It was challenging and it was about actually communicating very well to people how things were going with the budgets. There were huge challenges there and one of the things that I took on was more detailed reporting. So being able to provide really key information to management by developing a management information tracker to deliver balanced scorecard-type reporting, from all over the business meant I was able to issue the information that was required, which was fun and challenging at same time. It presented me with a few sleepless nights, but it did improve my IT skills no end.

On how to prioritise time between building a career, work, studies, & kids

It's really all about recognising what was most important and the things that were the most important were my job, my children, and my studies. So somehow I had to fit all those three things in. I know I left the husband out there but that was also important. It was about prioritising what I was going to do. Many of my evenings were actually taken up doing my studies. So instead of sitting watching TV I would study. The full-time job, there wasn't much I could do about that, because that was what I was required to do. Weekends were taken up spending time with the family because that too was important. There's a bit of time coming home from work, spending time with the children, putting them to bed, and then after the children had gone to bed that was my time to sit there and put my head into the books. Yes it was hard work, yes it was very tiring, but you don't succeed in passing the exams and getting the qualifications if you don't put that extra effort in. I know there were some people I was studying with at the time who were complaining about the amount of time they had to put into studying for the exams and these people didn't have children. I was thinking well I'm managing it, and I've a family as well, what are you complaining about? It's about stopping some of the things that you do for fun, because you can always do them afterwards. When you've a deadline to meet for an exam, if you work very hard leading up to that and once you've done your exams, actually then you've got free time to do the things you really enjoy doing. I will say that once the final exam was over it was such a relief that I'd never have to do another exam again. That's the reassuring thing, they do come to an end at some point.

On how we can improve the impact of our communications

It's great having a lovely report in front of you, that's accurate, to the point, but not if everybody fails to understand it. So you always have to understand who your audience are. In a previous role I was working with scientists who had different levels of understanding for financial information. The chief scientific officer could read a financial report, he understood it and didn't need anything explained to him. He was just happy to have something that was very clear and precise. Then some of the project managers actually needed to talk through the numbers and would ask what do these mean? What are you saying? So I'd have to take it back to basics and explain why I'd come up with the information I'd come up with from the information they'd provided me versus what was in the systems. That also helped me as well because I would learn more about what they did and also how their work impacted them in financial terms. It was quite an education to be able to take what I do, take what they do and then find some common ground where we could actually discuss the financial results in a format that they understood. It is so important to be able to take your very nice reports and them break into information that people can understand. Sometimes you just take a little bit of it and you explain it. I've been very fortunate with the places I've worked where people are not financial experts. I've worked with nurses in hospitals and some of them are in charge of budgets They're not really interested in numbers, what they need to know is can I buy this? Can I buy that? Have I got enough money to put an agency nurse in here if needed? That's what they were interested in. So the reports we used to present at the hospital varied from being basic and never really going into the numbers too much to where we would have more of a discussion about, *"what are you looking for? What do you need to make your roles a success or your wards a success?"* And then I'd be able to present answers to them. It's all about learning who your audience are, learning what information they really need, and doing the best you can to impart that information to them.

On how we can best futureproof our careers

Most of us in finance realise that some of our jobs could be done by a robot in the future, but it's not going to explain the reports, or sit down and listen to somebody to get an understanding of the information they require. So it's important that we develop our communication and soft skills to continue in employment as opposed to being replaced by robots.

On the best bit of advice Michelle has ever received

It's to break things down into bite-sized pieces so you can actually achieve things. When you have a challenge, to break it down so that you can actually set yourself achievable goals. A bit like how do you eat an elephant? Piece-by-Piece.

Recommended Resources

Article: *"Communication Dividend,"* Financial Management Magazine, June 2017, pages 52-53 (link)

Website: Accountancy Age (link)

Website: Accounting Web (link)

"Every time you hire somebody that's a major investment for you and your team. So really concentrate on making sure that everybody on your team knows more about something than you do."

Niall O'Sullivan
LI: niall-o-sullivan

Tags:
#best practice #change #soft skills #learning

NIALL O'SULLIVAN is currently Google Finance Director for Emea, responsible for the implementation & maintenance of financial controls and statutory reporting across Europe and Africa in a highly centralised model. Niall is also CEO of Google Payments Ireland. Niall has built an exemplary reputation for relentless execution of organisational change and complex cost reduction programmes. Niall has managed diverse teams of financial, legal, technology and operations experts across multiple geographies, and at Vodafone he managed a large team of over 2,500 people across 20 countries including 3 Shared Services Centres.

Niall is a speaker at many executive level conferences on change and transformation He also holds an ACA designation and lives with his family in Dublin, Ireland

On the ingredients for successful change drawing on his time at Vodafone
Obviously there needs to be a driving business need and realisation that the business has to change. Equally what helped was that Vodafone had a lot of really strong finance people, who were very Maths driven and hungry for information and precision around finance. There was a huge level of frustration because they couldn't get the information they needed. Equally it was very much in the post-growth phase and every point of margin was absolutely crucial, which meant the finance people came to the fore running the business. That ability to predict what cash flow was going to be to within a couple hundred thousand every year, it

just gave a huge assurance to the market. The business might be struggling and challenged in some areas but because of the discipline and accuracy, there was never a miss in terms of accounting issues or anything, despite all the pressure that was on the business.

On why the traditional accountant is gone but its skills are still crucial

I talk to my teams about it, the age of this traditional accounting is pretty much gone. Journal entries and that sort of stuff is just going to be gone. Month end processes will be completely automated in time, but how do you and what do you need to know to get to that position? You need to know how processes work, as well as process engineering. For machine learning and robotics to work you need to be able to tell these things what to do. A human still has to instruct them what the core task is and why. So our audit training is still absolutely crucial here. That ability to actually say, this is where the numbers come from, this is the data source and this is where it ties back to. The discipline of having your bank rec accurate at the end of the day. Having that discipline and then being able to explain to a machine, this is what you need to do. I think core accounting skills are now going to move towards understanding process engineering, being able to talk to IT people & explain what's important, what can be done and what can't. That is definitely going to be crucial.

On how to get the most out of best-practice sharing

I've always done a huge amount of best practice sharing. One of the things I used to do is have a meeting with a group six months or so after joining the business and I used to ask them: *"What are three things that we do better than your last company?"* And, *"What are three things that your last company did better than us?"* I've always tried to set the standards but there are always things that somebody else does better. So we must try to find out what is it that they do better than us? What can we learn from them and steal from somebody else? Finance people tend to be pretty good at sharing best practice. You go talk to somebody, they'll tell you what they're good at and what they're not so good at. Particularly when you're implementing systems people tend to share their stories pretty well. We did a lot of work with Hackett to find out who is world class. Thankfully there are now a few, we even got Vodafone into the world class bracket. At Google there are some things that we do amazingly well and there are some things frankly that need improving because of the dynamic of where our business is at. There are always things to learn from other businesses.

On the key skills required for us to remain relevant

Boosting your database and analytical skills is huge. Everybody talks about big data, it's a massive issue but somebody has to figure out what it means. With all those thousands of data points coming in, the task of making it real, looking and sensing the patterns, is very important. There's always going to be a huge need for change management and project management skills to be able to drive the change, since change is constant. Bots, artificial intelligence and machine learning, all those sort of things mean essentially that Finance has to go from where it is today to a different position. The core skills of understanding the process of how numbers get created, how a number gets into the end financial statements from the core processes and being able to explain which are important and which are not as key. In FP&A, it's more forward looking and this involves scenario building. That's fine, but what is the source of that data, and how reliable is it? Controls and compliance are a core area, and will become a more important skill as we try to outsource more and get computers to do more. People who understand this are saying hang on, the machine might make a mistake here and you'll have to be able to unravel how the mistake was made.

On being open to learning from others outside your own world

I've always been really interested in the innovation side but I think the thing is just to be open to finding out where other people are doing things better. Just be full of ideas. There's always somebody doing something better, and there's always somebody who has a solution to a problem you're facing yourself. So build your network and build your level of expertise with people outside your own world.

On the best bit of advice Niall has ever received

Hire the best people you can. Headcount is always going to be scarce, and modern companies really look at the headcount as being a real way of controlling the spend in a business. That certainly is true of all the big tech companies. Every time you hire somebody that's a major investment for you and your team. So really concentrate on making sure that everybody on your team knows more about something than you do. If effect, what skill do they bring that you know nothing about.

"The biggest gap we see between the maturity of the skills today and those required in finance going forward is in data & technology savviness."

Nilly Essaides
LI: nilly-essaides
WS: thehackettgroup.com

Tags:
#digital transformation #business partnering #agility #world class #change #talent

NILLY ESSAIDES is a leading finance and EPM thought leader with 30+ years of experience researching, writing and speaking about the role of the finance function and of financial executives within global enterprises. Nilly is a public speaker and industry expert on finance transformation, EPM and treasury topics.

Although originally from Israel, Nilly is currently based out of Salem, Oregon, USA.

On where the world class finance organisations are doing it better
We see several things that are emerging as the characteristics of world-class finance organisations. They have responded to the digital transformation challenge by increasing the automation level of their processes. World-class organisations are more highly automated, and that improves their process quality and efficiency. Automation is not just the cost play, but it's also an effectiveness play. Additionally, world-class organisations are much more in tune with their customer needs and are much more customer-oriented, what we call customer-centricity. They have better talent management programs and develop talent to fit what the business needs are and evolve staff skills in response to the changing needs of the business.

On the importance of agility

I think it's very important to think about this word agility in today's finance & accounting practices because finance must become more responsive to the rapidly changing external environment. The velocity of change is increasing and with that finance needs to be able to leverage its talent, its processes, and its technology so that it can become more agile and more responsive to that rate of change.

On where all this change is taking finance organisations

In the 30 years that I've been in this business I've never seen as much change happening as fast as it's been in the last 2 or 3 years. The upshot is that finance is becoming more of a strategic advisor and partner to the business. There has been a lot of talk about this in the past but not a lot of action. And I don't even think there is a clear definition of what partnership means. Traditionally, some CFOs have gotten involved in developing and executing on business strategy. But the function overall has been quite isolated, dealing only with the financials, doing routine reporting, and manually logging G/L entries, and performing cash applications, reconciliations, etc... . In fact, even if they wanted to, accounting & finance professionals were so bogged down in grunt work they really didn't have time to be strategic. But digital transformation is really changing the equation on that.

On where digital transformation can positively impact finance

In our 2019 key issues study there's nearly universal agreement that digital transformation will have a step-change impact on finance performance and will fundamentally affect the way finance delivers services to internal customers. We have a proprietary model that leverages our extensive benchmark database to calculate the performance enhancement opportunity for various business services functions, which takes us one step closer to analysing what automation does to performance using both efficiency and effectiveness metrics. The model uses a factor to estimate the size of the improvement opportunity if finance went closer to full-scale digital transformation for both peer and world-class finance organizations. The numbers are just in for 2019 and we found peer groups have the potential to shave 74% off their finance costs. World-class organizations, which we know already operate at a great degree of efficiency and effectiveness, can reduce their costs by 60%. Our data shows that while digitalisation is on the rise, technology investment is steadily declining, as old and expensive systems are replaced with faster-to-implement and cheaper to maintain tools. What is finance doing with the savings? It is redeploying them to activities such as business analysis, in line with its expanding role as a partner and advisor to the business.

On encouraging words to those scared of digital finance transformation

The implications for finance talent can be scary or can be exciting depending on who you are. A lot of people will be threatened by the changes and some will embrace them. Ultimately there's no choice because this change is happening. But finance organisations are far from being prepared. We had a finance talent survey last year and found that only half of finance organisations have come up with a talent strategy for the digital age. And less than half know what the new roles would look like or have the right talent in place. Some jobs will be eliminated, but eventually new roles will be created as well. They will require different skills. I'm doing a series of case studies that have developed very intricate and comprehensive talent development strategies. The common thread is that they really focus on empowering their employees to chart their own career path. They are offering the training, they are offering the support, the mentoring, the rotational programs, but they're telling their people, *"you are in charge of your career."* I think it's critical now more than ever that people realise that things are not just going to happen to them. They must take charge of their professional development if they want to be successful. even if it's intimidating. Look around and see what's available to develop your skills for what is going to be needed in the future.

On where the biggest skills gaps and opportunities are

The biggest gap we see between the maturity of the skills today and those required in finance going forward is in data & technology savviness. So, that is one area where you should go. But not that far behind is business partnering. It's important that finance professionals focus on both in their career development. By business partnering we mean the ability to work with business leaders, and the business units, to help them make decisions. Understanding the business and how it works is critical if you want to give advice about improving performance within that business context. I'm more excited about where we are today than I've ever been before, and I know a lot of finance executives feel the same way. I guess the ones who talk to me are not the ones who are intimidated by change but are the ones who want to leverage the change and make their jobs more meaningful because that's how they have an impact on business decisions and contribute to strategy development through the utilisation of digital tools.

On the best bit of advice Nilly has ever received

The best advice I have ever received and the hardest thing I've had to follow for me personally, is to maintain some kind of a life-work balance. I've been so passionate about my work and I'm sure a lot of finance and accounting professionals are in a similar position. But it's been hard to have a life that is separate from my work and for all of us with the advent of digital technologies work is just pervasive. It's with us all the time. I also work remotely, so work is around me in my home. I've been trying to keep some kind of balance, but I have to say in 30 years, I still haven't been able to do this very well. My managers are still on me for it. It's the one negative thing I get in performance evaluations *work less* which is kind of a strange thing to hear.

Recommended Resources

Book: *Thinking, Fast and Slow (2012)*, by Daniel Kahneman (link)

Book: *The Second Machine Age – Work, Progress, and Prosperity in a Time of Brilliant Technologies (2016)*, by Erik Brynjolfsson, Andrew Mcafee (link)

Website: The Hackett Group (link)

Website: Best Practices Conference (link)

"For example in the case of anything legal coming up you're going to get your lawyer right? So for anything financial, anything to do with your business, you should have them think, let's just run it past my accountant first."

Patrick Leavy
LI patrick-leavy
WS:farnellclarke.co.uk

Tags:
#engagement #translation #impact #educational finance #practice

PATRICK LEAVY is a manager at Farnell Clarke, a Norwich and London based digital accountancy firm that automates clients' bookkeeping as much as possible, allowing more time on advisory work to create more value for their clients. Patrick previously worked as a Schools Finance Advisor, Management Accountant and Bursar within industry and the public sector. Before moving into practice Patrick had a career performing and writing music, having been credited on 15 TV documentaries. Patrick holds AAT & ACCA designations, has a BSc in psychology and lives in Norfolk, England with his family.

On the common threads between finance and visual direction

There are actually some common threads. You're a specialist and you're working with people who immediately say *"I don't know anything about that"* but they need what you do. You are next a translator. You ask them what they need and then they come out with a load stuff in a completely different language. So in music they go, *"Hey look, I don't know what music I want but I want something which kind of feels like this and it's a bit like this other film."* They give you this whole thing which is non-musical talk and you have to translate it into music. Then you create the music and give it back to them saying, *"I think this is what you meant from what you said around what you needed."* So you end up interpreting their asks, a bit like a business owner or business partner has asks, based on what they say they need and you deliver that specific thing thereafter. So it's kind of similar in finance in that people have given me exactly the same language like, *"I don't know the first thing about Finance."* It's uncannily similar to, *"I don't know anything about music"* and they get really defensive. So your first job is to kind of say, *"Listen! Don't worry about all that, we're here to work it through together."* In effect, it's translating those two languages of business & finance or visual direction & music to bring them together.

On getting business partners to take immediate action

From the educational sector a good example is how I changed my approach to getting business partners to take action around their timing differences. I used to say, *"look at this, your numbers have changed, that means you need to start planning ahead, have you thought about the staff levels, etc...,"* that's how I used to do it at the beginning. And nothing was really taken on board. In schools' finance what you're funded on in this year is based on your pupil numbers the previous year. So it's lagging, which means you're always a bit of a step behind in terms of the data. And even when you say, lagged student numbers are going to have an effect, there is still absolutely no action taken, nobody does anything. In effect, you have to really spell it out. So, literally the minute you see them drop you have to be saying, *"Maybe we need to think about a restructure,"* which is a more painful outcome. They're very close with people they work with, teachers are like their soldiers out there in the field. They don't want to get rid of them, and I don't want you to be the bearer of bad news, so what can we do instead?

On the 3 main challenges facing Patrick's clients

The main one which is common to all small businesses is short-term cashflow. With the few exceptions of people who are really doing well it's more about what do I do with all this money, the investment side. On the most part we deal with businesses with a turnover between one hundred thousand (British pounds) and two million (British pounds). So they are kind of small, which means cash flow, and keeping on top of it is the main one. However there are three main problems that our clients face: the money issue, just worrying about whether they have the **money** to do it and pay themselves and their staff; it's time, so it's trying to win back some of the **time** for them and we do that through various efficiencies and trying to make things run more smoothly; and then just **peace of mind**, in general, trying help clients on any one of those or all three, cash, time and/or peace of mind.

On how to reduce the number of business failures.

I think the first challenge is to make sure that you or your firm becomes the first person they think of whenever they make any kind of move or if they're worried about anything in their business, that's the key thing. For example, in the case of anything legal coming up you're going to get your lawyer, right? So for anything financial, anything to do with your business, you should have them think, let's just run it past my accountant first. As opposed to only thinking about you when they want to think about their taxes or getting some compliance work done. I think that's the key, to change the perception they might have.

On how to get clients to engage more with their finance professionals

Stage one is being curious. If you go in with a mentality of us versus them, that is, *"They won't give me the details, I can't get the return done, Ahhh! What are these guys like?"* To instead thinking, never mind all that, *"First of all, why are they not doing all of that?"* If you really want them to engage, then it's about taking more of an interest in thinking about, *"What do they do?"* When you're speaking to the client, always in the back your mind be thinking to yourself, *"How can I help?"* Because there's a big skillset already there just not being utilised. So I think that's it, taking an interest.

Recommended Resources

Book: *How to win friends and influence people*, by Dale Carnegie (link)

Book: *The Art of Possibility: Transforming Professional and Personal Life (2002)*, by Rosamund Stone Zander and Benjamin Zander (link)

Book: *Thinking, Fast and Slow (2012)*, by Daniel Kahneman (link)

Book: *The Digital Firm: How to change your accounting firm to remain competitive (2018)*, by Will Farnell (link)

Podcast: Strength in the Numbers Show (link)

Podcast: The Cloud Accounting podcast (link)

Podcast: Cloud Stories (link)

Podcast: Generation CFO (link)

Podcast: Startup Stories (link)

"Stepping out of my comfort zone, doing lots of different roles, lots of different industries and with that I found that I really like the commercial stuff, I really like being in the trenches with the business."

Paul Murphy
LI: paulkevinmurphy
WS: 1000yearsofcareeradvice.com

Tags:
#commercial finance #career #comfort zone #LinkedIn

PAUL MURPHY has over ten years' experience working in commercial finance and business partnering roles across various industries at well-known brand names. He is also author of the #1 Amazon Bestseller "1000 Years of Career Advice," which interviews 100 graduates 10yrs out of university about their career paths and advice for a younger generation.

Paul holds an ACA designation and is based out of London, England

On how he broke out from the Big 4 into 'sexier' commercial finance roles
I left Big 4 as I wasn't a huge fan of audit, but it was great training in retrospect. I went into a media company in a financial control role and wasn't a huge fan that either. I wanted to go more commercial and to do this I'd always be on the lookout for new roles. All year round, not only internally but also externally in other industries. I'd always be on the lookout because getting the 'sexier' commercial roles would be tough. I always stepped outside my comfort zone and found that for me the best roles weren't necessarily a promotion within the company I was in already. If you go to a different company, you learn so much more. The status quo won't be the same, the politics might not be the same, etc, etc... . So I've learned a huge amount and my CV (résumé) is way better for jumping around a little bit. I think that's the thing you can do in your 20s, maybe not so much in your 30s. In your 20s the theme is to try

different things, roles that will push you more. Vary your skills by trying different things to figure out which bits you like and the stuff you most enjoy. Then everything else will just fall into place.

On some ins and out of commercial finance

I left financial control and went to a financial planning & analysis role that was very commercial. It was me business partnering with, 50-year-old directors and looking at commercial contracts, looking at how we drive down cost per train and utilisation rates in a warehouse. Then I went and did some big projects. So I did a billion (British) pound roll out of an ERP system where I was basically looking at cost saving initiatives. How could we outsource pieces of work? How could we pay our contractors less? How could we make pieces of the deployment overlap, to save some of that billion pounds for a rainy day? Then my current role is that big integration which again is about unlocking huge benefits and synergies by putting our heads together with the senior operations guys and saying, *"Okay is this the best use of this money for the company? If this was your money would we be doing this?"*

On critical advice to get into the more fun finance roles

It was kind of stepping out of my comfort zone, doing lots of different roles, lots of different industries and with that I found that I really like the commercial stuff, I really like being in the trenches with the business. So do some of that trial and error. Figure out what you like, you might like financial control. Once you figure out what you like then I'd advise try to find a person five or ten years older than you, within the role that you might like. So that could be a CFO, COO or just the next team or level. Then say, *"Okay, this guy has such and such experience, has such and such skills, do I have those? How do I pick those up? What do I need to get there so I can be at the interview table looking for a job like theirs?"* We didn't really have LinkedIn ten, fifteen or twenty years ago. Now you can type in and find out Head of Finance, Commercial Finance, CFO and a lot of guys have their CVs on there. And I'd encourage anyone of any age, go and find those people, have coffees with them. That's how to get into the more fun roles.

On why you shouldn't be intimidated by more senior professionals

I'm firmly in the business now, so I sit in the room with 20 very senior guys. They would come ask me business questions, all day, every day. The experience you get out of that instead of being in a stuffy finance department, it's just great and whetted my appetite for more commercial stuff. Don't be intimidated by people who are more senior than you. Very often they don't know the solution, they are just better at bluffing.

On the best bit of advice Paul would offer

If you can reach out to people who are five or ten years ahead of you, I wouldn't encourage people reaching out to those who are twenty or twenty-five years ahead. If you are a twenty-five-year-old and you reach out to a guy in his fifties who's CEO, he might not give you the best advice because the world's moved on since he was twenty-five. However, if you can get that guy or lady at the next step of the ladder and say, *"Okay, how would you advise me to go about my next three to five years?"* I think that's really the best advice I can offer anyone.

Recommended Resources

Book: *1000 Years of Career Advice: interviews with 100 graduates 10 years on from university, their career paths and lessons learned (2018),* by Paul Murphy (link)

Website: 1,000 Years of Career Advice (link)

"I think some people think you have to say yes to everything, but you don't. If you say yes too much then you're going to be exhausted so you have to have a strategy."

Paula Downey Jones
LI: paula-downey-jones

Tags:
#cash controls #aid agencies #trouble spots #career management #personal strategy #management accounting #mentoring

PAULA DOWNEY JONES is an award-winning CFO with over 20 years' international experience in providing value adding financial and commercial insight, leadership, and financial control for a variety of prestigious blue-chip organisations including Centrica, Honda and Coca-Cola. Paula qualified with The Chartered Institute of Management Accountants in 1997, is the winner of the 2005 Financial Business Leader of the Year (CIMA) and became a CIMA Fellow in Jan 2009. She became an accredited business coach with the Institute of Leadership and Management (ILM) in 2013.

On leaving behind the safety of management accounting for conflict areas

I've always been a big traveller and I was at a certain stage of my life. I wanted a change and the opportunity arose to be a finance manager in an aid agency. In Sudan I was working on a cross conflict program, then Sri Lanka, just after the 2004 tsunami, I worked in two locations: one part of the country was relatively safe, the other part I worked in, the east of the country, was still in the conflict zone with the Tamil Tigers.

My management accounting world up until that point had been in big companies and had never really seen the physical cash side of things and how it worked. It was a quite remote thing to me. When I got out to these places I was on my own with a laptop. Often there was no real finance or banking infrastructure, so cash suddenly became king and it was a completely different experience. The first couple of days when I was out there I was thinking about: How do I do this? How do I work the petty cash? I've never dealt with this stuff but actually I had to deal with it and it really opened me up to the operational side of things. It has given me a huge amount more breadth to roles and experiences since, than what I would have ever got out of staying in the world of management accounting within the finance teams at big companies. And I think the point on this is a lot of people just want to be in management accounting in big companies because that's the sexy end of finance, but actually it's quite a narrow area.

On carrying 60,000 US dollars in a backpack across borders and war zones to pay people's salaries and developing appropriate financial controls

I think one of my first roles when I was in Sudan was that I had to do the payment run. Now that part of South Sudan had been at war for many years so there really wasn't much of a finance or banking infrastructure there. So in order to pay people's salaries and things like that we hired a plane from Nairobi (Kenya). I went to the bank there and took out 60,000 US dollars in cash which I put in my backpack. I then travelled across Nairobi to get to the plane to take it to Sudan. Now one of the interesting things is obviously you can't do that every week. We had to pay people for the next 3 months but in a way that they received the money once they had earned it. Those types of financial controls were very interesting because you really have to think differently about them, because it is very remote and a cash only environment. When you're not there and it's pretty much all cash driven you actually get thinking more creatively when you face a lot of challenges which has helped me a lot.

On the confidence that comes from making your career work for you and the benefits of the winding road

The first point I want to make is that I've tried to make my career work for me rather than the other way around. I've never really been a slave to my CV. There's actually a lot of times I've just gone, *"I'm going to do it anyway,"* and then it turns out that it's worked out really well for me. I feel that everything always leads to something. So how do you prepare for something like this winding road? Well I don't know if you can but I think you need to open up your mind, be flexible and adaptable as well as thinking quickly on your feet.

Wherever you are with your career there are always things thrown at you that you may not have had the experience yet to take on or been able to look it up in a textbook to show you, *"Oh that's how I do it!"* It's really about having that core belief that you can do it right and get out there to make it happen.

On areas where Finance professionals can improve our value proposition

In no particular order what I would say is look at all your experiences as adding something to your development even any bad ones. I've had probably a more varied career than most but all of it has added to where I've got to now. I wouldn't have left University planning out to do it this way, it just happened but it has added to the value I offer.

I've found role models and mentors are great. If you're in a corporate environment, then relationships and politics are really key even though you might not want to have to deal with them, they are there. So I would choose a role model who is accessible and where you have visibility into how they interact with others.

A mentor can be a good experienced sounding board as to how you interact with peers. Additionally, the people who work for you are as important as your interactions with those who are more senior.

Emotional intelligence I believe has equal value to academic intelligence and the higher up the organisation you go the less it is about your technical skills and the more it is about how you handle people. There is no substitute for hard work, no matter how bright you are. At the end of the day you can't pull it off without actually working hard.

This next thing isn't for everybody but for me it works quite well, is to build yourself a personal strategy. So imagine or visualise what your ideal role is? What the location is? What the hours are? What sort of industry it looks like? And then once you have that in place it's easier to know which opportunities to say *yes* to and those to say *no* to. I think some people think you have to say yes to everything, but you don't. If you say yes too much then you're going to be exhausted so you have to have a strategy. You need to know what you need to say yes to and what you don't need to say yes to. I think that's quite important.

Also mistakes will happen, it's human nature. What's important is you don't beat yourself up about it. Now I'm the worst person at this, but this wasted energy can prevent you seeing how improvements or changes to a process could put you or your company in a much more superior position than before the problems arose. So win on that one. It's about not wasting a crisis but instead try to make most of it.

Finally, be aware of the impact of other people's perception of you as some people might perceive you in a way that is not what you intended and it counts. Maintain integrity, always try to do the right thing and asking for help is not a sign of weakness at all, it can actually be very valuable so I would definitely put that back on the list as well.

On the best bit of advice Paula has ever received

The winding path has made me feel more confident now. Knowing that doing this different stuff is okay and that I don't need to stay on that straight line. For me it has actually added to my CV (résumé) even though that was not the intention that I had at all.

Recommended Resources

Movie: This Is Spinal Tap (movie)

"Of course you bring your own culture, your own values, but you have to go towards the other people and understand how to bridge these, how to make it unique and how to make it happen."

Jean-Philippe Gauvrit
LI: jpgauvrit

Tags:
#business partnering #culture #change management #coaching #CFO

JEAN-PHILIPPE GAUVRIT has held several senior finance and leadership roles during a rich international career. Until April 2019 he was Nokia's head of Region Finance for the Asia-Pacific and Japan region. He has spent the last 20 years in Shanghai, Singapore, India, Paris and recently London. Leading change, creating teams and developing talents that have shaped his career and personal life. Jean-Philippe is passionate about role design and creation, professional identity and about the impacts of digital disruption on people and teams.

Jean-Philippe is a certified coach, a grandfather, speaker and writer as well as an avid photographer.

On the importance of unlearning and reinventing yourself
I felt a lot of excitement in having to reinvent myself every day when I got to meet people from different cultures, from different ways of working. I had to reinvent myself. You have to go and meet people. You have to learn and unlearn some of the things you learnt when you were for instance in France or in Europe, and find your own way with the people there. It cannot be done on your own. During the 20 years I stayed in the Asia Pacific region practically every day was a different day. Because every day I had the opportunity to connect with different people from different countries and I had to build teams from scratch by bringing people together. You have to go through this journey where of course you bring your own culture, your own values, but you have to go

towards the other people and understand how to bridge these, how to make it unique and how to make it happen. This capacity to unlearn a little bit of what you've learned and reinvent yourself to get a better connection with people was extremely important for me.

On the value of partnering with people with different logic & cultural ways

What was really exciting for me, whether I recall my time working in China, India or even other countries, is the opportunity for partnering. And I insist on this word, partnering, with people with different ways of thinking, with different conceptions of what time is about, with different ways ideas about working individually versus in a group, with different reactions when facing challenges and so on. If you approach this only with your existing tools and techniques, and what's already in your mind, then you might have some success. However, I'm not sure that this is actually the most effective way. In France, we are very cartesian, which means, having the reason behind something and thinking it through is extremely important. If you press the button then something should happen. Life is different now, and especially when you go to other countries. When you press the button something else might happen. It's easy to forget this, so you need to be able to say, *"Look maybe it's different and maybe someone else knows where to press and how to do it better."* Also, letting it flow is extremely important. You have to let things go, and say, *"Okay, that's maybe not the way I would have done it, but yes, let's listen to these guys who seem to know. Let's trust them, let's build this."* It's fascinating, it's difficult, let's be honest about it. I can remember the first years I spent in China for instance or the first time I was exposed to India but I learned a lot from these relationships.

On recollecting his first Chinese Board meeting

I remember the first time I was in a big Board meeting in China. So you can imagine a big room with a long, long, table, so much so, that you don't know exactly how many people were around it. Everything was extremely codified, you have the boss, and the guy just sitting next to the boss and so on. It's not like in Europe where you just come in and sit down. No! You have to be at your place. The flow in the way the meeting is done is different and you can only speak up at certain moments and so on. So I remember the first time I was in this kind of meeting, There was a topic that wasn't working for me, so I just did it in the western way, I just interrupted the conversation. All the other people around the table just stared at me, as if who's this guy? And it worked. The big boss, because he did not want to embarrass me engaged with me. However, someone came over to me after the meeting and said, that's not the way to do it. So then I said I need to better understand this.

On a lively interaction in India

In India I think it's the other way around. I remember meetings when there were very lively interactions, where everything is compromised, where you think you reach a point, but no, it's only the beginning for a new point to open and so on. I remember some meetings where actually we spent literally hours to come to what we thought was an agreement. We shook hands, it was late in the afternoon and everything was okay. However later that evening the customer came calling back and we had to do a new round for another two to three hours. Those are the kind of things you just have to let go and say, *"Well okay, that's the way we do business here, it's the way people work together."* So, let's not always come with our rigid views.

On connecting with local people to be more culturally aware

What is very important is to connect with one or two local people from the team and to get feedback, *"Is it okay? Do you have any recommendations? Can you help me to navigate through this?"* Getting this understanding of how it is meant to work is extremely important. You cannot invent it yourself; it can become extremely complex. Also, something important to bear in mind, especially when we talk about multi-cultural teams, is that it's not about building a French or European team in China. It's not about building a Chinese team with some international input. It's about building a different team, something which is one and unique by itself. You need to define how we are going to build together something which is not purely on your side, not purely on my side, but it's something a bit weird and unique.

On the distinction between change management and transformation today

As finance professionals we have seen a lot of changes and much more complexity in change management over the past ten years than when we used to do transformation in finance 15 years ago. I'm not saying it was easy, it was still about bringing out new tools, new processes and so on. Now it's totally different. It's much more complex, much more open to other functions, and much more open to different things. I realised a couple of years ago that doing transformation today in a very classical manner, actually meaning to simplify it in a top-down manner, actually didn't work in my own environment. Maybe it's working for other people, but when you're the CFO for 20 countries with different cultures and loads of complexity it is very difficult. So this question of approaching change management differently, bringing in a little bit more of the coaching skills, means that the approach you take will emerge gradually. Because if we want to be successful it has to come from the people. Who am I to tell you it's the right way to do it say in the UK, or the USA? Your team knows. So coaching is about bringing the ideas from people, bringing what you know and using this in order to change and transform.

On the best bit of advice Jean-Philippe has ever received

I was still very junior in my first or second job, it was very challenging, and one of the senior guys came to me and we had a debrief. He told me, *"You know, don't feel isolated, don't stay isolated, you don't know what you don't know, so you need to learn with others. You need to find someone who knows better than you know. And raise your hand. When there is something wrong, don't stay in your box, just open up and say Hey! I don't know."* I remember this conversation at that time, I was 25 or 26 maybe, and you say, *"Well, maybe he's right?"* But as you get older, you get it. Yes, you raise your hand and say, *"I don't know, help me."* Actually, it looks stupid but it's extremely important. And that's maybe why, by the way, 30 years later I'm on this coaching and mentoring journey.

"You can always look at something you've never done and be a little bit concerned or almost scared around taking on something new. Throw yourself into those things because those skills that you could develop in areas that might be more niche in finance now will be critical in the future."

Rakesh Sangani
LI: rakeshsangani
WS: proservartner.co.uk

Tags:
#consulting #practitioner #experimentation #vision #strategy #change management #transformation #digitalisation

RAKESH SANGANI is the CEO founder of Proservartner a global practitioner-led consulting firm whose commitment is to boutique style work, smaller teams and personalised attention to deliver operational transformation, cutting-edge technology, and problem-solving for clients. Rakesh is a regular contributor on LinkedIn and makes many appearances at conferences in Europe, Asia, and North America. He is also a chartered accountant, certified project manager, and holds a Black Belt in Lean Six Sigma.

Rakesh lives with his family in London, England.

On finance professionals being told to 'act more like a consultant'
If you've got to carry out some process mapping to better understand and improve your finance process, one approach is to bring in maybe one of the Big 4. You've got maybe graduates supporting this type of activity, they don't really understand the responses from subject matter experts, and they don't really understand the process. So you end up actually in the improvement stage maybe not getting a) all of the insight from the people that are talking to you; b) all of the improvements that you could achieve; and c) there's a credibility factor when it can be

frustrating for the subject matter experts (SMEs) when they are having to speak to a consultant that doesn't really understand what they do. Therefore, I think there's certainly value in having someone with that finance background, that knowledge of how it works and the experience of the role that finance plays within an organisation, to support organisations in a different way. Again if we take that process mapping example it's really being able to build the right relationship with the SMEs so they open up. Instead of them telling you what they should be doing they tell you what they are actually doing, as well as bring to light real world experiences and identify improvements that are perhaps very pragmatic.

It is interesting that finance people are being told to be more like consultants. Generally, consultants have a bad reputation, you've probably heard the story around the consultant will look at your watch and tell you what time it is. Although there are different types of consultants, there are ones that maybe just listen too much and play back what they're listening to, document that and show that to senior management. There's the other type who just have a boilerplate and drive you to that final answer and don't listen at all. In reality you need that balance of the two. I think that's relevant for finance practitioners because when organisations say, *"be more like a consultant."* It's really around bringing in best practice but also about contextualising it and listening and adapting it so that it works for that environment. I don't think you can achieve that with people straight out of university.

On advice for younger professionals who want to get that practitioner type experience fast

Certainly, I think experience counts for a lot and take the opportunities to learn about new things. Finance is undertaking so much change at the moment with the onset of robotics and automation. Finance within many companies have already adopted lean and six sigma techniques. With new skills being desired there are lots of opportunities for the younger professionals today. I would say don't be afraid to get involved in new things. You can always look at something you've never done and be a little bit concerned or almost scared around taking on something new. Throw yourself into those things because those skills that you could develop in areas that might be more niche in finance now will be critical in the future.

On why it's easy to be cynical of finance digitalisation and how to successfully bring it on board

I have to say this whole onset of digitalisation I have found fascinating. I've gone through a bit of a journey myself. I was very cynical at the start as there was lots of talk around how we can automate the whole finance function through robots. There was talk that 35% of jobs in the UK will be lost to robots in the next 4 years and there's a lot of hype around the topic. That really made me quite resistant around it. But over the last 3 years, after I really got more and more experience of it, you recognise that if you leverage it in the right places, in the right ways, then some of the robotics & machine learning tools, some of the artificial intelligence options out there, are really impressive and can provide tangible value within the finance function.

The problem we have today around digitalisation is that there's just so much technology out there today, we have ERPs, and obviously some organisations want to just optimise these. We have process enabling technologies and off-the-shelf tools that you could leverage. We have macros that you could create at the other end of the spectrum, you've got robotics, you've got business process management technology, you've got machine learning, you have artificial intelligence and all of these different types of technology. I think as a finance user it is really difficult to understand where you should start.

There's also a change of how you bring on new technologies. Growing up in finance functions, organisations would typically go through an assessment phase and a design phase which could last upwards of six to nine months. That needs to change. Additionally, leading organisations today are doing more proof of concepts, where they'll go through eight to twelve weeks of quick and dirty, does this technology work for our organisation and if it does then scale it up.

On the concept of low cost, quick and dirty, experimentation and the importance of overcoming our fear in finance of getting things wrong

It's not standard practice yet, however we should definitely be embracing those types of concepts more and more. It's the whole concept of experimentation. If you look at the Facebooks and the Amazons of the world they're running 50,000 experiments a day. They're trying out lots of different things because they see it as critical to their growth and I think in finance sometimes we don't like to experiment because of the fear of getting things wrong.

You have to have that mindset to begin with of, *"Okay, we're going to do this low-cost quick and dirty proof of concept. It may succeed, it may fail. But at least we know whether this technology fits our organisation and helps solve a particular business problem."* We see different types of organisations at the moment, some are embracing that. I think they'll do very well. But there are some that are still very scared of failure and scared of doing a proof of concept for any new technology. They would rather go through that six to nine months assessment phase.

On the importance of Finance knowing it's why?

When we carry out this type of vision and strategy work, we are in essence asking six questions for the finance function. We are asking why does finance exist today? What is the purpose of finance? That's a really important question because if you don't answer that question then the rest of the business is expecting the finance function to do a lot of things. They're expecting the finance function to be innovative, to have high internal customer satisfaction, to reduce cost via continuous improvement, to have the best process, to have a great control environment, to standardise processes and ways of working, to have engaged people that want to work at the company and are really excited about those opportunities, etc, etc, etc … . The demands on Finance become a little bit unrealistic because suddenly you have to deliver on all of these things. So I think more and more finance functions are realising, okay it's impossible to try and do everything and what we need to do is prioritise. What we need to do is stand for something and that's really *the why*, which is, are we the finance function that is going to be a business partner and provide strategic business value to the rest of the organisation? Or are we the finance function that's just going to be performed at the lowest cost? It's really understanding where finance plays in that spectrum so that *why* is important.

On setting really clear objectives to drive customer satisfaction

We must set really clear objectives and measures of what it is that success looks like in finance and then also understand our customers. So if we talk about business partnering, who are the customers? Who do we influence around this organisation to make sure that finance is seen as a valuable service? So that *who* is really important and so too is understanding what their perception is of finance today? How many finance teams have embarked on a customer satisfaction survey to get the opinions of their stakeholders within the organisation on how finance is performing? However that's a very important thing to do, to really get a view of whether our measure of good is consistent with what our internal customers think of us.

On why "better never stops"

With finance undertaking so much change it's really important to not be afraid of some of the ambiguity that you may find. Because to be successful in finance in the future you really need to have a mentality around **better never stops** and look to improve the ways of working, not just across the finance function, but also in the rest of the business too.

On the best bit of advice Rakesh has ever received

It was based on an African proverb, which was *"If you want to go fast go it alone, but if you want to go far make sure you do it together."* That really resonated with me because early on in my career when I wanted to achieve something at pace I would not always involve all of the people around me. I felt they were maybe not able to operate at the same pace, so that would frustrate me and I wanted to get things moving and move things forward. That advice really helped me because I recognised actually, by taking that approach, I can only go so far. By taking the team, and in a broader sense organisations with you when you are taking this journey, I think that becomes a lot more powerful. I've taken that into my work as well, so when we talk to finance leaders it's also around involving the business to make sure that they take the whole organisation into account on a finance change program rather than just finance going it alone.

Recommended Resources

Book: *Good To Great (2001),* by Jim Collins (link)

Book: *Traction: Get a Grip on Your Business (2012),* by Gino Wickman (link)

Website: Proservartner (link)

"We cannot fight every battle. You can't be defensive in every scenario, because you're never going to come across someone who is going to agree with everything you say all of the time."

Ranu Sharma
LI: ranusharma

Tags:
#prioritisation #stakeholder management #relationships #volunteering #business partnering

RANU SHARMA is a high calibre finance professional with over 10 years' experience and a proven track record of delivering financial initiatives and building key relationships with business stakeholders. From carrying out successful external supplier negotiations, leading numerous high profile projects to supporting multi-million pound business divisions on a global scale, Ranu has gained a huge amount of experience in Commercial Finance. She is a Senior Finance Business Partner, heading up the International Operations & Technology cost division at the recently acquired Mastercard Subsidiary, Vocalink. She is also a public speaker and actively motivates young youths via charities such as Working Options in Education, Inspiring the Future and most recently, a mentor for The Girls' Network.

Ranu holds a CGMA designation, has a degree in Management Accounting from Brunel and is based out of London, England.

On the importance of developing relationships

I cannot emphasise the value and importance of human connection enough, it's so important. James Comer once said that *"no significant learning can occur without significant relationships."* I have watched colleagues over the years do the bare minimum when it comes to communicating with their stakeholders. Just simply sending emails and claiming that their job is done, is in my opinion not being a true business partner. No business stakeholder will be interested in even opening up an email from a person they don't know or have a good relationship with. Therefore in order to be an effective business partner, good healthy relationships are key.

On why some find it easier to dive into business partnering

It depends on the individual. If the individual is already a 'people-person', has that natural ability to build relationships and makes that their focal point, I think they're going to find it easier to dive straight in. If you have an individual that perhaps isn't so sure and needs to learn more about themselves before they learn about others, then I'm not saying they can't become a great business partner, of course they can, but they might just have to take a few pre-steps, if you will, to gain an understanding of the kind of people they're working with and adapting to the different characters. Some stakeholders can be easy, whereas some can be tougher than others.

On an approach to dealing with difficult stakeholders

My theory is 'killing it with kindness.' I genuinely believe in that because I can't tell you how many people I have come across that have made me sit there and think, *"Why am I dealing with you?"* You can get some people that will forever complain and sometimes even accuse you of not getting something done on time. You must look at the bigger picture, look at what we're trying to achieve, what we're trying to work towards and ask yourself how can we come to a compromise? We cannot fight every battle. You can't be defensive in every scenario, because you're never going to come across someone who is going to agree with everything you say all of the time.

Essentially you need to take a step back and think, *"Right, I've a difficult stakeholder here, they're not happy with this situation, so how do we challenge that?"* Rather than try to defend your position to the other person by saying, *"Oh, but you said you wanted this, that and the other."* It might be better to say, *"Okay, let me try and understand you, rather than trying to be understood. What is it that you think they need? What is it that we can do to try and fill that gap?"* Stakeholders in the business partnering world are your customers and need to be treated that way. It doesn't mean you have to lie down and take everything that comes every which way from them. It simply means that you have to be a bit calmer, more rational and don't put up a defence. Instead, try to understand why they are saying the things they are saying, where they're coming from. Attempt to find a way to collaboratively work with them, gain that trust and give them what it is that they need. Aim for what is going to be a value-add and then it becomes a 'win-win' situation because you're happy your job is done well and they're happy that they're getting the results that they need.

On an approach to prioritisation

One thing I have learnt is that if something can't be done, ask yourself *"what is the impact of that not being done?"* If you could attach a monetary value to an impact, so for example, if a stakeholder said, *"I need a report for my management committee meeting on Friday and the report needs to show the actuals that we have achieved to date, what the rest of the forecast is going to be and I need it by Wednesday,"* Then on the same day you have got another stakeholder who says, *"I've got a deal negotiation with a supplier, it's a multi-million pound deal and we need the analysis done for it otherwise we lose the deal."* Imagine both of those stakeholders are screaming at you, sending emails with exclamation marks which are sitting in your inbox. What do you do?

Here, it is all about taking a step back and prioritising; I've X number of people in my team and Y amount of stuff keeping my team working. So, I need to be able to delegate, and I need to be able to delegate effectively. To do this, I need to be able to understand what is up for grabs and what it is that we're going to lose if we don't do certain things in a certain order? We need to be able to quantify that opportunity or loss. In the example above, it's pretty clear if I don't deliver the report that shows actual performance, the monetary impact is pretty much nil as it is reporting on the past. You then have the other side, with someone who has to negotiate a business deal with a supplier that is worth millions of pounds. If we don't do the analysis in a timely manner with the correct degree of accuracy, we could lose money, so it's pretty obvious which one we work on.

On how volunteering has helped Ranu in her professional career

There is no more valuable currency than the feeling of being able to give back and change a life. If I know that even out of 100 students, I've helped positively change one life, that's another life changed. I've been working with young children and I've learned to help them to communicate better, how to come across in a way where people take them seriously, and help them become a better version of who they already are.

On the best bit of advice Ranu has ever received

Always remain humble as no one is better than anyone. Everybody has to understand that we are all deserving of mutual respect. Let's be happy for each other. If one is more successful than another let's celebrate that success. Let's learn from each other and work together to be better. Let's be Better Together, as burning out another person's candle doesn't make yours any brighter.

Recommended Resources

Book: *The Secret,* by Rhonda Byrne (link)

Documentary: *Blue Planet series* (link)

Website: The Girls Network (link)

Website: Working Options (link)

"I see there is no option that you either as a CFO try to do everything and get stuck in the middle again or you start splitting it up."

Richard E. Reinderhoff
LI: reinderhoff

Tags:
#Strategy #CVO #Business Planning #Forecasting

RICHARD E. REINDERHOFF is an experienced Board Advisor helping the management of corporations with their strategic planning & execution, in effect bridging the gap between Finance & Strategy. Richard is a regular contributor to 10+ Finance publications leveraging his many career experiences gained at corporations from 3 continents, ranging from Finance & Operations departments in Brazil, to Consultancy in the Netherlands, leading carve-out, turnaround and MBO, setting up Risk Management Functions and redesigning FP&A processes, as well as leading finance teams through economic turmoil and business crises.

Richard holds an MScBA from RSM Erasmus and lives near Rotterdam, the Netherlands with his family.

On using 'projects' to budget with as opposed to a chart of accounts and how to capture quick wins

I structure the budget in a different way. I do not use a chart of accounts but I use projects [accounting]. All the spend is put into an area or strategic part. Each project has its own chart of accounts, say for an Internet marketing campaign to improve market penetration, but also goals. Sometimes there are quick wins, for example a government changes a regulation, which can happen very quickly. As such, you should always have some money left in a project to be allocated to other areas or to capture those opportunities that unexpectedly come up.

On how to close the gap between Strategy & Finance
Avoid telling management what to do. My background is in strategic management so I know a lot of frameworks that other finance professionals don't, but it's not necessary. It's what management talks about, it's what they understand, and you have to stimulate their understanding. Rather than just criticise A-B-C, instead of being the guy who always says no, be the one who always asks *why*?

On splitting Finance into operations (Chief Accounting Officer) and strategy (Chief Value Officer)
What we have today is that Finance is in a changing environment. I see there is no option that you either as a CFO try to do everything and get stuck in the middle again or you start splitting it up. I really see the opportunity in getting the finance operations and transactions part separated from let's say the business development part. Then you have the operations which is about control and compliance, but also data. Data have to be perfect and who could be better than the department with trained accountants or financial professionals for managing it. The CFO I think would like to be much more active in the business and needs to be much more involved on the strategic side so we talk about a Chief Value Officer. In this role they really add value to the Board and what has been happening, for example in the last 10 years, is that we now have for technology and data, a Chief Information Officer (CIO), for risk management there is a Chief Risk Officer (CRO) which is usually under the governance of the CFO.

Why not also have for accounting a Chief Accounting Officer in charge of accounting. Then the CFO's antennae can be liberated to work on business development. Think about the circular economy, think about being more available to explore new areas within your business, being better able to look forwards. And to do so you'll want to have perfect numbers to base decisions on, which is where the CAO can help.

On why business planning is a key skill.
Forecasting is a central theme, so you have to understand business planning. In turn you have to understand what is impacting the forecast. You have to think about scenario planning, whether the exchange rate is going up and down? Or Brexit, if there are trade barriers that get put up, what will happen to the supply chain? What will happen to your customer? What if interest rates go up? Which actually happened to our

clients, which impacted our level of supplier credits. There are a lot of things happening, so be aware of the external elements to get a sense of what's happening to the business. That's why we talk about business planning before doing any financial planning & analysis.

On the importance of following up and asking questions of management on their concerns

Predictions! You have to talk to management on their ideas and not your assumptions or your [favourite] subject. Ask them what is happening? What are you worried about? Let's say they are concerned about their supply chain systems. Perhaps there might be some opportunities for you to help.

The best bit of advice Richard has ever received

In business expect anything! Anything can happen in 5 minutes. Your whole world can change.

Recommended Resources

Documentary: The Corporation (2003) (link)

Book: *Case in Point 10: Complete Case Interview Preparation (2018)*, by Marc Cosentino (link)

"So often if we say the word mental health the imagery that people come up with in their minds will be those of mental ill-health, or mental illness, or anguish of black and white photos with people with their head in their hands, of people struggling and that's not health, that is ill-health."

Rob Stephenson
LI: robstephenson
WS: inside-out.org

Tags:
#mental ill-health #stress #wellbeing #stigma #anxiety #opportunity cost

ROB STEPHENSON is founder of InsideOut, a social enterprise with a mission of ending the stigma of mental ill-health in the workplace. Rob has a strong and personal interest in mental wellbeing and is also the Chief Catalyst at BetterSpace, a technology start-up with the mission of stimulating investment in preventative mental wellbeing solutions. Rob has lived and worked whilst managing bipolar disorder for as long as he can remember. Rob conducts speaking engagements on his personal experiences and ideas as to how we can facilitate change.

Rob is a chartered accountant, an accredited Firstbeat Lifestyle Assessment Provider, a certified coach and Level 2 Certified British Cycling Coach. Rob is based out of London, England.

On signs of potential mental ill-health in others
The signs can be quite individual, but actually in looking at ourselves we can see things like: changes in our sleep patterns, where we're finding it difficult to get to sleep; it's a full on waking up in the middle of the night and we're ruminating about things that are going on in work; or if we find it very hard to switch off to focus on our family, to be present in the activities that we're doing outside of the workplace.

There's a lot of signals that can show perhaps we're heading towards burnout. Physiological stress is your flight or fight response. It's the stress hormones that we are biologically trained to release if our lives are in danger. But the problem is now we're not running away from sabre-tooth tigers. Instead we're getting emails, deadlines, clients, audits, year ends, all these things that are causing stress. What we're not doing so well is allowing ourselves to recover from those periods of stress. If you use the example of the sabre-tooth tiger, if we run away and hide and the tiger goes away then what do we do? We rest, we digest, and we recover. In the workplace it's often we're going from one stressful situation to the other.

We have a unique opportunity in the workplace. We see people for eight plus hours a day regularly. We do notice changes of behaviour, we can notice if someone is looking and acting a bit more reserved, is not contributing in the way they might normally do, or might be contributing too much. For me in a manic period, with my bipolar disorder back, I might want to have the last word all the time and my ideas need to get out there. So we can see these changes in behaviour but because of stigma what we don't do generally is say, *"Actually are you okay mate? How are you doing? You're not looking yourself today. Can we go for a cup of coffee or tea to have a chat about it?"* Instead what we're doing in the workplace is we're saying, *"Yeah, Hi! How are you doing?"* and then someone says, *"Yeah! I'm good, I'm fine, I'm alright,"* it's a ritual it's a greeting and it's not asking that question and answering it honestly.

On 3 things to do to recover from stress at work

Stress can lead to things like anxiety or burnout if we're continually not allowing ourselves to get those moments to balance the stress. So some of the simple stuff like, are we taking a break from our desk? Are we taking our lunch outside in the park on a sunny day? Are we going for a walk in the middle of the afternoon just to break up the day? It's little things actually that can make a big difference if we do them consistently.

On the stigma of mental ill-health and the opportunity for organisations

I think we need to be clear on what we're describing, and I think we need to be clear on what mental health is. So often if we say the word mental health the imagery that people come up with in their minds will be those of mental ill-health, or mental illness, or anguish of black and white photos with people with their head in their hands, of people struggling and that's not health, that is ill-health. If we're talking about physical health immediately we think of vibrancy, we think of athleticism, we have healthy people. The brand of mental health has been a real problem and we've an obligation to try and change the brand of mental health because it links to a fundamental issue that people in our society have come to believe that it's binary. We're either mentally ill, or we're mentally well. Most of us are meant to be well so we don't need to worry about mental health and those poor unlucky people who are mentally ill, there's a stigma attached.

Now, actually the most important statistic I think that exists is one in one. 100% of us have mental health and if we accept that, we can then get into the thought process that we can influence mental health, like we do to influence our physical health. How we can both look after ourselves and how we approach mental health in the workplace. Because mental health is not just about looking after the people who are struggling with mental ill-health. The agenda is about wellbeing, it's about mental fitness, it's about the health of our minds. Actually what are we using in finance functions and companies to do our jobs? It's our minds, yet most of the focus on management is on our physical health, with health insurance, etc... . So if we can get over the fact that we all have mental health, we all have good and bad days, we all experience things like bereavement, relationship breakup, which will impact our mental wellbeing. The question then is can we create the type of cultures in our workplace that allows us to prioritise mental wellbeing and try and move up that curve towards the thriving category? Because I think that this is one of the biggest performance gains we can make as organisations and for the people within them.

On how mental health is affecting the company's bottom line

If you look at the costs of mental ill-health in our workplaces I think the latest estimate for the UK economy as a whole is, 105 billion (GBP) annually, which is a staggering number. However if you look at the costs estimated in the Stevenson-Farmer review of mental health in the workplace, *"Thriving at work."* It was estimated something like 46 billion (GBP) was attributable to employees. If you break that down further, the biggest element of that was presenteeism (17-18 billion GBP). So people are doing their jobs, they're turning up, but they're underperforming because of mental ill-health. That number far exceeded the numbers for absenteeism (8 billion GBP) and staff turnover (8 billion GBP). The cost for every employee in the workplace is put at 1,500 GBP per year.

On making sure to prioritise our wellbeing because it will pay in dividends

I'm sitting in my cycling attire because I'm about to go on a bike ride that I've scheduled in. So make sure in our days we prioritise something that we do for our wellbeing because it will pay back in dividends. For me it's a bike ride, but it could be just as simple as going for a walk at lunch time. Do some of that and we will be happier, more productive, and ultimately higher performing people.

On the best bit of advice Rob has ever received

It is okay to talk about your mental health and if you are struggling it is okay to talk about it. Because what I've noticed is that when I was struggling but keeping that to myself there is an added pressure that is put upon your shoulders of trying to be something you're not at a time when you are really struggling. This then becomes a vicious circle that makes how you're feeling worse and the guilt of phoning in and saying, *"I've got a bad back today and I'm not coming in."* When in fact I'm struggling with my mental health. It just actually makes what I'm going through harder to deal with. We're challenging the stigma and we're trying to create cultures where it is okay to talk about mental ill-health. So the best bit of advice I've received is that it is okay to talk about your mental health and your mental ill-health.

Recommended Resources

Book: *Depressive Illness: The Curse Of The Strong* by Dr. Tim Cantopher (link)

Paper: *Thriving at work. The Stevenson / Farmer review of mental health and employers.* (link)

Website: Inside Out (link)

Website: Samaritans Wellbeing in the City (link)

Website: Heads Together Campaign (link)

Website: The Minds At Work Movement (link)

"It's just helping them focus on the items where they can make changes and see an impact on the bottom line."

Robin Kiziak
LI: robinkiziak

Tags:
#business partnering #relationships #confidence #meetings #operations #comfort zone #impact

ROBIN KIZIAK is a Finance Manager at Wickes and previously a long-time finance professional at DHL. Robin shares with us his experiences of challenging his introverted nature to go out and walk the shop floor to build new relationships and make an impact in terms of his own effectiveness but also for his business partners.

Robin is currently based out of Northampton, England.

On the hidden challenge with email

The confidence piece is certainly something I wasn't great at in my early career. I was one of those typical finance people, if there is such a thing, very introverted, quite happy to sit in my office, and get told these are the numbers from last week, put the reports together and distribute them. I suppose it hasn't been helped by email, because email is a way of getting out of talking to people. I could email a report so I never got to speak to anyone. It's brilliant, that's the way I would approach things, but today improving confidence and building relationships has become so much more important as I've gone through my career.

On how to practically develop confidence in building relationships

I had started in a new job, so in effect I had a fresh slate. I had been in DHL for ten years or so, so wherever I moved around people already knew me. When I came into Wickes it was a completely new environment. I could set out from the start that this is how I'm going to do things. I really pushed myself out of my comfort zone to get to know people and start building relationships straight away. Before I would sit in the background and wait until I was needed. So that's where I made the biggest step in my career so far.

On four relationship building steps

The first time you do it feels difficult, but once you do it you realise that people aren't as bad as you made them out in your mind. A useful list of relationship building steps I got from CIMA starts with asking questions about other people, because people like to talk about themselves. Then show an interest in what they are saying. It makes sense because if that is what people like doing, then let's build on that to see what happens. Then finally seek an understanding of where they are coming from, what their values are, what they see as important in the business. The big word is collaboration at the moment so then just start cooperating with each other. So if you need a favour, that's where you start building the trust and the relationship grows.

On how to use weekly meetings to scale your impact

We have weekly meetings, so the operational guys get to know what a P&L is and how they can impact a P&L. We try to track all the metrics, we look at run-rates and trends so that when we come to doing forecasts then we know potential areas where we can perhaps improve, or cut out a bit of fat from the budget. I think that's key, because a lot of operational people, below a 'Head Of' level wouldn't really know what a P&L is. They just go about their day job, which in logistics and distribution is just to get the boxes out the door. They are perhaps not as focussed on the P&L as we would be, but they need to have an interest in it because as soon as they can understand how they can impact it, it helps everyone. It also helps their development as well because if they want to progress in their careers, P&Ls and understanding finance is going to play a big part in that.

On how to change the perception of Finance as being in our "golden towers"

Before I walked the floors there wasn't someone on site as often as I am. So their view of finance was just people sitting in their golden towers somewhere, putting a few numbers into a laptop and that's their job done. I've got to give credit to the Head of Distribution at interview because he was a big advocate of wanting to see more visibility of finance on the shop floor. He wanted to see me in the business educating his operators on how they could impact the finances and see what they could do to impact and help achieve the overall business objectives. I think it's made a big difference to them and how they see things, such as, we're not telling you to get rid of something for the sake of it, but because the volumes not there.

On why it's important to challenge your business partners

If you can give them that challenge, *"Look, this is what you did last year or this is what you did last month, why are we not hitting those highs this month?"* It's just helping them look at things in a different way, because their focus is just on churning the business, picking the boxes and getting the boxes out the door. It's helping them focus on the items where they can make changes and see an impact on the bottom line.

On the best bit of advice Robin has ever received

Every day is a school day. You're always learning something new every day and especially in finance. It's pushing yourself out there, pushing yourself out of your comfort zone each time, and you'll find something new.

Recommended Resources

Article: *To create value you must walk the shop floor*, by Robin Kiziak & Anders Liu-Lindberg (link)

Article: *Is Business Partnering A New Trend*, by Phil Spall (link)

"I would never walk into a manager with a problem without having two to three solutions for it. I can only do that if I know what's going on in the business."

Sabine Prenslev Christensen
LI: sabine-prenslev-christensen

Tags:
#business partnering #courage #Navy #influence #relationships #comfort zone

SABINE PRENSLEV CHRISTENSEN started her accounting & finance career working within the renewables sector before eventually deciding to do Military Service, which later on led to a stint in the Finance department of the Danish Navy. Sabine also volunteers with the Red Cross teaching children Mathematics and Danish.

Sabine holds a degree in International Sales & Marketing, a Graduate Diploma in Accounting & Finance and is based out of Denmark.

On actions unknowingly holding us back from becoming more influential

Many of us just sit behind the screen doing the numbers, running the report, handing it over and not thinking about it anymore. However this is stopping us from developing. We're stopping ourselves from getting more into the business. It's preventing us from being a part of the decisions that are being made. So knowing what our bosses want to know, both what they need, or is nice to know, means we have to develop relationships, not only with our customers, but also with our bosses, their peers, the other leaders and so on. The thing is that when you get to the point, where you know what kind of information they need to make the best decision possible. The work you have been doing to get there is very useful and valuable because you are cutting down the time cost involved. You're driving value by helping identify the best decision and the relationships you develop with management actually helps you become involved in more decisions and discussions.

On some simple actions on leading up and leading down

Being in the Navy, there's so many levels of managers and people working it's kind of hard to understand where you are. I was in the middle of the hierarchy. I had a lot of people under me sailing the ships as well as over me saying what they have to do. My job involved completing reports where I had to get all of my information from the lower levels and bring that up to the higher levels. Often the lower levels used to delay their reports because they had no idea what was going on and they were also too busy sailing and so on. So I simply opened my office door and went out to visit them and told them, *"You're delaying my report, so what's up?"* They said they didn't get the information either. After that I started to visit them more often and they started calling me more regularly too because from that moment I really understood the additional workloads my asks were putting them under, which were enormous. Just by picking up the phone, sending an email, or visiting them we cut down the time cost and our relationship improved enabling me to more easily consolidate my reports. It also meant that I was always ahead. Whenever one manager asked me for anything, I knew what was going on. I knew what the cost would be, and I knew what kind of things we would have to do to improve whatever was going on.

On the importance of the courage mindset

It takes courage to go out there. Sitting behind your desk and looking at the numbers is quite a safe area. So when you go out of your comfort zone and actually meet the customers they will be looking to you for your knowledge about the numbers. You get a whole new view of how the business works and doing that is so important for understanding the numbers. I would never walk into a manager with a problem without having two to three solutions for it. I can only do that if I know what's going on in the business. I think that it is so important to get out there, to get away from the screen and just go and learn in the business, as well as to build those relationships which help you to know what's going on in the business and how it works.

On the unique challenges of working with the military

When you're in the Navy or the defence forces you get money from the governor and you have to make the best value from it. It's a big challenge because working in the Navy is where no two days are the same. It changes all the time. You have this amount of money (budget) and you have to do the best for it. That means you have to be ahead all the time and be in front of whatever is going to happen, A very good example is on a little line in one of our regulations where I found that you can actually convert certain activities into additional budget. It had never been done before so I went over to my manager saying, *"Hey by the way we can actually get some money here."* He was like *"No way. Are you sure?"* So I said Yes, and you know what, that's a challenge I accepted. I then took it to my customers saying we've an opportunity here, so let's go for it. And they were like, *"you're crazy, it's never going to happen."* So I thought that's like having a double-challenge. The bottom line was that with their cooperation and a finance report I developed over the next three months, we actually gained back a double digit million DKK sum for our Department's spend. It was a big success because it was the first time anyone had actually done it. It was in the regulations, but nobody had dared to do it. It only succeeded because I had such a good relationship with my customers and with my managers. They had my back all the time even though they were shaking their heads until we succeeded. I was quite proud of all the people involved. I challenged the system and sometimes you have to go out, be brave, have the courage to look up from your screen and not just sit there behind your screen.

On how you gain respect by having the courage to say 'No'

Actually one of the things that I've earned the most respect for in my finance work in the Navy is my courage to say 'No.' I mean you're standing there in front of a highly ranked commander and he's just looking at you, shaking his head thinking, did she just say *'No'* to me? As far as I was concerned, as long as he knows the reason why I said *No*, he can still say yes., I really don't care as long as he knows what's going to happen. Just the fact that I'm standing there, being a woman, not in uniform and being in finance, saying *No* to a commander, is unusual. So have the courage to trust in your skills. I knew what I was doing. I knew how things were going to turn out if they said yes. I knew what the future held and what costs there might have been from going ahead with this decision. Saying *No* actually gained a lot of respect.

On the best advice Sabine would give younger finance professionals

I think that it is very important for the future to know how the business works. I know that building the right relationships across the organisation is very important and I think you should not be afraid of going out there and having meetings with others. I once invited some of the highest levels in the Navy to join me for tea and everybody was like, *"they don't have time for you."* Well actually they did and they were quite interested in what I had to say because in finance we can add value from the bottom-up. So believe in your skillset, believe in what your analysis is saying about the future. Don't be afraid of being wrong or having everybody shaking their heads because they knew something you didn't. Instead, you can say, *"Okay, nobody told me, so thank you."* Just take the chance and go out there. The future is changing all the time, today is not tomorrow, and maybe your job is not there. So to remain relevant in finance you have to always be looking up from your screen.

Recommended Resources

Article: "A Business Partner's #1 Skill: Listening!" (link)

Article: "How did I reduce 1000 hours per year with one simple task" (link)

"If you said that finance is really an art more than a science but the data side is a science it tends to lead to two different mindsets."

Simon Harrison
LI: simon-harrison-dtb
WS: deeperthanblue.co.uk

Tags:
#IT #tech skills #data skills #SQL #Excel #big data

SIMON HARRISON is operations director at Deeper than Blue Analytics and has had over twenty years of experience within senior commercial finance roles, including experience of reporting to Billionaire business owners. Simon has also made significant improvements to business performance in a wide range of areas from Financial process, to business processes, leveraging management accounting and analytics including SQL, data visualisations, scorecards, IBM Business Analytics, Tableau, PowerBI.

Simon holds a CGMA Designation and is currently based out of Sheffield, England.

On an opportunity between IT and Finance to add more value

When I had responsibility for IT initiatives one thing I did was getting finance's spreadsheets really connected into our financial system, so they could be pulled straight into spreadsheets rather copying and pasting. They thought it was amazing, but it wasn't really. There's millions doing this around the world. It feels like a gap and an opportunity. I've felt that for most of my career people don't really get the most out of what can be achieved with the tools they already have.

On why we're not getting the most value out of the tools we have in Finance

I would point the finger really at the people who put the tools in. I've been there, I've been sat in that chair, and you're being bombarded with new information and you probably take half of it in. Then you probably learn another 25% of the capabilities and you're left with the final 25%

that you've never learnt because there's nobody prompting you to learn it. So you're really probably getting 75% out of the tools you've got. And that's why there is a big market for sharing that information because a different person might know another 75% when compared to somebody else. Getting people to share and collaborate on it will help spread the word and get everyone on the right level.

On the areas Finance can focus on to improve their tech and data skills

Learning simple basic database concepts. So what is the table? What is a basic join? What is a query? Real basic level SQL. When I was at Sports Direct, one of the things I got my team to do was to write an introduction to SQL package which gave people some simple little exercises. Every new entrant into my analytics team there did this if they'd never come across SQL before. And even if they had, they all found it useful and got up to speed with the principles very, very quickly. I would say that after six months of working with it people are really up to an advanced analytics level after beginning from a standing start. So it can be done, it's just about recognising the need to teach people.

On the main areas to be open minded on what IT can teach us on

What I find with IT, the DBAs the SQL developers they're absolutely fantastically highly skilled at data, but they're not so good at answering business questions and putting the two together. Once the IT guys understand what you're trying to do, which isn't easy to get them to understand because they don't think that way. If you said that finance is really an art more than a science but the data side is a science it tends to lead to two different mindsets. So the IT guys can teach the finance analysts how to get the data out more efficiently, how to deal with rogue bits of data because no one has got perfect data, and how to deal with the data cleansing. I've probably wasted far too many hours of my career cleaning data, particularly when there's a whizz in IT showing you how to do it faster.

On why there is a natural barrier between IT and Finance

There tends to be a natural barrier between the two departments I think, one won't let the other one in and the other one won't let them see the business data, and I'm like:

Me: *"C'mon guys. We're both trying to achieve the same thing."*

IT: *"I can't give you access to that data because you might change it."*

Me: *"C'mon no I won't."*

One idea to overcome these barriers is to start by working together on the smallest project, it just gets the ways of working going.

On the main challenges data is causing businesses

It's really about how to handle all this massive influx of data that's starting to come from your traditional sources. But now we've got this concept of big data where we've got rafts of unstructured data that are difficult to work with unless you've got the skills, the talent and the systems to merge that in with the rest of your data and see what patterns can be drawn from the external factors. For example how does the weather affect the demand for your products?

On how Excel can be used for rapid prototyping of data requests

If I'm starting a new project, instead of using SQL, I would generally knock up a model in Excel of a very small subset of data to demonstrate what I'm talking about. It's a quick, easy, prototyping tool for things like that.

On the best bit of advice Simon ever received

It's even more important now given that technology delivers new opportunities. In fact something I was reading this morning is that people studying their degrees today, by the time they are finished, there will be new jobs that didn't exist when they started. The pace of change is so quick you're starting to go down a career path that you don't know what it is yet. You've got to keep on learning.

Recommended Resources

Website: FP&A Trends Blog (link)

Website: Deeper Than Blue (link)

"When I'm talking of an interim I don't mean a contractor going to do a BAU role, what I'm talking about is ... going into, here's a bundle of mess, here's where we want to get to, we don't know how to get there, can you help us, type of thing."

Simon Kelly
LI: simonmkelly

Tags:
#international #interim #influencing #resilience #Sales #flexibility #failure

SIMON KELLY is a pragmatic delivery focused and "hands on" leader with an emphasis on relationship management across all levels. As a leading finance interim Simon has delivered process optimisation, restructuring and transformation projects, enhancing the analytics and providing thought leadership to deliver winning solutions. He has a track record of delivering around People, Process and Technology perspectives with a focus on improved efficiency and cost outcomes.

Simon holds an ACMA CGMA designation and lives with his family in Reading, England.

On two steps to consider when taking on an international assignment
Find somebody that is really good and has been to that country, area, or whatever you're looking at. Find a really good connection that can talk about the culture and talk about the nitty gritty stuff that you kind of forget. For example, what are the sleeping accommodations like? What's the cost of living? Those sorts of things, because some of those you might think are not too different to London, and then you get there, and *Oh crikey!* It's extremely different. Really do the research well and understand where you want to go, but maintain that flexibility because other things open up and you get to experience different things. I think the second part would be to really be sure around the role that you want

to do. I would always recommend if you want to work aboard and are post qualified a couple years, to really stretch yourself in terms of the roles that you apply for. They are much more forgiving internationally around promoting people and giving them much more senior roles than you'd get in the UK. And that's where the work experience and that's where the benefits really come from. So if you're going to do it, then those are the 2 things I would probably try and focus on.

On the biggest thing Simon learned about himself on his international move

I think the biggest thing I learned about myself was probably that I can do an awful lot more than I thought I could. By that I mean different things. I'm always an amenable guy. I talk to lots of people, hierarchies don't phase me or anything like that, they never have. However, I'd always question the people and stakeholder management side. Was I really influencing there? Was I really getting them to my way of thinking? Was I getting them to the conclusions that I wanted to get them to? And in Saudi because I was dealing with princes, and the royal family, and people like that, because some were working in these roles. When I was at NSN who were owed a huge amount of money by them. It wasn't as if they would never get paid. It was like that because the princes weren't being courted in the right way. They were the influencers. And that's where I learned I can actually do an awful lot more influencing and I was a much better influencer than I had realised. Because you are thrust into a situation where there is a really big outcome at the end of it and I think that was my biggest learning.

On what distinguishes interims from a BAU contractor role

I love being an interim. I love the change, the opportunities, the non-BAU, the key project elements of what you normally get in terms of an interim. To be clear, when I'm talking of an interim I don't mean a contractor going to do a BAU role, what I'm talking about is an interim being a proper interim, going into, *"here's a bundle of mess, here's where we want to get to, we don't know how to get there, can you help us type of thing."* That definition is quite important I think because there are lots of people that call themselves interims but they are just going to do a BAU role, they just happen to be on a day rate or contract rate.

On the three key qualities to be successful at interim roles

Would I recommend it? You have to have a certain amount of resiliency, you have to have a certain amount of perseverance and you have to be extremely confident that you can manage your energy really, really well. One of the things that I didn't realise it was a thing until I got the chance to meet Sophie Devonshire, is that energy management was a thing that I had been doing without realising I'd been doing it. You need to be able to manage your energy when you're an interim. I've been fortunate enough to have next to no time off between assignments and I've not been out of work for a really long time or anything like that. But that brings its own challenges in terms of getting tired and things like that. So when managing your energy I think you need to understand that if you want to be a successful interim, when you go into it, you have to be prepared to not have a holiday if opportunities arise and you want to take those opportunities.

On the benefits of embracing failure & salespeople

I was extremely fortunate in my first few roles that I had really good bosses and they were extremely supportive if I did make mistake or if I did make an error or I said something I shouldn't have said. They were 100% supportive of what I was doing. However the key bit for me was the fact that I was constantly working with salespeople and business development people and those guys are totally different animals to finance people. We talk about accuracy and we're talking about that it's 100% right. Salespeople talk about accuracy and it's maybe 20% right, the rest of it they can fix. That's not being disparaging about salespeople, that's what they're good at, that's what they work with. So I think early on having exposure to salespeople and senior salespeople and directors, seeing how they worked and seeing what they did, and what didn't work. Learning what they wanted was flexibility and what they didn't want was a complete answer. They wanted options and that enabled me to go in with a different mindset.

On the importance of a data governance competency

Everybody talks about analytics, automation, AI and all the rest of it. But that's only as good as the data and the data governance that you've put over all of that stuff. It's become a core role now. It used to be well I'm going to get a 50,000 row ledger extract and I'm going to manipulate that to give me what I want to see. I've seen it, graduates that come in and you go to them, *"Right, this is what we do to extract the data."* And they look at you and say, *"Well that's a really slow way of doing it, it's not very automated."* They then spend the day looking at it and come up with something where you end up with a little drop down box and you can tell it what you want and it will give it to you. Then you think *"Oh my God."* I think it's a generational thing. Every generation gets better at using the tech and the tech is moving so fast. However I think having data governance as a core skill is going to become even more key as we move into a much more automated AI world.

On the best bit of advice Simon has ever received

"Trust yourself because you're not stupid." It was from a boss who was amazing, I would always be sitting in the meeting and everybody would be talking and I'll be going in my head, *"why don't you do this?"* But I'd never say anything. I'm sure there's lots of people that do that and I'm sure there's lots of people that still sit in the meeting, think about something, and they don't say it. Then two or three weeks later somebody else says it and everybody goes, *"Oh my God that's amazing,"* and you sit there beating the hell out of yourself because you didn't speak up when you could have earlier. So trust yourself because you're not stupid is probably the best bit of advice because it's enabled me to question and challenge. Again that comes from being confident, and it comes from experience and it's something to learn. However if you feel that you've got something to say and you think that thing is relevant, then say it. What's the worst that can happen?

Recommended Resources

Book: *Superfast: Lead at speed,* by Sophie Devonshire (link)

Book: *Intuition Pumps and Other Tools for Thinking,* by Daniel C. Dennett (link)

"I don't know what happened but something inside of me, just like a fire inside to make this work sparked it, because I'm absolutely loving it and I feel like I should have done it years ago."

Wendy Thomson
LI: wendy-thomson
WS: blueboxaccountants.co.uk

Tags:
#practice #entrepreneur #failure #numbers #entrepreneur

WENDY THOMSON owns the Blue Box Accountants Ltd. She helps women to set up and run their own businesses. Working with many different businesses over the last two decades Wendy can tell you how to build your new business from tiny beginnings into a success to be proud of. She is also the owner of My Three Cats, a cat-sitting business. Wendy also holds a degree in Accounting and Finance, an ATT designation, and is based out of Warrington, England.

On the learning from the companies that failed which gave her ideas on how to better run a business
I actually learned as much about how not to run a business, as I have on how to run a business, because the companies that I worked for, that have actually failed, I can see exactly what went wrong. Having had those experiences I can obviously use that going forward to advise people how not to do it now. In finance obviously I had a full picture of what was happening in these businesses, and on the outlets that were not performing and all I could do was break it down and explain it to the owners. They did everything that they could as well but there were all sorts of factors out of their control. You need to have a very strong business model to make it work.

On Wendy's decision to run her own business
I've always had a burning desire to have my own business somewhere deep down, but it was just never really the right time amongst all those

different jobs. I also did all the usual family stuff. I got married, had two children, and then subsequently got divorced. I was a single parent for a while, I got a new partner and it's all those things happening at the same time. It just seems that now, whether it's that all the stars have aligned, or maybe it just seems the right time to do it. I have had other small businesses on the side throughout. When the kids were first born I set up a business with a friend making baby blankets and a cat business. I don't know what happened but something inside of me, just like a fire inside to make this work sparked it, because I'm absolutely loving it and I feel like I should have done it years ago.

On the value of LinkedIn for getting more clients and inquiries

I was going to all the networking events, but I needed to get out there more. For me LinkedIn has been working really well. I had an account on LinkedIn for years but I've just never really used it. I didn't really get it so I decided that I needed to learn how to use it properly. I did a five-day challenge four months ago and started to understand it more. For me that's where most of my leads and inquiries are coming from at the moment. I kind of put myself out there as this gin drinking, cat loving accountant. I get told off for being a little unprofessional sometimes, but I'm actually engaging with loads and loads of my ideal clients out there and it's really helping me. I just post about things that pop into my head throughout the day and there seems to be a lot of people out there who connect with me through that.

On challenges that clients are facing and dealing with the numbers

I tend to find that people are quite nervous about numbers and figures. Now I don't know whether they really like to admit it but I think that if you are starting a new business, you are sort of expected to have a financial plan. You're expected to know exactly what your forecasts are. And a lot of small business owners are just not confident that they understand how to do that, but they don't know who to go to, to ask. If they went into a truly traditional office-based accountant and said that, they'd feel like they would be laughed at. Whereas I'm very much like, look you don't have to know anything until you tell me what you want to do. I'll help you do it, I'll get you set up with a simple accounting system that you can understand that makes it easier for you to invoice your clients and collect your payments. I'll do your returns for you and I'll just support you. People just seem to like that. I mean it goes back to being at school again. There will be people who will say, *"Oh I hate maths, I can't do it. I don't get it. I don't understand it. I failed my maths."* I think that almost carries on into adult life. You can have all the creative ideas in the world and you can have these amazing ideas for business, but you can still be quite nervous about actually: How much to charge? How much to pay for this, that and the other? That's where I'm slotting in. I just advise these people who seem to appreciate my fairly down to earth approach. I find working with people, with their own businesses absolutely fascinating. So I'm really interested to hear about their business, how it works, and what I can do to help them make it better. They seem to be the issues that I find that clients are having at the basic level.

On embracing technology to help finance & accounting professionals as well as clients run their businesses and lives more easily

I don't think I would have set up my business without embracing, for example, the likes of Zoom for online meetings and cloud-based accounting systems. There is so much technology now that allows us to basically run a business from our own living rooms. I'm embracing everything I can find that will make life easier for me. I think particularly some of the old school accountants really need to use that to keep up with the changing world.

On the best bit of advice Wendy has ever received

Just to be yourself, because if you're not being yourself then you're giving a false image of who you really are.

Recommended Resources

Book: *If I Did It: Confessions of the Killer (2008)* by O.J. Simpson (link)

Website: Blue Box Accountants (link)

USEFUL RESOURCES AND INDEXES

Index of Key terms

Index of Recommended Resources To Read

Below is a list of the most popular reading resources in alphabetical order with their number of recommendations underlined in brackets.

Books

(4) *Good to Great: Why Some Companies Make the Leap...and Others Don't"* by Jim Collins (link)

(4) *The Audacious Finance Partner: Reveals The Key Factors and Skills for Business Partnering Success*, by Andrew Codd (link)

(2) *Give and Take: A Revolutionary Approach to Success (2013),* by Adam Grant (link)

(2) *How to win friends and influence people*, by Dale Carnegie (link)

(2) *The Art of Possibility: Transforming Professional and Personal Life (2002)*, by Rosamund Stone Zander and Benjamin Zander (link)

(2) *Thinking, Fast and Slow (2012)*, by Daniel Kahneman (link)

(2) *What Got You Here Won't Get You There: How Successful People Become Even More Successful (2012),* by Marshall Goldsmith (link)

(1) *1000 Years of Career Advice: interviews with 100 graduates 10 years on from university, their career paths and lessons learned (2018)*, by Paul Murphy (link)

(1) *16 Things High Performing Organisations Do Differently* by Don Yaeger (link)

(1) *7 Habits of Highly Effective People (2001)*, by Stephen Covey (link)

(1) *7 Strategies for Wealth & Happiness: (2009)*, by Jim Rohn (link)

(1) *A Curious Mind: The Secret to a Bigger Life (2015)*, by Brian Grazer and Charles Fishman (link)

(1) *A River Sutra 2007,* by Gita Mehta (link)

(1) *A Rogue Economist Explores the Hidden Side of Everything*, by Steven D. Levitt, Stephen J. Dubner (link)

(1) *Absolute Honesty: Building a Corporate Culture That Values Straight Talk and Rewards Integrity (2003)*, by Larry Johnson and Bob Phillips (link)

(1) *Accelerate: The Science of Lean Software and DevOps: Building and Scaling High Performing Technology Organisations,* by Gene Kim and Nicole Forsgren (link)

(1) *Add Then Multiply: How small businesses can think like big businesses and achieve exponential growth*, by David B. Horne (link)

(1) *Behind Every Good Decision: How Anyone Can Use Business Analytics to Turn Data into Profitable Insight (2014)*, by Piyanka Jain (link)

(1) *Beyond Budgeting: How Managers Can Break Free from the Annual Performance Trap*, by Jeremy Hope and Robin Fraser (link)

(1) *Black Box Thinking: Marginal Gains and the Secrets of High Performance: The Surprising Truth About Success (2016)* by Matthew Syed (link)

(1) *Bounce: The Myth of Talent and the Power of Practice (2011)* by Matthew Syed (link)

(1) *Kiss Your BUT Good-Bye: How to Get Beyond the One Word That Stands Between You and Success (2013)*, by Joseph Azelby and Robert Azelby (link)

(1) *Leaders Eat Last: Why Some Teams Pull Together and Others Don't (2014)*, by Simon Sinek (link)

(1) *Leadership and Self-Deception: Getting out of the Box*, by The Arbinger Institute (link)

(1) *Lean In: Women, Work, and the Will to Lead (2013)*, by Sheryl Sandberg (link)

(1) *Linchpin: Are You Indispensable? How to drive your career and create a remarkable future (2010)*, by Seth Godin (link)

(1) *Managing Transitions: Making the Most of Change (2009)*, by William Bridges and Susan Bridges (link)

(1) *Maverick!: The Success Story Behind the World's Most Unusual Workplace (2001)*, by Ricardo Semler (link)

(1) *Michelle Obama: A Biography (2009)* by Liza Mundy (link)

(1) *Mindset – Updated Edition: Changing The Way You think To Fulfil Your Potential (2017)*, by Dr Carol Dweck (link)

(1) *On China*, by Henry Kissinger (link)

(1) *On The Shoulders of Giants: 33 New Ways To Guide Yourself To Greatness 2008*, by Rhondalynn Korolak (link)

(1) *Originals: How Non-Conformists Move the World Book* by Adam Grant (link)

(1) *Prediction Machines: The Simple Economics of Artificial Intelligence (2018)*, by Ajay Agrawal (link)

(1) *Pre-Suasion: A Revolutionary Way to Influence and Persuade*, by Robert B. Cialdini (link)

(1) *Pricing Value: The art of pricing what your accounting clients value most 2019*, by Rhondalynn Korolak (link)

(1) *Protect Your Profit: Five Accounting Mistakes and How to Avoid Them*, by Elizabeth Hale (link)

(1) *Radical Candor: Be a Kick-Ass Boss Without Losing Your Humanity*, by Kim Scott (link)

(1) *Reinventing the CFO: How Financial Managers Can Transform Their Roles And Add Greater Value (2006)*, by Jeremy Hope (link)

(1) *Resilience: Hard-Won Wisdom for Living a Better Life (2016)*, by Eric Greitens Navy SEAL (link)

(1) *Rising Strong (2015)* by Brené Brown (link)

(1) *Sales Seduction: Why Do You Say Yes? 2012*, by Rhondalynn Korolak (link)

(1) *Search Inside Yourself: The Unexpected Path to Achieving Success, Happiness (and World Peace) (2014)*, by Chade-Meng Tan and Daniel Goleman (link)

(1) *Secret Life of Trees*, by Colin Tudge (link)

(1) *Start With Why: How Great Leaders Inspire Everyone To Take Action (2011)*, by Simon Sinek (link)

(1) *StrengthsFinder 2.0: A New Upgraded Edition of the Online Test from Gallup's Now Discover Your Strengths (2007)*, by Tom Rath (link)

(1) *The Richest Man in Babylon,* by George S Clason (link)

(1) *The Second Machine Age – Work, Progress, and Prosperity in a Time of Brilliant Technologies (2016),* by Erik Brynjolfsson, Andrew Mcafee (link)

(1) *The Secret,* by Rhonda Byrne (link)

(1) *The Subtle Art of Not Giving a F*ck: A Counterintuitive Approach to Living a Good Life 2016,* by Mark Manson (link)

(1) *The Wall Street Journal Guide to Information Graphics: The Dos and Don'ts of Presenting Data, Facts, and Figures (2013),* by Dona M Wong (link)

(1) *The Whole Story: A Walk Around The World Paperback (1997)* by Ffyona Campbell (link)

(1) *Traction: Get a Grip on Your Business (2012),* by Gino Wickman (link)

(1) *Tribe of Mentors (2017),* by Timothy Ferriss (link)

(1) *Triggers: Creating Behaviour That Lasts–Becoming the Person You Want to Be (2015),* by Marshall Goldsmith and Mark Reiter (link)

(1) *Trump: The Art of the Deal, by Donald J. Trump, Tony Schwartz* (link)

(1) *What Is Your WHAT?: Discover The One Amazing Thing You Were Born To Do (2013),* by Steve Olsher (link)

(1) *What They Don't Teach You At Harvard Business School (2016),* by Mark H McCormack (link)

(1) *When Coffee and Kale Compete: Become great at making products people,* by Alan Klement (link)

(1) *Who Moved My Cheese?: An Amazing Way to Deal with Change in Your Work and in Your Life (1998),* by Spencer Johnson and Kenneth Blanchard (link)

(1) *Work Less, Make More: The counter-intuitive approach to building a profitable business, and a life you actually love (2017),* by James Schramko (link)

(1) *Work Wise (2010),* by Rahul Kapoor (link)

(1): *You Are Born to Lead: Reflect, Adapt, & Make an Impact Right Now (2017),* by Christine McLaren and Kelly McCleary (link)

(1) *You Can't Teach a Kid to Ride a Bike at a Seminar: The Sandler Sales Institute's 7 step system for successful selling (1995),* by David H Sandler (link)

(1) *Your Brain at Work: Strategies for Overcoming Distraction, Regaining Focus, and Working Smarter All Day Long* (2013), by David Rock (link)

(1) *Zero to One: Notes on Start Ups, or How to Build the Future (2015),* by Blake Masters and Peter Thiel (link)

Articles, Reports & Whitepapers

Index of Recommended Resources To Watch & Listen

Below is a list of the most popular resources mentioned for videos, documentaries & podcasts mentioned by the guest mentors.

Podcasts

#SITN Strength in the Numbers Show (link)
Cloud Stories (link)
Generation CFO (link)
Superfast Business (link)
The Cloud Accounting podcast (link)

Videos

B Inspired (link)
Developing a growth mindset with Dr Carol Dweck (link)
How Great Leaders Inspire Action, TEDx, Simon Sinek (link)
How to be the Luckiest Person in the World | Lindsay Spencer-Matthews | TEDxUQ (link)
How to start a movement Ted Talk (link)
Robert McKee - The importance of storytelling in Business - Seminar 29th November 2013 (link)
TaxStreets Global (link)
What Synapse Do (link)

Documentaries

Blue Planet series (link)
Planet Earth: The Complete Collection: (2006) (link)
The Corporation (2003) (link)

Movies

Apollo 13 (link)
This Is Spinal Tap (link)

Index of Recommended Resources To Visit
Below is a list of the most popular websites mentioned to visit

#SITN Portal (link)
1,000 Years of Career Advice (link)
Accountancy Age (link)
Accounting Exam Coach (link)
Accounting Web (link)
Add Then Multiply (link)
AICPA-CIMA (link)
Authenticity Resolved (link)
B Inspired (link)
Bearing Point (link)
BeastBI (link)
Best Practices Conference (link)
BFAN (link)
BizStreet.biz (link)
Black Female Accountants Network (BFAN) (link)
Blue Box Accountants (link)
Businest® (link)
Centage (link)
Certified Corporate FP&A Professional (link)
CFO University (link)
Data crossroads (link)
Deeper Than Blue (link)
DISC Test (link)
eeCPA (link)
Entrepreneurs' Organisation (link)
Fast Track Trade (link)
Financial Modelling Institute (link)
Financeseer (link)
Flexxus (link)
FP&A Experts (link)
FP&A Trends (link)
FPA Group (link)
Generation CFO (link)

Gilchrist & Co (link)
Heads Together Campaign (link)
Inside Out (link)
Intend to Lead (link)
Investopedia (link)
Jenny Okonkwo (link)
KAI Test (link)
Leaders In Finance LinkedIn Group (link)
Make the SHIFT™ (link)
Mark Lee (link)
Model Citizn (link)
OptiBPO (link)
Optim2 (link)
Proservartner (link)
Samaritans Wellbeing in the City (link)
Sequel CFO (link)
Simply Glin (link)
Supercharged Finance (link)
Synapse (link)
The Business Partnering Institute (link)
The FSN Network (link)
The Girls Network (link)
The Hackett Group (link)
The Minds At Work Movement (link)
The Numbers Guys (link)
The Outperformer (link)
The Vitiligo Society (link)
True Colours Test (link)
Working Options (link)

Index of Topics Covered

Create Your Own Index

As mentioned in the introduction to get the most out of this book it is important that you absorb what is useful for you and construct a career that is also uniquely your own.

So I invite you to make notes of your favourite insights, a-ha moments of clarity, key quotes, next steps, reflections on how you can put it into practice, and it might even help to put in the page number too.

For example:

P83 Idea on blocking out personal development time (Stan Besko)

Next step: block book 60 minutes on Friday mornings in calendar and then schedule in specific learning opportunities (i.e. Microsoft Teams; White Papers on Advanced Analytics, Psychology, ...) with last 15 minutes to summarise and internalise key learnings.

LI message Stan to thank him for insight.

Different ideas will resonate with different people in different ways. I'd love to know what you're taking away from this book. If you'd care to share take a pic and share with us on LinkedIn (@sitnshow), Instagram (@sitn) or Twitter (@andrewSITN). I see and reply to quite a bit.

Happy notetaking!

Andrew

Acknowledgements

Firstly, I must thank all the guest mentors whose advice, stories, and hard-won lessons are the essence of this book. Thank you for your time and your generosity of spirit that has left a lasting legacy of helping others in our accounting & finance profession to find a better path and meaning in their careers.

To the rest of the #sitn team, Pia, Wei Chien & Mitan for putting up with my idiosyncratic ways. The podcast wouldn't exist, and I wouldn't be able to do any of the rest without you. For my team at Dell, thank you for keeping Finance Fun. You all rock!

To Rory, I appreciate all your efforts in helping turn this book idea into a reality and keeping up with my deadlines. You passed with flying colours.

To Katie, words cannot express how much your help and support mean to me. Love you to the Moon and back!

About #SITN (Strength in the Numbers) Show

The #SITN Show (www.sitnshow.com) is a popular accounting & finance podcast listened to in over 150+ countries around the world.

Getting an accounting qualification or finance certification is one of the best things to do to make a difference in our society. It potentially gives us a position from which we can help businesses make better decisions for the good of their customers, suppliers, communities, colleagues and yes owners and other financiers too. We can help increase the opportunity for all. So #SITN was established to leverage the value of mentoring:

1. To elevate the influence, impact, value, and difference we make for our organisations; and
2. To have more fun, rewarding, and meaningful careers in accounting & finance.

In this way we make it more accessible to everyone in our profession, regardless or geography, professional affiliations, status, gender, etc…

The fundamental premise of #SITN is that despite for all the challenges our profession is facing into, the seemingly accelerating rate of change, the new digital technologies and business models, we still have the ability to share with each other practical advice & experiences on what works well and what doesn't, so that we can all plot better paths forward.

Every Thursday we release a professionally produced podcast with a 30- to 40-minute interview that has been recorded with a guest mentor relevant to the finance & accounting profession. These guest mentors share their real success stories and hard-won lessons which are not found in any textbooks or on LinkedIn profiles. Together with the interviewer they deconstruct their experiences into the key strengths, qualities and practical 'baby' steps that others can also follow. On Mondays there is the popular #SITN Monday Memo which is a 5-minute debrief on a topical issue or useful piece of practical advice in accounting & finance.

The show is accessible via: iTunes; Stitcher; Spotify; YouTube; and Soundcloud, with detailed time-stamped show notes, key quotes, resources & ways to connect with guest mentors at www.sitnshow.com.

About the Author

ANDREW CODD is a bestselling author, speaker, coach, trainer and podcaster, regularly contributing finance thought-leadership via the top-rated Strength in the Numbers Show (#SITN), listened to in 150+ countries worldwide, helping create more influential finance professionals who solve meaningful problems for their organisations. He has over 20 years' experience in leading and effectively developing Global Finance and Sales talent at recognizable brands like Pepsi, Three, Virgin and Dell in a variety of countries across different continents.

Currently Andrew is a senior member of Dell's Aftersales Finance Operations, which is responsible for partnering with Sales teams across the world to optimise the return from its $5bn global support services portfolio. He is also President of AVF Worldwide which delivers customised end-to-end managed learning solutions and analytics software that helps Finance & Sales teams drive measurable top- and bottom-line improvements at mid-sized recurring revenue businesses.

Andrew graduated top of his faculty at University College Cork, holds an MBA with distinction from Manchester Business School and is a Chartered Global Management Accountant. He is also a registered Mind Coach and a licensed NLP Practitioner.

When not writing books, podcasting, coaching, speaking or running a business, Andrew can be found enjoying the treasures of the Wild Atlantic Way with his young family in the southwest of Ireland.

Getting in Contact

Please message your feedback on the book or requests for coaching, speaking and customised training workshops to support@avfww.com.

Multiple and Bulk Order Copies

If the ideas and advice in this book have interested you and you see the motivational value of the mentors' experiences to gift and distribute to your team and staff, then you can enquire about ordering multiple copies. In addition to availing of special bulk purchase rates and discounts, for these larger purchases the author, diaries permitting, can also be made available speak at your event or hold a sixty minute 1:1 Q&A with you or your team. Contact info@avfww.com to enquire further.

Value Creation & Capture Diagnostic

There is mounting pressure and growing expectations on finance & accounting teams across the world to add more value to their organisations. In response the author has made available for a limited time a free proprietary diagnostic tool at www.avfww.com.

After completing thirty-six reflection questions this diagnostic tool helps you deconstruct and identify your strengths as well as areas of potential opportunity to improve the momentum of you and your team's value creation and capture activities.

THANK YOU

Printed in Poland
by Amazon Fulfillment
Poland Sp. z o.o., Wrocław

53498885R00223